Daughter of
BLUEBIRD

GINA CAMPBELL

WITH

LYNNE GREENWOOD

GREAT N-ORTHERN

Dedication

To all my 'special' friends, in no particular order, plus the Ladies of Moor Allerton Golf Club who have shown me the true value of friendship, loyalty and how to restore, maintain and keep one's own self-worth.

Avril
Linda
Sue S.
Sue B.
Sue W.
Sam
Nora
Etta
June
Jane
Denise

Last but not least it is for my father, Donald Campbell CBE, whose lasting memory I shall do my very best to ensure is upheld.

Great Northern Books
PO Box 213, Ilkley, LS29 9WS
www.greatnorthernbooks.co.uk

Every effort has been made to acknowledge correctly and
contact the copyright holders of material in this book. Great
Northern Books apologises for any unintentional errors or
omissions, which should be notified to the publisher.

ISBN: 978-0-9572951-2-4

Design and layout: David Burrill

Printed and bound by CPI Group (UK) Ltd, Croydon, CR0 4YY

CIP Data
A catalogue for this book is available from the British Library

Day of destiny: January 4, 1967 and Bluebird's fatal crash at Coniston (above). The similarities to my father's crash and my own at Holme Pierrepont in 1984 were uncanny (below).

Acknowledgements

Many people mentioned here have influenced my life in one way or another and I thank them all. I would like to thank Lynne Greenwood, who has become an enormous part of my life since we first met when she interviewed me for the *Sunday Times*. Her understanding, dogged determination and attention to detail has ensured this project was completed. I would also like to thank her husband, sports writer Andrew Collomosse, for his advice and expertise. And to thank my 'family' here in the UK and in New Zealand who are always there for me, and Sue Stone, for 'knowing' me!

Lynne Greenwood is a freelance journalist and writer for national newspapers, including the *Sunday Times*, *The Times* and *Daily Telegraph*, and a former staff reporter on the *Daily Express* and the *Daily Star.* She lives in Hebden Bridge, West Yorkshire.

CONTENTS

DAMON HILL OBE

I don't know Gina Campbell very well, which might sound like an odd thing to say before introducing Gina Campbell's book! But in another sense, I know Gina Campbell very well indeed.

We share a similar legacy: the famous speed-loving father, the tragic accident and growing up in the shadow of a deceased national hero.

And another odd connection, as Gina has reminded me: we both appeared on a TV programme in the last millennium called *Whose Baby?*, a sort of *X-Factor* for privileged babies. Strange old world, entertainment!

Famous names can be troublesome things. They prefigure you. They create expectation and scepticism in equal measure. They make it difficult to see yourself; to be sure you are being yourself. They can make things confusing, especially at a formative age. I think it takes a long time to become the real person inside the famous name, maybe longer than it might have done otherwise. The name, you have a right to. But the fame? What have you done to deserve it? After all, you are not your father. These questions niggle.

And then you throw in loss, a violent accident, grief, broken families. It's a lot to sort through.

Then there's the BIG question: What was it (is it) that can be so alluring, so inviting, so important that one's father would gladly risk death, would willingly risk leaving you behind to cope without him? What the hell could that be? Why do that? Why risk everything? How could you do that to the ones you love the most?

Bruce McLaren, the F1 driver who gave his name to the McLaren F1 team, famously wrote his own epitaph. In the final sentence of his 1964 autobiography entitled *From the Cockpit*, he wrote:

"To do something well is so worthwhile that to die trying to do it better cannot be foolhardy. It would be a waste of life to do nothing with one's ability, for I feel that life is measured in achievement, not in years alone."

This is a noble philosophy, but scant consolation to those left behind. But Bruce was only 27 when he said that. He had no family, either.

So what drove Donald to press ahead, into the wide blue yonder?

If you were Gina, you would have to try to find out. Wouldn't you?

In the play *The Blue Bird* (1908), by Nobel Prize-winning writer, Maurice Maeterlinck, the play that so inspired Sir Malcolm Campbell that he painted his racing car blue, hence all the Bluebirds that followed, a fairy visits two poor children and urges them to go and find the 'Blue Bird'. When they ask her why, she says it is for her little girl who 'wants to be happy'.

It is curious, that Gina finally found *The Bluebird*, isn't it?

Gina's story is one of amazing courage and perseverance, qualities her forefathers were rightly admired for. She has honoured the Campbell name in her lifetime already. I think this book is testimony to the existence of what my friend George Harrison called 'the love there that's sleeping'. Perhaps that's why we do all these crazy things?

Congratulations Gina. I think it's pretty obvious whose baby you are now.

Damon Hill, OBE
Formula One World Champion 1996,
Son of Graham Hill, OBE, twice F1 World Champion.

Foreword by
SUE STONE

Those of you who have never had the privilege of meeting Gina Campbell, could be forgiven for thinking that she has a very outgoing, confident and assertive personality. The reality could not be further from the truth.

The 'Campbell' dynasty has proved to be a double-edged sword: on one hand Gina has had the honour of being Malcolm and Donald's granddaughter and daughter, but on the other the burden of proving herself and not letting the 'Campbell' name down.

Her own racing achievements and public life are there in the history books, but make no mistake the records that she broke in her own right only came about because she showed incredible grit, determination and a deep inner strength.

I am luckier than most – Gina is one of my closest friends. This gentle, unassuming woman has shown me endless warmth, love and laughter. Underneath her public image shines a true lady who has a quiet vulnerability and self-doubt.

Gina has a natural skill of putting anyone she meets at ease, giving them her undivided attention; a special gift of touching the hearts of all who come into contact with her.

She is a very private person which is why I feel blessed that she has allowed me to become a part of her inner life. I believe that my dearest friend will also have a place in your heart by the time you finish this book.

As a reader, you will learn that over the years she has had many ups and downs, but she will always be able to hold her head up high whatever life throws at her; after all she is a 'Campbell.'

Sue Stone is Managing Director of Fresh Knowledge, a company which specialises in providing assistance for alcohol abuse and its prevention. To find out more visit www.freshknowledge.co.uk

INTRODUCTION

My father, Donald Campbell, was buried 34 years, eight months, one week and one day after he died. And the date we chose for the funeral? September 12, 2001 – one day after the world-shattering events of 9/11 when the terror attacks in America killed 2,996 people.

I had been through so much in organising the funeral, trying to make sure everything was just right, as he deserved. When September 11 happened, for a fleeting moment I thought: 'Why today?' That's not meant to sound churlish – I honestly think anyone who had planned a parent's funeral for the next day would have felt the same. My father meant every bit as much to me as each of those people did to their families.

Television companies had planned to transmit part of the funeral service and the church had been taken over by camera positions and sound systems. But after September 11, virtually all the news people vanished.

I never expected to be at my father's funeral. A long, long time had passed since January 4, 1967 when, as he attempted to break his own world water speed record, his boat *Bluebird* took off over Lake Coniston, plummeted back down and then sank.

It's with some sort of irony that my father died in that spectacular way because he felt an overwhelming sadness about the way his own father, Sir Malcolm Campbell, died in his bed after suffering a stroke. Father found it almost shameful.

My grandfather was a record-breaker, too, setting nine world land speed records in his car *Bluebird* before turning his attention to water and setting another four records.

Many of his contemporaries, including compatriots Sir Henry Segrave and John Cobb, had died in a blaze of glory attempting records of their own and yet he died after a stroke. He was also losing his eyesight and was physically diminished. That had a massive effect on my father, who was 27 at the time.

However, for my father, death was his finest moment, an eternal moment. I'm positive that had he died this year (2012) aged 92 there would have been a column inch in the news pages of the *Telegraph* and perhaps something on the obituaries page. Instead he immortalised himself, whether he wished to or not.

At the age I am now, I have friends with elderly parents still alive, and all you hear from them is terrible sadness. They see their parents, people who have looked after them, nurtured them, slowly decaying in front of their eyes.

To me that must be desperately sad – yes, they've had 40 extra years with them, but can they turn round and say they have brought wonderful pleasure, when it does eventually become torment? The sadness those people feel, I'm never going to feel. Is that a bonus?

I lost my dad when he was a handsome man in his prime, everything going for him. And what might have been the alternative? To witness him as some, sad, dribbly, incontinent old man, suffering all the degrading things that none of us want to happen to us.

I'm going to say I was lucky, which is probably the wrong choice of words. However I do feel quite passionate that my father's life turned out that way. He always said that he wanted to die making love to a beautiful woman and I say he died at the hands of a beautiful bird. It's a bit of a cliché now but it's a fact.

I was 17 when he died. Life was just starting for me.

SIR MALCOLM CAMPBELL

'One warm September afternoon in 1897 a small boy, hands in pockets, mounted on a large bicycle came careering down Chiselhurst Hill in Kent. He hurtled beneath the railway bridge and terrified the life out of two old ladies preparing to cross the road. Never, as they later testified, had they ever witnessed such awesome speed. Another and more effective witness of the account was the local Constable. The offender was promptly hauled into Court and charged with furious riding. A crusty old Magistrate glaring sternly over his spectacles, summarily dealt with the young culprit. "Fined ten shillings, and let that be a lesson to you not to go so fast in future, Malcolm Campbell."'

This is the first paragraph in the book *The Eternal Challenge*, which my father started to write but sadly never finished. It might well explain the start of the Campbell family's love of speed. (Further extracts are at the end of this book.)

The first 38 pages of the manuscript, neatly typed on A4 foolscap pages and held together with metal clips inside a battered orange folder, include many stories about Sir Malcolm, who died in 1948, nine months before I was born.

But I soon began to hear the extravagant stories about his life, not just his nine world land speed records and four world records on water, which are so well known, but the amazing adventures which also defined him.

My father described him as "a courageous, colourful character; a dynamic, dominant, personality. You could love him, you could hate him, you could never forget him." I know that my father never did forget him and was always striving to reach the standards he knew my grandfather expected of him and to match his achievements.

In a similar way, I know that I have always been influenced by my father when it comes to competition. Even now, at such simple times like when I am playing golf and standing over a putt, I can sense some pressure. I am telling myself: 'Come on girl, your father would expect you to hole this one.' There was never any place for second best.

Grandfather broke his first land speed record in September 1924 at Pendine Sands in Wales with a speed of 146.14 miles per hour – 11 years later he reached 301.13 miles per hour at Bonneville Salt Flats in Utah. His first water speed record followed in September 1937, on Lake Maggiore in Switzerland, reaching 126.33 miles per hour. And his final record was established on Coniston Water in the Lake District in August 1939, with a speed of 141.74.

But some of my grandfather's exploits away from official record-breaking were just as amazing and often very funny. Like the time in 1910 that he built his own plane and attempted his first flight. He started the project after being inspired by a film of the Wright Brothers with their primitive aeroplane in flight. And he was spurred on by a cash prize of £1,000, offered by the *Daily Mail* newspaper owner Lord Northcliffe, for the first mile-long circular flight by an all-British machine.

So Grandfather, who by then was an underwriter in the City, rented a barn on the edge of a strawberry field near Orpington in Kent and spent every evening there after he finished at the office, working with a local carpenter he employed to build his plane. He chose a Sunday in June for the trial flight when unfortunately lots of local people turned up and stretched out across the field which was to be his runway. They had objected to his plans from the moment they knew what he was up to and claimed they were entitled to be on what was a public footpath.

But of course they were not going to deter Grandfather. He started the engine, his friends who were holding the wings let go and he began to run down the sloping field. He pulled back the joystick and lifted a few feet in the air before sadly crashing back to the ground seconds later. The story goes that when he emerged splattered in red, everyone immediately thought it was blood - but in fact it was squashed strawberries!

Even though he bought a bigger engine and rebuilt the plane that year, it never really got off the ground. Meanwhile others were picking up prizes for flying from London to Manchester and England to the Continent and so he became disillusioned. That's when he turned to cars and motor racing.

Then there was his search for pirate treasure on the Cocos Island off Costa Rica. Imagine making that journey in 1926. Apparently he always said his interest in buried treasure started when he read Rider Haggard's book *King Solomon's Mines* as a child but then, after the First World War, he started to read any book he could find on pirate gold.

He linked up with his old friend Bill Guinness – his real name was Kenelm Lee Guinness – who had already sailed down the West Coast of Africa in his yacht called *Adventuress* and they agreed on an expedition to Cocos Island. They had read and researched that the hidden treasure, which could be worth as much as £20 million, was from the city of Lima which, when it was threatened with capture in 1821, had removed all its riches to Cocos. Their expedition arrived at the Island in February 1926, but it seems they quickly lost interest when they realised that a 'clue' to the treasure's whereabouts, which they were relying on, simply led them nowhere.

It was in 1931, after he had broken his fifth land speed record at Daytona Beach in Florida, that Grandfather was knighted by King George V. A banquet was held at the Mansion House in London in his honour when he returned from the States. Four years later he set his final land speed record, this time in Utah.

His achievements are still celebrated in various Halls of Fame in the United States and I have been invited to three of them, in St Louis, Birmingham, Alabama, and Daytona.

In June 1994 I went to Talla Dega in Birmingham, where grandfather was among the first men to be inducted into the International Motorsports Hall of Fame there. His *Blue Bird V* was there for the ceremony, although it had not been restored at that time – it was so salt-encrusted that the bodywork looked grey, not blue, and it seemed as though mice had been nesting in the seats. The local paper came along and I was photographed with the car.

Then, a couple of years later, the BBC, who were making a

documentary, invited me to go to the Daytona USA Hall of Fame at Daytona's International Speedway circuit where there was a stand named after my grandfather. *Blue Bird V* had been completely restored by then and looked better than new. While I was there, I was also interviewed for American television by none other than Ronald Reagan Junior, son of President Reagan.

He was delightful. He had trained as a ballet dancer but later became a talk show host and magazine journalist. I understand he never really shared his father's politics, much more of a liberal, but in 2011 he published a biography of his father entitled *My Father at 100: A Memoir.* I asked him what it had been like living in the White House and in the shadow of arguably the most powerful person in the world and I'll never forget his answer. He simply said: 'That's like asking a tomato what it feels like to be red'!

After Grandfather returned from his final land speed record, he decided he needed a bigger house and he and my grandmother, Lady Dorothy, moved to Headley Court. It was a Georgian mansion with over 80 acres of parkland, high up on the North Downs in Surrey, a beautiful house.

Sir Malcolm was married three times, first to Marjorie Knott in 1913, then after his divorce, to my grandmother, Dorothy Whittall, in 1920. She had two children, my father Donald, born in September 1921, and his sister, my aunty Jean, born a year later.

But he divorced Lady Dorothy, whom I remember visiting us at my first home at Abbotts and who spent her last years in a nursing home, and married his third wife, Betty Nicory, in 1945. I never knew her.

My grandfather died in bed at home on New Year's Eve in 1948 after suffering a stroke on Christmas Eve. He was 63. In those days, people's illnesses and conditions were not publicised so much. Today, if a man as famous as Sir Malcolm Campbell suffered a stroke, it would be in the papers, you'd maybe see him in the wheelchair. Then they managed to keep their dignity, keep it private, but it's not the same now.

My father often recalled that Grandfather opened his eyes on New Year's Eve to see the family in his room and said: 'What are you all doing sitting here? Don't you know it's New Year's Eve? Get the champagne out.' Then he closed his eyes – it was almost his last breath. My father could not understand how he knew it was New Year's Eve because he'd been in a coma. Extraordinary.

For the rest of his life, my father used to go into terrible depressions at that time of year. At Christmas he tried so hard to make it fun, buying loads of presents, and throwing a party in the house on Christmas Eve.

Leo Villa, who was both my grandfather's and my father's mechanic, and his wife Joan would always be there along with whoever was high profile in our lives at that time. And then after Christmas, Father seemed to sink into that terrible depression until New Year's Eve.

His father's death had such a lasting impression on him and he used to say he was heartbroken to see the man who had been such a hero so ill, so diminished. But Sir Malcolm was not diminished. My grandfather established the Campbell DNA.

Chapter 1

LONG RED FINGERNAILS

It must be the most difficult thing for any child to say: that she has no love, respect or true caring for her own mother. But, even worse, that a mother holds no emotion for her own child. It is so unnatural. But sadly, in my case, this was the plain and simple truth.

When my parents divorced, I think when I was nearly two years old, my mother found a place for me at High Trees, a boarding school-cum-residential home, where I lived for two to three years, 365 days of the year. She could find no place in her life for her only child and this was the convenient alternative. To this day I'm not sure whether my father knew exactly where I was all the time – later in life he said he thought I was with my mother at her mother's grand estate called Lock in Sussex. But on reflection I think he must have had a good idea and he certainly knew by the time he married for the second time. I must have been about four years old when his new wife Dorothy came to collect me from High Trees.

Dorothy told me later that when she drove up in her black Ford Popular, saying she was my mummy, come to collect me, I replied: 'Not the one with long red fingernails.' That must have been my only memory of my real mother. She also said that the matron of High Trees told her she had read in the local paper that my father had married and so rang him to tell him that her school had his little girl.

My father had married my mother Daphne Harvey in 1945, totally against both sets of parents' wishes – her father tried everything to stop her. And I was born four years later and named Georgina Dorothy Campbell. My dad always told me that my mother hated being pregnant. She tried gin and hot baths, the supposed way to induce an abortion, and wore a tight corset around her stomach to disguise the pregnancy.

Apparently she was totally disappointed when her baby was a girl and I'm sure my father would have preferred a boy, too.

But the marriage didn't last long and my parents divorced after my father found Daphne in bed with another man. He was the local vet whose name was Donald Balls – isn't that wonderful? At least she kept the Donald. My father had been out for the evening in London with his brother-in-law Brian Hulme, married to my dad's only sister Jean, always known as Buddy. Initially they had arranged to stay the night at their club but changed their minds later and decided it would be better to go home. So not only did my father find his wife in bed with Balls, but Buddy was also there to witness it! Even today whenever I meet up with Buddy, he always recalls this incident, which, I was told later, had a huge psychological impact on my father.

Apparently after the divorce, my mother was recalled to court by the King's Proctor for failing to disclose her misconduct with two men when her undefended petition was being heard. The decree was allowed to stand and at that stage my mother was granted custody of me.

Soon afterwards she met and married a man called Tony Turner who worked in the Foreign Office, although what he did there, I have no idea. By that time my father was embarking on his land and water speed records with the *Bluebirds*, following in the footsteps of his father. High Trees must have seemed a good option for a young child. The school, mainly for children of Army families, was a nasty 1900's red brick building – it looked like the typical house that a child would draw, oblong in shape with four windows and a central door. It used to have those metal window frames which created bubbling paint and condensation, always condensation.

I spent a lot of time looking out of the front window and I have two strong memories from that room. One is of gazing out at a climbing frame on the lawn, watching a squirrel weave in and out, except I didn't really know what it was then. And the other was of haring into the room – I was a real tomboy – falling and hitting my eyebrow on the tiled fireplace. There was a huge spurting of blood and I screamed and screamed, more from the horror of the blood than the pain. You can still see the scar now.

I cannot really remember the routine. I know there were always stout women around, matronly types with bosoms melded to their stomachs. There wouldn't have been any love or affection or praise, that's why I'm a bit of a tough cookie and very independent today. Rather than look to somebody else to do x for me, I will struggle round and do it myself – it's almost a conscious way of saying I do not need anybody. I'm a permanent fetcher and carrier for everybody around – by the time someone vaguely starts to look for something, I've found it and given it to them before they've had chance to stir.

I'm sure all the children at High Trees were girls, I don't remember any boys, and we slept together in a dormitory. Nor can I recall many lessons but I know when Dorothy finally took me home, she was surprised at how well I could read.

We seemed to spend a lot of time outdoors. There was a bridle path down the side of High Trees and we used to go for walks, little gaggles of kids all hanging on to each other. It's a wet part of Surrey and there's lots of clay, so wellies were the order of the day and so when Dorothy asked for my 'things', all she was given was a pair of wellington boots.

My father remained a mystery to me and I never saw him all the time I was there. I never went home for weekends or holidays. I vaguely remember my mother visiting with a very tall man, who must have been Tony Turner, who was well over six feet tall with a great big shock of red hair. I'm tiny now but I was an absolute scrap then and he looked like a giant. I'm sure she would have brought him along as a bit of a party piece – 'Oh do come and see my daughter.' I wonder what on earth he thought.

It was 1952 when Daddy married Dorothy McKegg, a New Zealander who came to the UK with a group of students and watched him with *Bluebird* at Lake Coniston. He swept her off her feet – she said she was a virgin when they met. Because she was from a big, warm family, she could not believe I was living at High Trees and she insisted on bringing me home. Dorothy was very loving and I soon adored her. Yet she said that at first I did not know what affection was. When she said: 'Give me a cuddle,' I said: 'What's a cuddle?' I had never known them.

When she collected me, we drove to Little Abbots, a small cottage in the village of Leigh, near Dorking, where they lived. It was a black and white timbered one up and one down with an extension, like a little arm, for the kitchen and my tiny bedroom. Downstairs was a small lounge, with a dining alcove area, and my father and Dorothy slept upstairs. The house had wooden doors inside which opened with big fat latches – you pulled down on a piece of leather which looked like a shoelace and it lifted the latch.

We had quite a big garden and an orchard along the drive, which was probably about 200 yards long. There was a wooden barn-cum-garage with a flight of wooden steps up to my father's office, which had pictures of aeroplanes on the walls, signed by Neville Duke, a friend of his. He was a famous fighter pilot in the Second World War, who was decorated for gallantry and later became one of the world's best test pilots, breaking the sound barrier in the Hunter Hawke.

My father had a dog called Maxie, a big, black shaggy Labradoodle – half standard poodle, half Labrador – which he once took with him when he went for dinner at Rules restaurant in London. When the waiter rather pompously said: 'The restaurant is only for diners,' my father replied: ' My dog is dining,' and promptly seated Maxie on a chair, tied a napkin round his neck and ordered him a three-course meal. Someone was quick enough to take a photograph which I understand was framed and hung on the wall in the restaurant for quite some time afterwards. Maxie took an instant shine to me and followed me everywhere and slept on my bed.

Alongside the drive was a field belonging to the house next door, which usually had a pony in it. I used to sit on the fence trying to encourage this pony to come to me so that I could climb on its back. I managed it sometimes and was thrown off at least once which made my father angry with me. Behind the garage there was a chicken farm and I used to wander all around there too. Today parents wouldn't let their kids have that freedom but I was a great wanderer.

Dorothy soon took me out to buy me some clothes and she remembered I asked her if they were for me alone because I had been used to sharing from a communal pile of clothes. We must have looked like a bunch of bloody urchins at High Trees. She also used to take me to London in the car – it seemed to take forever and I was always carsick. She took me to see all the sights, the Changing of the Guard, to various museums and art galleries. Having spent all her life in New Zealand until then, Dorothy just loved the culture and history of England.

After leaving High Trees, I started at a day school in Redhill, where the one incident I remember is having a polio inoculation. But soon I became a boarder at Dunottar School, a big imposing house set in huge grounds on the edge of Reigate. It all looked very grand with tall trees and big lawns – it's still there. We wore grey divided skirts and yellow T-shirts.

We slept in dormitories, which we were not allowed to leave at night so you had to pee in a po under the bed. That's where I swallowed a hair grip, a kirby grip, one night when we were all in bed. I was holding it in my teeth and I swallowed it by mistake. One of the girls had the sense to go to the matron, God knows what time of night it was, saying Georgina had swallowed her kirby grip. Matron came bustling in, the lights go on, everyone blinks. Then the headmistress arrived. My dad must have become a bit famous by then because I seemed to be receiving star treatment, although I don't think she really believed me. She said: 'Stupid girl, of course you haven't swallowed a kirby grip.' She started stripping the bedclothes to search for it.

Finally she decided I had to go to hospital so a taxi was called and I was bundled in, still in my nightclothes, along with the headmistress. It was probably the only time I'd been out there in the dark and it was spooky. As we drove away I could see faces at the big window which overlooked the drive.

All the way to Redhill General Hospital, the headmistress was ranting and raving: 'Stupid girl, you'd better not be lying. You couldn't have swallowed it.' She wore her hair pulled back into a bun and silly little spectacles. She looked just like Granny in TV's *Beverley Hillbillies*. I was totally bemused, thinking what's so serious about swallowing a kirby grip? I can remember X-rays and men in white coats disappearing and then the radiologist coming in with the X-ray, which showed the kirby grip nicely lodged in my insides. And I can remember the look of horror on her face. I was so impressed. I'd never seen an x-ray before and this thing had taken a photograph of my gut.

That night I was transferred to a private hospital called Smallfields and our family doctor turned up. There was no room for me in a ward so they put a bed at the end of a passageway, next to a radiator and some French windows, and arranged screens round so I had a little space. Maybe in those day it was private hospitals which didn't have enough beds – now it's the NHS! I could watch everyone coming down the passageway, nurses with bedpans, people scurrying.

The radiator was very important after they started to feed me cotton wool sandwiches – real cotton wool in between bread and butter, which was meant to wrap itself around the kirby grip so it didn't damage any organs. Everything I passed I had to do in a po so it could be dissected, in the hope the kirby grip would find itself out in a natural way. Can you imagine having to chew cotton wool? So I used to munch away, pulling out the cotton wool and stuffing it behind the radiator. How could you possibly eat cotton wool?

They kept X-raying me and the kirby grip was still lodged against my spleen, so eventually I was carted off to the operating theatre. I was really scared then and when I came round from the operation I was so sick. I was awfully poorly, and apparently I was one of the early children to have penicillin, something to do with possible lead poisoning, they said, so there must have been some kind of lead in kirby grips in those days.

All this time my father was in Ullswater, accompanied by Dorothy, where he was making an attempt on the world water speed record. And on July 23, 1955, a couple of months before my sixth birthday, he broke the record at 202.32 miles per hour.

A few odd people came to see me – friends of my father's I guess. Ironically, a patient in one of the rooms was a fellow called 'Goldie' Gardner, a racing driver – one of the Bentley Boys – who had accompanied my grandfather to Daytona Beach in Florida for one of his world land speed record attempts. He also knew my dad so I used to go and sit on his bed and talk to him. I was in hospital for quite a considerable time because it was probably more convenient for my dad while he was up in the Lakes. I didn't question it at the time and only now do I realise how extraordinary it was.

Eventually I went back to school where much later I swallowed half a bloody button. I must have had a habit of putting things in my mouth – I used to bite my nails something rotten. I was put in a dormitory on my own and again was told I was a stupid, stupid child and ordered to poo in a pot. They hoped the button would come out. When it hadn't appeared after a few days, guess what? I found a button, broke it in half and pushed it in the poo so I was let out.

I was a bit of a devil at school, or let's say adventurous. Once, another girl and I decided to run away when everyone went into morning prayers. I used to run away, just for the fun of it. We went a hell of a way from Dunottar, through the town, under a railway bridge and up to the top of Reigate Hill. It's got to be a good three miles. When we reached the top we saw the games mistress in her car, looking for us. I can remember thinking we'd just flogged our guts out reaching the top of a steep hill and now we have to go back down... Ironically, my grandfather Malcolm Campbell used to live at the base of Reigate Hill, in the house where he died.

The only subject I really enjoyed was geography. I could sit through most lessons and not absorb a thing because I was a daydreamer, mainly dreaming about ponies and horses, I was pony mad. When the teacher asked me something, I would look at her with a glazed expression and stutter – I had no idea. I was in a world of my own. I loved games. We played netball but I was never hugely good at it which depressed me because I like to be good at what I do.

By now I was becoming aware of what my father did, not least when the *Bluebird*'s engine arrived in the garage at home. It looked absolutely huge and lay on an RSJ, a rolled steel joint, tied to the floor. Sometimes my father would fire it up and I was told to come out of my bedroom which was in line with the jet blast. The local bobbies would be there because I suppose my father would have to inform them it was going to happen. It made a terrific noise and I can visualise Leo Villa, my father's engineer, leaning on the fence with the little hair he had all standing on end with the blast. I think it was something of a party piece for my father – he was a bit of a showman. Or maybe I am being unkind and he fired it up as part of the work Leo was doing on it.

It must have been around that time that I first was taken to Lake Coniston. It took forever to get there, probably two days from the south to the Lakes in little old cars which chugged along. To me, *Bluebird* was just a boat, although it didn't even look like one, but I suppose I was a bit blasé; kids today would have been so much more informed. I didn't have a clue what it was all about. Nobody had sat me down and said your father breaks water speed records in this boat.

But he broke one record on my seventh birthday, 19th September 1956, with a speed of 226.5 miles per hour. Everyone was thrilled and delighted but it all happened in the blink of an eye. My strongest memory is of someone with a live broadcast microphone coming up to me and saying: 'Well Gina, isn't that the best birthday present you can have?' And I said: 'Oh no, I'd much rather have a pony.' By that stage my father had promised me a pony if I stopped biting my fingernails.

My father was definitely becoming a mover and shaker. He had met Marlene Dietrich, the Hollywood film actress and cabaret star, who gave him a cowboy outfit for me so then Dorothy bought me a bow and arrow to add to my Wild West kit. It was in that same year, 1956, that my father appeared on the BBC's *This Is Your Life* programme, presented by Eamonn Andrews. Because the programme makers always kept it a secret from the person involved until the very last moment, my father thought he was going along to a book signing. I stayed at home with Mr and Mrs Botting – he was the gardener at Abotts and his wife helped Dorothy in the house – and we watched it on our little grainy black and white television. TV was a fairly recent phenomenon and I think we were really posh to have one – the Bottings wouldn't have had a TV.

There was never a suggestion that I should appear on the programme - kids were not allowed on TV then, you had to have an Equity card in those days. They arranged for a little boy about 12 or 13 years old, to play the role of a boy who wanted to meet my father and have his book signed. Years later in the 1980s when I had a coffee shop in Lymington, a man came in and introduced himself and said he was that child. At the time he had been a child actor and had an Equity card.

The Conservative MP Edward Du Cann, who was a friend of my

dad's, and the Crazy Gang, a bunch of zany comedians who included Bud Flanagan, were guests on the programme. My father once took me to see them at the Victoria Palace and we had front row seats. I took my shoes off and sat on my feet, which is something I still do, when all of a sudden one of them came down, took my shoes back on stage and made me go up and get them. People don't believe this but I am shy. As a young person, and even now, I'd happily sit there and not say a word. I hate people scrutinising me – I have a desperate inferiority complex, instilled in me by my dad who was always picking holes in me.

I was almost detached watching him on television. Did I look at the programme and think: 'That's my daddy?' I didn't really know him. In fact I don't have a poignant memory of first meeting my father.

Usually my dad was quite formal. He never displayed any affection towards me, never put his arm around me, never sat me on his knee, never praised me. In fact it seemed all he did was criticise, belittle me. He criticised my laugh in particular, said I sounded like a bloody donkey and then he would mimic the 'ee-ore, ee-ore' sound. Maybe that's why I don't laugh out loud a lot now.

But I know his character was formed by his own father. Grandfather died before I was born and my father and his sister Jean were his only children. His obsession with speed meant he was a renowned racing driver before my father was born and he broke the World Land Speed Record for the first time in September 1924 when Daddy was three years old.

Apparently Malcolm wanted to be the master of whatever he did, even down to competing with his children to prove he was better at anything they did together.

The only one bit of fun I remember having with my father at Abbots was when we gave Maxie a haircut. We lifted him on to the table in the garden to give him a bath and a haircut. He hated it but it caused much hilarity. But my dad was absolutely paranoid about truthfulness and always told me that if I had done anything wrong, at least to have the guts to own up. Like the time I threw sticks in the pond behind Abbots for Maxie, something I knew I shouldn't do because he came out all filthy and stinky and shook water all over the place. He had been in the water one day, when Daddy spotted him and caught me out.

He was very strict about behaviour and manners too and a great believer in spanking. He used to exact that punishment quite regularly if I was naughty. I was so scared if I knew it was that time again that I used to wee myself and he would tell me to go to the toilet and then to my room to wait for him. Then he would come and administer the punishment. He used to put me across his knee and spank me with his hand on my bottom. I remember screaming, but whether that was in pain or just a tantrum I don't know. I do know that today this would be viewed very badly, and is even now against the law, but in those days we were brought up in such a different way.

Dorothy told me she hated it but had no parental rights. Years later she looked back in horror that she allowed him to do it but at the time she had to stay well away. My father would say: 'I will handle this.' You did not argue with him in that mood. But then that was the way he had been brought up by his father.

By that stage my father's and Dorothy's marriage was in difficulties. One day Dorothy actually packed her bags after a row. I ran to her with my pack of Coronation money – about five coins in a thick polythene pack which children were given to celebrate the Queen's Coronation in 1953 - which was my pride and joy. I said she could have it if she would stay. Dorothy said it broke her heart and she stayed for a while longer.

Chapter 2

TWO BOILED EGGS, PLEASE

By 1957 I had left Dunottar for another boarding school, Knighton House School at Durweston, near Blandford in Dorset. It was close to Bryanston public school. My father was a great believer in boarding school education, he thought it taught children to have more respect for their home and their parents and also helped to give them a sense of team spirit, loyalty and self-preservation. I agree with him now because it does create something of a 'them and us' mentality with 'them' being the teachers, the matron and the other staff and 'us' being the kids. It's not really like that but it does make the kids all pull together, making sure they protect each other, a bit like the old trade union mentality of one out, all out. I look back on my boarding school days fondly now and think they instilled into me much of my outlook on life – and of course, without being too cynical, my father's lifestyle made it very convenient for him to believe in them.

He arrived at Knighton House one day to take me home for half-term with a very pretty girl called Colette, whom he introduced as his social secretary. I think that's a wonderful euphemism for 'girlfriend' but it sounded very plausible to me at the time! Then, in the car, he told me that I was going to America with him in a few days' time and that I would not be going back to school for the rest of term, which I guess might not go down too well these days. Then, in the same breath, he mentioned that Dorothy had returned to New Zealand to see her family and wouldn't be coming back. But my excitement over an extended trip to America and not returning to school completely distracted me from the news about Dorothy. That sounds terrible now but to a small child, it was a case of priorities!

A few days later, on June 20, 1957, we boarded the *USS United States* liner at Southampton to sail to New York. Colette was with us and Leo and Joan Villa and other members of Dad's team. The *Bluebird* was sitting very proudly on the deck as precious cargo and I suppose it caused a bit of a stir. I'm sure some passengers knew who my father was but I wasn't aware of any fuss around him. I had a connecting cabin with my dad and the whole journey was the height of luxury travel and so exciting for me, as it would be for any young child in those days. The entire trip was full of 'firsts' for me.

The ship had two pools and Leo spent a lot of time teaching me to swim during those six days – he was so diligent that by the time we reached New York I was pretty good. But I must have been a real nuisance, wanting to spend the entire trip like a fish. One day it was deemed too rough to swim safely as the water sloshed backwards and forwards with the movement of the boat and while I was so unhappy having to forego my swimming, Leo was probably delighted with a day off at last.

We were heading for Canandaigua in upstate New York, one of the finger lakes off the Great Lakes, where Dad was going to make an attempt on the water speed record. The Lake itself was huge – you could not see from one end to the other or even across its width – and there were lots of ski boats and speedboats of all sizes running around it. It was very much a holiday place for upstate New Yorkers and we stayed in a place called Redwood Lodge, a sort of B&B, I guess, which had a little chalet in the garden where I slept with Dad and Colette. It can be very hot in upstate New York at that time of the year and I got terribly sunburned after my first couple of days spent around the Lake. I had to lie in a darkened room, smothered in calamine lotion, which Colette came in to apply. She was a pretty girl, dark, plumpish – my father didn't like skinny women; he used to say: 'Who would want to cuddle a broom handle anyway?' But she was very kind to me then. I feel awful that I didn't miss Dorothy and I didn't even realise that my real mother was just not in my life at all. Just then, it was Colette.

The place was called the Bluebird Theme Park, which held British-style 'ceremonies' – someone had brought soil from England for the site and visitors would pay a few cents to go round the park. There were

Coca-Cola machines all over the place and a guy would go round every day filling them. I was obviously quite wily because I would follow him and say: 'I put a dime in there yesterday and nothing came out!' Then he would give me a bottle free. I'm sure he knew all about my little trick, but he gave me them anyway.

There was a beautiful old mansion house in the park, home to a man called Howard J. Samuels, an American industrialist and statesman who was a special adviser in the administrations of three Presidents – Johnson, Ford and Carter. He was also president of the Canan Lake Promotions and he and his wife Bobbie invited me to stay with them and their family. They had lots of children – eight I think – and I went to school with them which was so different from anything I had experienced. I even had a beautiful, flowery satchel with zips and bangles hanging from it, unlike the awful brown, ugly satchel I used back home, with jangling clasps and straps which split.

Every morning in the classroom, the Stars and Stripes was raised and all the kids and the teacher sang the national anthem with their right hand clasped firmly to their heart. No one dared even flutter an eyelid during the ritual. School was fun, though, and seemed so less strict than in the UK. After school we would all go to the YMCA, where we played games and sports, went in the gym and had great times. I was in seventh heaven.

On the bus back from school, I became friendly with another family who, on reflection, were I think what the Samuels would have called 'rough.' They didn't approve of my friendship with them. But the family had loads of horses and ponies and soon I was riding 'western style' with them across the fields and even though it was all new to me, I soon picked it up. We'd ride to what they called Death Valley, which had a huge rope swing across a ravine, and they told me stories of people being killed there, which scared me a lot and gave me nightmares about the eerie place. One day their father shot a dog which came on to his land, he shot it right in the eye, it was absolutely horrible. I knew it belonged to a family down the lane and I went and told them.

I had no real idea what my father was doing, although I did hear the word 'work' mentioned quite frequently. That didn't mean a lot to me but it would have involved a lot of shaking hands, raising awareness of the Lake and its virtues and, of course, preparing *Bluebird* for the record attempt with all the testing and trials that that involved. My father's work was clearly different from that of other kids' parents, who were doctors, dentists, shop managers and assistants but somehow I didn't see it that way at that age. Anyway I barely gave it a second thought because I was having such a good time with the Samuels family. They grew their own corn on the cob and we used to pick it in the garden, cook and eat it. I had my first taste of peanut butter, too, and chocolate spread, lots of goodies that kids love but which we didn't have in post-war Britain, where they would have been unaffordable luxuries.

My father made several record attempts on the Lake during our stay. I sometimes mooched around the building which had been built to house *Bluebird*, where there was a gantry to roll her down into the lake. I saw a few runs – you can't help but notice because it's so noisy – but I just know it never went right and, in fact, all sorts of things went wrong. There were a lot of pleasure craft on the lake and they could not police it sufficiently to stop the washes from their boats. With hindsight it was probably ill-conceived. They later took the Bluebird to the Canadian National Exposition for two weeks and we were there on my eighth birthday. There was a wee party and all the guys who worked for Dad gave me a little watch, with a card saying 'from the team.' It is the only birthday party that I can remember as a child.

It sounds idyllic now but where was my dad? Where was my mum? I remember Dorothy, Colette, later Dory Swann, a very glamorous model who went to live in America, various girls – I cannot put a name to all of them. Would they care about me? I'm sure they thought, 'Bloody little brat,' but they had to accept I came with the territory if they wanted to be with this superstar. I bet they wished they'd had the odd sleeping tablet to slip into my drink to keep me quiet when it wasn't convenient for me to be around.

I don't remember any affection, caring, love. I didn't have my father's love, I probably didn't love him, but I didn't half respect him. If he said jump, it wasn't a case of why, it was how high. I knew what was right and wrong and I truly believe that kids don't have to think for themselves today, everything is piled on the plate and shoved in front of them.

When I look back now, conceitedly I think I was lucky; lucky not to have all that schmaltz, feted with fancy clothes and toys, because I think I'm a better person for that. It's made me into the person I am. At least I'm not some wishy-washy spineless creature, I'm not scared by what the big wide world has to throw at me. I'll make my own decisions.

On reflection too, I believe my father did the best for me in the way he knew how. He didn't praise me, he didn't participate in my life, but what difference would it have made? It might have made it even harder when I lost him. One could say he did not get close to me for knowing one day I might lose him; but I don't believe that.

I flew home with Leo and his wife Joan and by the time we landed back in the UK, my father was living in an apartment in Dolphin Square in central London. The apartments had a swimming pool and a very glamorous girl called Sabrina used to swim there. She was a model and a minor film actress – as famous as Katie Price is today – and there were always people in the restaurant overlooking the pool, watching her. I used to be shy about swimming there and I would never go at lunchtime because there would be people about. I never wanted to be watched then and I still loathe being watched now. When I play golf, if there are people round the first tee, I'll run out quickly and tee off... I hate being scrutinised, I'm very susceptible to scrutiny. I'm very sensitive to criticism too, which must stem from those years.

I was still a boarder at Knighton House, which, happily for me, gave riding lessons, as horses and ponies were so important to me by then. In class we wore grey divided skirts but if we were out in the grounds we had to wear red dungarees so you stood out like a sore thumb. It became really fashionable for your dungarees to be as faded as possible, not bright red but a nasty mellow pink with patches in the knees – that was your street cred. Girls who were leaving would sell their dungarees and there was a squabble as to who got the oldest, most faded pairs.

That's the school where I got the other scar on my head when I smashed into some iron railings. We used to give each other rides on a pair of metal gates which would swing round and while we were waiting for games, we'd pile all these girls on the gates and push it through180 degrees. This day, someone must have slid the handle out because I crashed against the railings, blood everywhere, and I broke my nose and damaged my knee. There were girls practising Christmas carols in one of the school buildings at the time, me hollering like a stuck pig outside and suddenly all these faces at the window. These huge shrieks of horror interrupting the school carol singing, not from the pain but from the blood; I really have a thing about blood. I ended up at the hospital and came away with little butterfly stitches across my head.

All the girls had lovely tuck boxes – an old chocolate box or biscuit tin with their name on. They were kept in a locked cupboard and the girls had to stand in line and the teacher would reach down each box and allow them to take a Kit Kat, a Mars bar, a Crunchie, but just one, not the whole box. I didn't have one so I used to stand there waiting for someone to give me a bite. Every letter I wrote, often to my dad's secretary Rosie Pielow, I would say: 'Dear Mrs Pielow, could you send me some sweets please?'

It wasn't because of any meanness on my dad's part, just a complete oversight and the lack of parental involvement. I was out of sight, out of mind, pay the bills and get rid of her to school. I often used to inherit cast-off school uniforms because there was no-one consistently at home to make sure I had what I needed – new blouses, a new skirt. Everyone else would start the term in nice new stuff but not me.

It was that year, on Christmas Eve 1958, that my father married his third wife Tonia Bern and there I am with a silly short fringe because the nurse had cut my hair to stitch my forehead. I wore a pale blue coat with a little collar. Tonia was a singer and actress, terribly glamorous, the exact opposite of Dorothy, and they were married at Caxton Hall Register Office – I remember Tonia trapping her finger in the car door after the ceremony.

The wedding breakfast was at The Savoy and I sat next to Terry Thomas, the actor.

When the waiter came round, frightfully posh, and asked me what I wanted for my meal, I said: 'I think I'd like two boiled eggs, please.' And Terry Thomas said: 'What an amazingly good idea, I think I'll have the same.' What a prize memory!

But then my father and Tonia went off to Courchevel on honeymoon. They left me at home – well you can hardly take your daughter on your honeymoon – probably staying with some of Dad's friends. I was a bit like an exhibit – I came out when it was appropriate and was put back in the box when it wasn't. People could say I didn't have family love or the stability of a home, but I believe I was extremely privileged. What I lacked in one department – and I was not aware I lacked anything then – I gained in wonderful experiences.

How many kids ate boiled eggs at The Savoy at their father's wedding breakfast or sailed to America in the early 60s and went to school with the children of an American statesman? How many attended the Princess Grace Ball in Monte Carlo with their father, when Sammy Davis Junior and Lena Horne provided the entertainment? I was 13 or 14 at the time and I don't remember their startling performances but I remember being there. Now when I go to Monte Carlo and look up at the pink palace, I think: 'I was there'. Yet I never had a family birthday party, except that one in Canada, which is why it had stayed in my memory.

Soon after his honeymoon, we moved into a beautiful house south of Reigate called Roundwood, so named because it stood in around ten acres of land completely surrounded by – yes, a wood. Apparently he had always admired this house but for some reason hadn't been able to buy it before. It had lots of outbuildings too and a circular drive with a cherry tree in the middle, the most fabulous gardens designed in the style of Capability Brown, with dozens of rose bushes. And it had a petrol pump in the garden – it was always known as the house with the petrol pump.

I loved it there. For an adventurous child it felt like an Aladdin's cave with so many places to explore. It was a lovely old house, miles from anywhere – not by today's standards but the nearest neighbours were a way away. Reigate was the nearest town, which was then just a little two-lane place. There was an oak-panelled dining room where we had a painting of a beautiful nude leaning against a tree. She was very voluptuous but the picture was tasteful and in a huge ornate frame. My father used to make a big business of carving the meat in there for Sunday lunches – there were great big stains of fat splashes on the panelling – and he'd glance up at the painting and say she reminded him of a woman called Marjorie Brown. She was the second wife of David Brown, a friend of Dad's, who had bought Aston Martin and Lagonda in the 1940s but he also made gear boxes for the *Bluebird CN7* car. The DB series of Aston Martins, like the one driven by James Bond, were named after him, using his initials. He was knighted in 1968 so they became Lord and Lady Brown. One day when someone was looking round our house and commented on the painting, I said: 'Oh yes, that's Lady Brown.' My dad had said she looked like her so often that I thought it was her. Out of the mouths of babes and sucklings, eh?

My father also had an office in the house and the telephone number was Norwood Hill 16 but to make a call you had to ring and speak to the operator first. As time went on we got really posh and had two numbers. If the phone rang at Roundwood he'd often ask me to answer it and to always ask who was calling. I'd tell him and he'd ask me to make some excuse if he didn't want to speak to them. I'd be frightfully polite and say: 'He's indisposed.' My father used to say that when he was in the privacy of his own home, just because someone wanted to speak to him, didn't mean he wanted to speak to them. It's fair comment – the telephone and the mobile phone have become complete commands in our lives and he wouldn't allow that.

There were also staff quarters on the third floor and a lovely sitting room with a TV for them behind the downstairs kitchen which had a row of old-fashioned bells which went ding-dong to tell them which room was calling. We had staff there all the time; once we had a Belgian couple Louis and Julia Goossens – Louis liked a good drink. Tonia found them when she was visiting her father who owned a hotel in Knokke in Belgium. Then a Spanish couple – he was called Vincente. I had some happy times there.

Roundwood is where my father bought me my first pony called Columbine, although the first evening after she arrived, she broke free and galloped all over the beautiful gardens and undid in ten minutes what it had taken the garden designer years to perfect! I used to ride her down a bridleway, about half a mile down the road from Roundwood, past a place called Stumblehole – it's still there.

It was at Stumblehole that by pure chance, I finally met up with my mother again. At school I had received birthday cards saying 'love from mummy', which I always knew were not in Dorothy's writing but would think nothing else about it. And there would be Christmas presents, supposedly from Father Christmas, which I realised later must have been from her. It was only later too that I learned that my father was fiercely protective of her trying to make contact with me, but strangely I never asked about her, I was never curious. She never came to see me although her mother – my grandmother – visited me once or twice. I think she probably felt some sort of sadness that her daughter could just discard her own child in such a callous way.

However one day, when I was out riding, I saw huge building works going on at Stumblehole – apparently it was to be a state-of-the art stud farm. It was owned by a woman called Jennifer Biggs – and she was big! A while later, my father told me he had been invited to the grand opening of Stumblehole and he wanted me to go with him. It was out of character for my father to take me with him – he was a 'children should be seen and not heard' person but he knew I loved anything to do with horses.

It seemed to me that there were hundreds of people there although I don't remember any other children. I was just a scrap of a child anyway and everyone else looked huge. After a while I noticed a woman who was staring at me for a long time and I told Daddy. He looked across and then looked down to me and said: 'That's your mother. I think we'd better go and say hello.'

She was with her second husband, Tony, a huge man, in contrast to my mother, who was tiny like me. I think he later was honoured in the Queen's Birthday Honours List. It was the most extraordinary occasion – Dad was with Tonia and the five of us joined up for the rest of the evening. It was bizarre but I couldn't understand why everybody wasn't having a good time. How naïve can you be?

I overheard my father saying to Tonia that from here on in, life would be trouble. It turned out that my mother and Tony had also bought a stud farm, Hill House Farm, not four or five miles away from Roundwood, over towards Newdigate. So from then on it became torment for me as a child because she now decided that she wanted to see me. I'd ride over to her place and instead of my pony going into the wooden shed that was its stable at home and quite adequate, she would be led into a big foam-lined stable, groomed and her tack all cleaned while I had a cup of tea before riding home again. It was like visiting an aunt or something…I never slept a night there as a child.

But she told me that if I kept my pony there, it would have this treatment all the time. Of course all I wanted was the best for my pony and to hell with anything else. So I'd go home to my father and say that Mummy says I can keep the pony there. And he'd say: 'Well, take the bloody pony there if that's how you feel.' And then as soon as I told Mummy that Daddy said I could bring the pony over, she would change her mind. She would always have an excuse: 'It's not really convenient at the moment, dear, we haven't got a spare stable.' But then I didn't see that as a fob off, I saw it as a genuine excuse.

Another time, I think around 1961 when my father was going off to recce Australia as a venue for his record attempts, he said it would be a very good idea if I went to stay with my mother. I knew I could take the pony and thought it would be wonderful. He said he would ring her to sort it out and told me to pick up the extension, but not to interrupt. And when he said 'do not' do something, he meant it. The phone rang and the conversation went:

Dad: 'Daphne?'

Mummy: 'Yes, Donald.'

Dad: 'Tonia and I are off to Australia in 10 days' time and thought it would be a wonderful opportunity for Gina and the pony to come to you, seeing as you have the facilities and you've been telling her how much you'd love to have her there. She could help you around the place and with the horses – she's just dying to come.'

Mummy: 'Oh well Donald, no, no. I'm terribly sorry that wouldn't be at all convenient. I have problems with the cleaner and with the stud at the moment – the stud groom is away. No, no, I'm really very, very sorry, it just wouldn't be convenient at all. It just can't happen.'

Dad: 'OK Daphne, I just thought you might say that. Goodbye.'

He hung up and said to me: 'That's how much your mother wants you.' He obviously wanted me to hear it for myself. And it may sound strange but I cannot remember feeling hurt. I was one of those kids, and I'm still like it as an adult, who took whatever life threw at me. I don't ever look too deeply into anything, I just accept it. I think that's a legacy of my early years.

My mother never had a hair out of place – I know she went to bed with rollers in her hair. She was tweedy, wore brogues…and the red nails. And the house was pristine – annoyingly you'd get up from your seat and when you came back, the cushions would have been plumped. And Tony was just as bad as she was, prissy, prissy.

And yet they had these fucking dogs, Chihuahuas and Pekinese – they even started breeding Chihuahuas. The dogs would sit there and yap every time you got up from the chair. I love dogs but somehow I detested these. They weren't dogs, they were like rats. One was called Belle and my mother would French kiss with these dogs. I don't mind a dog giving you a lick, but she'd sit there with the dog with its tongue in her mouth and vice versa. French kissing with the dogs! I couldn't believe my eyes. Tony was as bad. Somehow my mother had this ability to make every man she was with end up as bad as she was and behave in the same way. Extraordinary – she had an incredible hold on men. My father hated her, hated her, hated her by that time and that was because he had truly loved her. I'm told you can never truly hate someone you have never loved.

There was a very strict routine at the stud. At about 4pm there would be the grand bringing-in of the horses. My mother insisted on dressing herself up in the groom's-type outfit with headscarf and green wellies, which she would then discard in the garage when she came back. If I was very lucky, I could go with them but even with my knowledge of horses, I wasn't allowed to touch. I would walk behind like a lame duck. I'm sure they thought I was much too stupid as a child and the horses much too valuable for me to be allowed to do any more.

Once that was finished, she would say: 'Right, Tony and I are going for our bath now – we bathe together.' They were always terribly lovey-dovey, they would sit right next to each other on a huge sofa and hold hands; he would light two cigarettes, one for her, and they seemed absolutely together. But it turned out that it was all a sham. She later told me it was a complete façade – they slept in separate rooms and came to loathe one another.

I didn't know that then, of course, so it came totally out of the blue when she told me one day, when Tony was away, that she was having an affair with the guy who sold them corn and hay. And she wanted me to meet this man, her lover. So she drove me in the car to a café, a popular little place right on the high stretch of the road out of Dorking, which goes up over the Downs and there we met this lover – I cannot remember his name. She had even bought him a sports car. He had lost the sight in one eye, which my mother said was as a result of the excitement of this new love!

Dad was away at the time but as we had staff, I had stayed at home. So when he arrived back from the States, the first thing I said to him, as any child would, was that Mummy's having an affair with a man and I've met him. I recounted the story and I could see him killing himself with laughter behind his eyes. So he picked up the telephone and called her to say he thought we'd better discuss the daughter's future, and could Daphne come over. I'll never forget that evening, with my mother and Tony, my father and Tonia all sitting in the lounge when he calls me in and says: 'Did you tell me, Gina, that your mother is having an affair?'

My mother is gobsmacked – Tony doesn't know anything about it. Talk about a situation. I burst into tears, it was awful. I have to say yes. I can't even think of words to describe the atmosphere. Tonia's pissing herself with laughter and I'm sure my father is, too. My mother is screaming in hysterics. Tony says: 'We don't have to sit here and listen to this.' But my father carries on. 'You tell me you've met this man, Gina?'

'Yes Daddy, yes Mummy, I have haven't I?'

My mother has to admit it and they leave.

My father had relished every moment – he loved it, watching her squirm. He told me later that he needed to know that I was telling the truth because he knew she was the most appalling liar and did not want me to be a chip off the old block. But this time she had no choice but to come clean.

I don't think her marriage ended there but all of a sudden all her horses were gone, except for a couple of special ones. She turned all the stables into pigeon lofts and bought extraordinary exotic pigeons and doves from all around the world. She later had all the gardens laid out with tortoise pens – she had all these weird and wonderful fads, which passed as fast as they came. When I look back, her whole life was like this; she jumped from one situation to another.

My situation was about to change, too, because I did not go back to Knighton House after the summer holidays. There was a General Election in 1958 and when my father found out that the headmaster was a Labour politician, he was so incensed he took me away. He was a staunch Conservative and could not accept that a man running a private school for girls, most of whom were never going to have to work, was standing as a Labour candidate. Whether that was the only reason he took me away, I'm not sure.

So my father found a school where the head said she would take my pony. But having driven down there with the Land Rover, the trailer and the pony and unloaded, she then said my pony had to be kept outside. My father had a row with her and within two hours we were loading up again and going home. So instead I went to The Warren in Worthing.

I hadn't been there long when a girl about my age, but a stout girl, much bigger than me, came up to me and said: 'I'm Susan, I'm your cousin.' Imagine that – I didn't even know she existed and I certainly hadn't met her before. She was Susan Gamble, the eldest daughter of my mother's sister Pat, but because my mother just wasn't in my life, I didn't know any of her relatives. That just shows what a dysfunctional family we were. Sadly Susan has died now but her two sisters and brother, also my cousins of course, all live in the Bahamas now.

It was from there that me and a school friend Carol Bass – we must have been about 13 – had a bit of adventure when we decided to ride over to her parents' summer cottage at Wittering one day instead of going to lessons. Our ponies were kept at the commercial stables next to the school so we went through the wicker gate, saddled our ponies and rode off. But it was further than we thought and because it was a winter afternoon it started to get dark and began to rain. Before long we had no idea how to get back to school. We were wet, cold and hungry so when we saw lights in a large house off the road, we rode up the drive.

It turned out to be a stately home called Parham Park and the door was answered by the butler. We said we were lost and wanted to hire a horse box to take us and our ponies back to Wittering. He went away to make us a cup of tea, served in china cups. He kindly rang a couple of people with cattle lorries but when he had no luck he decided to call the police. Before too long, two police patrol cars arrived – and the owners of the house who had been out for the evening came back too. The police drove us back to school and the generous owner offered to stable our ponies for the night. It turned out that staff at the school had panicked when they discovered we were missing and they handed out a pretty severe punishment. We were not allowed to ride for weeks, we were denied any other privileges and, worse, made to take our meals with the seven-year-olds in the junior school.

Chapter 3

VIENS ICI POUR UN CAFÉ, MA PETITE

By the time I was 15, I had moved to yet another school, Iford Manor in Lewes, which was known as a top class riding academy. It was owned by a lady called Miss Nelson who all the girls thought was obviously gay. Her friend was Miss Wilson and they were known by us as Willie and Nellie. All the girls brought their ponies and we had to get up early in the mornings to look after them. We'd have academic lessons in the mornings but spent the afternoons with the horses, not just riding but going through the formal British Horse Society courses.

Miss Nelson was strict, strict, strict – everything had to be just so and she would inspect every last sheaf of straw which had to be flat and banked. Your pony would be tied up and she would inspect the rugs, the grooming, everything. You'd lay your pony's bed so it was immaculate and then the bloody thing would whip round and scuff it up – you'd pray she would make the inspection when it was perfect. Although the discipline was immense, it didn't seem out of the norm to me because my father was a real disciplinarian.

We used to give riding displays and we competed regularly against other schools, including Benenden – we would go there and they would come to us. This is where I came across Princess Anne – I wasn't particularly conscious of her being a princess, she was always known as PA. When I met her again at Buckingham Palace in December 2011, when I was invited to a reception hosted by the Queen to celebrate Exploration and Adventure, I reminded her of those days. I remember two other girls who were there – Fiona Forbes and Vanessa De Quincey – who I really used to look up to because they had the best ponies. Fiona's married name is Marner and she is now one of Europe's top bloodstock photographers – I know she specialises in posed portraits of horses.

Although I didn't see much of my father while I was there, when school broke up for the Easter holidays in 1963, I was told I was to fly out to Australia where he was going to make his second attempt on the world land speed record. That's how life was – one minute I was in school and life revolved around ponies, the next I was heading off across the world.

My father's first attempt on the land speed record had been back in 1960 at Bonneville Salt Flats near Salt Lake City in Utah where, in 1935, his father had become the first man to exceed 300 miles per hour. That was to be the last of my grandfather's amazing nine world land speed records. My father's car, another *Bluebird* of course, was designed by Ken and Lewis Norris and was officially known as *CN7*, as in Campbell Norris. It was built in Coventry at a cost of £1,000,000, the most expensive car of its time.

Bluebird CN7 was to be unveiled in a huge blaze of glory at a special day organised at Goodwood race circuit, owned by Lord March, in May that year. The week before, my father had taken it to Tangmere, a small airfield near Shoreham, just as a trial to make sure everything was in working order. It was a beautiful sunny day at Goodwood and there were thousands of spectators and dozens of press photographers and reporters. And my father actually managed to negotiate this huge jet-engined vehicle round the track, which considering it only had a four degree lock each way, was a pretty special achievement. He drove it under power and, with an idling speed of 180 miles per hour, did not use the throttle at all. Apparently he had to keep the brakes on the whole way round.

His actual send-off was almost as spectacular, at a specially arranged dinner with lots of friends at London's Café Royal. During the evening his solicitor Victor Mischon produced a new will which had to be signed and witnessed – would you believe by members of The Crazy Gang, a group of entertainers who were friends of my father. It sounds pretty dramatic now but I suppose my father knew there was a chance he might never come back.

So off he went to Bonneville Salt Flats and while he was there, I was down in Sussex staying with some friends who ran a kind of summer holiday camp for kids, but all based around horses. I spent my time riding, going to gymkhanas, having a great time. Then one day, I think it was September 17, just before my birthday, as soon as I came in from the ponies, they told me we were all going to the cinema and whisked me off in no time. I couldn't understand it because they'd never mentioned the cinema before. But it turned out that my father had had a massive accident which had hit the papers and they wanted to keep me away from it.

Little did they realise that their great ploy to shield me from it was to completely backfire because there, on the Pathé News, was my father's accident. His attempt ended when the car left the track, where marks showed she was airborne for 275 yards before bouncing four times and sliding to a standstill. I saw him walk away from the crash but he had a pierced eardrum and a fractured skull although by the time he reached hospital his only concern was how soon *Bluebird* would be ready for another record attempt. That was so typical of him, he never seemed to dwell on the risk to himself, but in fact the car was totally written off.

But he was also hurt psychologically, very badly and, in my opinion, what hit him was that he knew it was his own damn fault. He tried to make 101 excuses about the oxygen mix being too rich so many feet below sea level, but what experience did he have at driving a car at over 360 miles per hour? I don't think anyone knew exactly what went wrong but I don't think that my father could quite stand up tall enough to say it was human error. He shuffled round it, but never really admitted it.

He was pretty miserable when he came back and he received a lot of criticism but Sir Alfred Owen, a Midlands industrialist, agreed to build another Bluebird. He said if my father was willing to make another attempt, he was willing to build another car. It was very low and sleek and interestingly, this time it was designed with a tail fin to give it a bit more stability. The first one didn't have that tail fin.

While the new *Bluebird* was being built, my father was up and down from home to Coventry to monitor its progress and he would sometimes take me with him. I remember sitting in the car once, waiting for him, and seeing the spire on the new Coventry Cathedral which was finally put back in place in April 1962. But because my father was a qualified pilot and had his own plane, first a single-engined Comanche and later a twin-engined Piper Apache which he based at Redhill aerodrome and then later at Gatwick, we would usually fly up to Coventry.

He had always wanted to fly and set his heart on being a fighter pilot in the RAF in the Second World War. He almost made it. But after he was accepted as a trainee with the humble rank of A/C2, the RAF number 964147 and a uniform, a medical revealed that he had a heart murmur as a result of suffering from rheumatic fever as a child. His pleas to be sent for aircrew training were rejected and he went home to civvy street in despair. But he later trained as a private pilot and loved to fly whenever he could. If he was going to Brighton, he'd fly to Shoreham; anywhere he could fly to, he would.

He flew Tonia and I down to the South of France once, but what a long day! We flew from Redhill to Lydd, then cleared Customs, Lydd to Le Touquet, cleared Customs again and then Le Touquet to Vichy. All this time you're just sitting in a small chair and God forbid that you want to go to the toilet. Usually Dad and Tonia would sit at the front with me behind, but sometimes Tonia and I would change places and we could just manage to shuffle past each other. It was like being in a bubble, you couldn't really stand up. I think we were only allowed to take ten pounds in weight of luggage each.

We had some food at Vichy and were then planning to fly on to La Bocca, the small airport at Cannes, when my dad was warned that the weather was pretty rough. But, typical of him, although he was very safety conscious, if someone said he couldn't do something, he was off. So off we went. The weather was dreadful, we were bouncing around like a cork in a rough sea and we had to turn back. I was terrified and I think that's why I'm scared of flying today. We had to wait till the weather improved and then we flew on to Cannes.

Another time he flew us to Geneva to go skiing – he wasn't licensed to land at Courchevel, because you needed special training to negotiate the mountains, the approach and landing on snow. When we arrived at Geneva and hired a car, he was warned that he would never make the drive to Courchevel that day as the smaller roads were snow covered and pretty much impassable. But, no, typical Dad, we set off, snaking up the hills, with him cursing the car for not holding the road, me in the back not daring to look down at the long drops to either side, until we finally made it.

When *Bluebird* was finally ready at the end of 1962, and my father was fit again, the team decided the next attempt would be at Lake Eyre in Australia the following year. He asked his friend Ken Burville, an ex-Squadron leader, to fly the plane out to Australia for him and Ken bunny-hopped his way half way round the world, through Asia, to get there. In contrast, I was taken to Heathrow Airport by my father's secretary Rosemary Pielow with my ticket, a suitcase and some traveller's cheques. I probably felt quite important – after all how many kids in their teens flew to somewhere like Australia in those days?

I flew out there with David Wynne-Morgan, my father's PR man, who spent most of the flight fast asleep. We had a stopover in San Francisco, where I had to share a hotel room with him. He went out for a night on the town and I remember him coming back, banging and crashing into the room and collapsing on the bed. In the middle of the night we were broken into and all David's money, his watch and his jewellery were stolen. We slept through the whole thing and in the morning the police said we were damn lucky we stayed asleep. I'm sure there were currency restrictions then but I know I had to cash some traveller's cheques so that we had some money between us.

His girlfriend at the time was a famous model called Primrose Austin, photographed by all the top names including Terence Donovan. She had been out to Australia with David on a previous trip and spent some time in the house my father had rented on the beach at Brighton in Adelaide, because the team had been back and forth. Apparently they had a huge row one day, completely fell out and when Tonia got back to the house, Primrose had scrawled in lipstick all over the mirrors in the bathroom 'f... off you bastard.'

When I arrived, I was told straight away not to go into the water because they said someone had dived into the sea there once – God knows when once was – and never came up again because a shark had grabbed her. I was probably told that just to scare me because I was rather prone to trying something I'd been told not to do but this time I took notice of their warning.

My first sight of Lake Eyre was from the plane. You cannot imagine the enormity of it, around 450 square miles, about a third of the size of Wales. In England, there cannot be anywhere where you can look and look and look and see nothing. But at Lake Eyre there was just this enormous expanse of nothing, no vegetation, no trees, just flies, trillions of flies that you couldn't possibly avoid. The saddest thing was that the children who lived on the sheep station nearby all had sore, infected eyes because when the flies came near their faces, instead of wafting them away, they rubbed them into their eyes.

It had not rained at Lake Eyre for many, many years, leaving the lake bed rock-hard salt, ideal for my father's land speed attempt. But there were so many traumas that year – and although it hadn't rained for so long in that part of Oz, as soon as he arrived in March, it rained, and rained, and rained. Australian army engineers built a causeway across the marshy area around the edges of the lake to take the equipment across and that in itself was a nightmare. And the salt bed is not a uniform thickness – in one place it's thin, in another thicker – and at times vehicles fell through the salt crust, a bit like going through ice. My father made a documentary film about it – he was good with a cine camera. He took the 20-minute film to the Venice Film Festival and won an award. I still have a copy of it.

The nearest town was Marree and we lived on a sheep station called Muloorina, owned by a man called Elliot Price and his wife. He'd built houses for his sons and daughters all around and there were sheep pens and barns, but strangely we never saw a damn sheep!

When my dad and everyone descended on the place, we lived in caravans. It was basic, basic living with outside dunnies, the Aussie slang for toilets. There were about 20 of Dad's personnel and it was the job of Tonia, Leo Villa's wife Joan and me to look after them. These men had to have their clothes washed, their beds made, sheets changed, food prepared – that was our daily routine. It was hot, dry, dusty and the chores could take you all day. I was really a glorified charlady but I had been brought up to do what I was told to do and Tonia was a martyr about the whole thing, she revelled in being one of the boys and even took the nickname Fred.

It was a godforsaken place. There was no shade and when the rain came, the lake flooded and the *Bluebird* would be in the water. Once I remember everyone rushing down there in the dark in Land Rovers and my father deciding to drive her off the lake under power, no headlights. Just imagine – here was probably the most expensive four-wheel drive that had ever been built, and maybe that is still so today, and it had to be driven in the dark through this maelstrom, across the causeway which was just dirt – the risk of *Bluebird* toppling over was enormous. At the time I probably thought 'big deal' but on reflection, I realise the emotion and tension and stress that must have built up. Sure enough the lake was flooded in the morning.

Then there were the winds which could be severe. We once had a real mad dash to get the aeroplanes off the lake because a tornado was coming and it would literally have just picked them up and smashed them to pieces.

My father just bundled Tonia and me into his plane with Tonia next to him and me in the back. He was such a diligent man normally and would always spend time checking every single thing before he flew but on this day it was a case of 'get in and let's go'. He said we reached 1,000 feet but I don't know how high we were when suddenly there was a noise like an explosion and the door blew open. It didn't flap right back but everything loose in the plane went woosh and disappeared. I just felt as though the flesh on my face and my hair were being pulled back. Tonia and I managed to grab the door and hold it in the gap – we all did our bit. My father knew to drop the plane down although it felt like it was descending like a stone. It was pretty scary. We managed to reach Muloorina and it felt more like landing in a helicopter. I think that's something pilots do if there's a problem, just drop down.

By mid-May it was clear the lake was not suitable for any more attempts, so it was time for most of us to head home and I travelled back with Leo and Joan Villa as chaperones. I think my father and Tonia stayed on in Australia. However, he returned soon afterwards to stories of how everything had gone wrong and he was pilloried in the newspapers. Sponsors withdrew and there were rows and recriminations.

But he was determined not to give up and he returned to Australia the following year and achieved something no-one else had ever done. After setting a new land speed record in July, he became the only man to hold both the world land and water speed records in the same year when, on New Year's Eve, he set a new water speed record at Lake Dumbleyung in Western Australia. That is some feat.

I didn't go with my father on his return trip to Lake Eyre. Instead I was having my own adventures. My father sent me to the South of France, where he had some friends called Pam and Neville Flower, who lived in Mougins in the hills about 15 minutes from Cannes. Because my grandfather had sent my father to France to learn the language, he decided it was a good thing for me to do as well, so I was to live with the Flowers as their au pair. They were English but spoke very good French and I'm sure my dad paid them to have me. She had this fine, blonde hair, so long that she could sit on it, and she used to sunbathe topless, which I thought was a bit shocking then. They had a little boy called David, I think he was three, and at that time I thought he was completely obnoxious.

They lived in a small house on a teeny lane with a kind of outside garage, which was where I slept. On regular days I would work in the morning and then in the afternoons, Pam would drive me down to Cannes in her Mini where I went to the Berlitz language school on the Croisette. The Flowers spoke French in the house but that wasn't really teaching me.

When the lessons were finished I couldn't wait to get out on the beach. Sometimes I would lie my way on to the private hotel beaches and other times go round to the public beach. I remember one day going into a hotel to go to the loo and when I walked into the lift, Yul Brynner was already in there. He was such a big film star at the time – he'd starred in *The King and I* and *The Magnificent Seven* – and absolutely unmistakable. Eventually, after I'd topped up my tan and when it was time for me to prepare David's tea, I'd make my way back to the Flowers' house on the bus.

That's also where I lost my virginity. I met this man – not a boy, he was a lot older than me – called Gerald, the French pronunciation made it sound so much more romantic! On one of my rare weekends off, he decided to take me to the islands off Cannes, Les Iles de Lerins, and that's where it happened. We lay in a little clearing in the sun, hidden from anyone else who may have strolled past, and then when it was all over, we jumped in the sea. But it was the biggest non-event – I thought afterwards: 'Is that it?' When I think back now, I cannot believe the risks I took then.

I began to think I was being treated as something of a dogsbody at the Flowers and I think we had a bit of a fall-out, so I decided to look for another job. By then I was able to speak some French and I found a job with a French family, a delightful lady with three little boys under the age of seven, who was expecting another child. They lived at Gap, much further inland, and I remember taking myself there on the train. I felt I had to do nothing but washing and cleaning, washing and cleaning but I did it. I've never been afraid of hard work, even if I haven't always enjoyed it. I have recollections of family meals around an enormous table – there seemed to be dozens of people, all their extended family.

Then in the summer holidays we were all shipped off to somewhere near Marseilles, to a lovely house with a beautiful garden. They had a Citroen deux-chevaux, a 2CV, not the easiest car to handle. I hadn't passed my driving test but I could drive and in the mornings they'd send me off to get the bread, with the kids in the back. I just had no fear at all – I wouldn't even think of doing it now. I was only 16. Sometimes I'd take them for a quick swim in the sea before we went back.

I didn't stay long with that family after the summer and returned to the Flowers. I remember going back to Cannes on the train and being fascinated by women peasant farmers with chickens on their laps and a goat or two. The Flowers had moved house by then to a place down a little dusty track, just outside Mougins. When I was hanging the washing out on the line, there'd often be this old boy a couple of gardens away who was always poddling around.

He'd shout to me: 'Bonjour ma petite, viens ici pour un cafe.' And I'd always reply: 'Je suis tres occupe'. I mentioned it to the Flowers, that the nice old man kept talking to me and they said he was a famous artist called Picasso. Isn't that incredible? It didn't mean a thing to me then. I wish I had said: 'J'arrive' and got a little etching!

Then there were one or two fun part-time jobs I found myself in Cannes. One was with a rather shabby old Englishman with a shabby old boat which he used to charter for the day out to the islands. I'd be his little waitress, making tomato and mozzarella sandwiches and salads, catering for his guests. He was a miserable old git but he had an old Mini which he used to leave parked by the quay near his boat. On the days I didn't work for him, me and a bunch of pals I'd got to know would wait until we saw him leave harbour, then hot-wire his Mini and race off to a go-karting track at Cannes La Bocca. We'd enjoy the go-karts and then drive back before his regular time for returning from the islands. I got up to some awfully naughty things.

I'd finished with Gerald – he'd have picked up some other little vulnerable virgin when I left for Gap and Marseilles. But I formed a relationship with a Dutch man who was the captain of a yacht, called *Vega*, which looked enormous. I can't remember his name but, like Gerald, he was a lot older than me. All his pals came and kipped on the boat and occasionally took the boat out. He actually gave me a ring but I lost it later in London.

My father and Tonia came down to the South of France around that time and I went to stay with them in their hotel. I told them I had a boyfriend with a yacht and as I knew where it was in the harbour, I wanted to show it off to Tonia. So we went out and walked up and down the quay looking for it, but he'd obviously sailed off into the sunset and I was broken-hearted. It was probably one of my first experiences of realising that nothing is for ever. Suddenly, without telling me, he left. C'est la vie!

At the end of their stay, I was going back to England and my father was going somewhere else, back to Australia I think. We were all packed up in the hotel to go to the airport on two different flights and my father had the most chronic attack of indigestion, so we couldn't leave that day. We stayed on in the hotel and the next day we all flew to Paris together; I was going one way, my father the other. It was still warm, so maybe October time. Paris became fogbound and we were both in separate departure lounges and we could peer through the glass wall at one another but not get together.

Next time I saw Tonia was back in London and after my French escapades, she wisely suggested that I should start to take precautions, use some kind of contraception. But I never liked the idea of taking the pill. She also told me that if I ever needed that kind of help, to go to Dad's secretary Rosie and a year or so later I did just that.

I had been in France when my father broke his land speed record. He reached 403.1 miles per hour to become the first man to beat the 400mph barrier in a conventional four-wheel vehicle and I read about it in an English paper. That may seem strange to people now but it was pretty normal for me, my dad had often been on the opposite side of the world from me.

Then the whole *Bluebird* entourage headed off to Lake Dumbleyung in Western Australia to attempt the water speed record. Apparently they had to travel 1,600 miles from Adelaide by train. Again he was beset by various problems and it took until almost the last minutes of the year, on New Year's Eve, before he finally broke the record at 276.3 miles per hour. It seems ridiculous to say that I hardly have any memory of where I spent that Christmas and New Year, which seems so awful when it was my father's greatest achievement. Although 20 years later I finally made it to Lake Dumbleyung when I was invited to unveil a granite memorial there to commemorate that very special world record.

I'm almost sure I spent that Christmas with good friends of my father's, Bill and Betty Coley who lived in St George's Hill, near Weybridge in Surrey. Their house was very posh, like walking into Buckingham Palace, because probably in those days they were the nouveau riche. Bill and his father were top class scrap metal dealers with a business in Hounslow, near Heathrow, and had a contract to break up all the old aircraft, including the TSR-2 which was developed as a Cold War strike aircraft but scrapped in the mid 1960s because of rising costs. At the time it was top secret.

The Coleys had two children, Christopher and Mary, and once or twice the family took me on holiday with them for a few days. Bill drove an Armstrong Siddeley Sapphire, the poor man's Rolls-Royce of its day, and they once packed us three children in the back with their grandma,

Bill and Betty in the front, to drive to Brixham in Devon, a place my Dad loved too. We got down into the West Country – it was a long drive in those days – and when we stopped, they discovered that Granny was not in fact just asleep, but that she'd died! She had been sitting there quietly; we all thought she was snoozing. They put her in the boot and Bill drove to the nearest town, parked and all trooped off to the police station – it was like something out of a Charlie Chaplin film. I was about nine or 10 so just went along with what was happening without really realising the seriousness. A policeman said he'd come back to the car with us, but when we reached the spot, it had been stolen! Needless to say it wasn't too long before it was found abandoned – the car thieves must have taken one look in the boot and fled.

My father adored Christopher, who was a very bright boy and a star pupil at his public schools. His nickname was Kit but my dad used to call him The Bosun. He was the son my dad never had. We were never boyfriend and girlfriend but we held hands and created a few heart flutters, and it was kind of assumed we might marry one day.

But sadly Christopher was killed in a car accident on the A30 at Hartley Wintney, near Horsham not long after my father died. I think he was about 21. My father's secretary Rosie rang to tell me. It almost destroyed the family. I didn't go to his funeral, didn't do the right thing – it haunted me afterwards. I was working as a live-in girl groom in Hampshire at the time and I had no-one to take me by the hand and arrange for me to go. I was very upset but I don't remember crying with grief. Whether it was because I had not come to terms with the loss of my father I don't know, but I don't like myself for it.

Chapter 4

HE'S HAD A TERRIBLE ACCIDENT

When I finally, finally left school, I spent a few months at St Godrick's secretarial college in Hampstead, learning basic shorthand and typing. I hated it, loathed it and would come up with any excuse not to go. I'm not sure whether it was my mother's idea for me to learn a skill but that was never my father's philosophy. His was very much based on the school of life which is why he sent me to France.

I didn't stay at college for long – I suppose I was guilty of a lack of tenacity and I just wanted to do everything. I felt as though I had so much to do and so little time. I had a Christmas job at Fortnum and Mason in the gift department which used to be downstairs. One day we were told to come in looking especially smart the following morning when it turned out that the Queen was coming to do her Christmas shopping! So the store was of course closed to the public, I think from 9 till 10. It was fascinating just to stand there and watch the Queen walking round, pointing to what she wanted, followed by the staff who wrote down each item. She had such a wonderful air and she very politely nodded to us.

On another day I was standing in the department, dreaming, watching a woman trying different handbags over her arm, looking in the mirror and then trying another one. Then all of a sudden she just walked away with one of them and I spotted it. We had been given a drill to ring the store detectives and I remember they caught this poor woman hightailing it down Piccadilly with the handbag, she even jumped on a bus. And we are talking about an expensive handbag - I think the word 'crocodile' came into the equation.

Then I had another rather more unfortunate incident – a bit of an understatement really. Almost everything in the store was displayed on tables covered with crisp linen tablecloths, very starched. So as I walked between two tables, the tablecloth stuck to my clothes and sort of followed me – and, yes, so did the contents of the table. And it was glassware, no doubt crystal, dozens of beautiful glasses went crashing to the floor. Make no mistake, I did some considerable damage. But they were so nice about it, told me not to worry and explained they were insured for it all.

When Christmas and the sales were over, I looked round for another job and found one at British Eagle International Airlines which was run by a man called Harold Bamberg, a wealthy, polo-playing, bit of a playboy type of fellow. The offices were in Conduit Street, off Regent Street and I was in the charter department, filling out forms.

I was sharing a flat with Jenny and Cherry Loosemore, the daughters of a good friend of my father's, Ralph Loosemore. He ran a marine business in Shoreham-by-Sea and was very involved with the powerboat committee of the Royal Yachting Association. He and his wife Peggy and the girls were regular visitors to Roundwood and when I reached my teenage years, I would go down to Shoreham some Friday nights and enjoy my first taste of misspent youth. The sisters were both a bit older than me and introduced me to an early version of the 1980s' Sloane Ranger lifestyle. I was just 16 but they'd take me to bars, introduce me to boys. The car of the moment was the MGB GT and we judged the boys on how new and shiny their MGB was.

The sisters were already working in London when I started at College and then at Eagle Airlines and I went to share their tiny flat in Earl's Court where we all slept in the one bedroom. Sadly Jenny died when she was quite young but I am still in touch with Cherry.

I used to take the tube in to the Airlines office and one morning I came up the stairs at Piccadilly Circus and there's my father sitting in his E-type Jag at the traffic lights – God knows what he was doing there. He spotted me, knocked on the window, asked where I was going and told me to jump in. Then he drives to the office, walks in with me and the next thing I know, we're in the boss's office having coffee and biscuits. Suddenly from being in the typing pool, I'm up in the owner's and director's office. It turns out he and my father are best buddies and no doubt my dad had a hand in getting me the job. It's quite sweet really, I was totally unaware of just how famous my father was.

Now of course I know the extent of the circles he moved in. The visitors' book from the house, which goes back to my grandfather's era, gives a great insight into their lives and friends. It holds some fantastic names including the Maharajah of Baroda, who bought Headley Court, my grandfather's grand house, and there are lots of names from the racing world, big business, journalists all signed with a proper pen and ink.

By that time my father had moved from Roundwood to Prior's Ford, a bungalow right on the river Mole near Leatherhead, which is now a block of flats called Campbell Court. I discovered that when I went back a few years ago. I'm almost sure he sold Roundwood for money reasons but at the time I wasn't really aware of the details.

I'm not sure of the figures but I think he gave around £12,000 for Roundwood. That figure seems a joke today but I know he sold it for somewhere over £30,000 which means he would have made quite a lot by today's standards.

It was at Prior's Ford that I had a massive row with Tonia, I think about something stupid like shampoo. Tonia used to get on my case and see how far she could push me. Tonia was either all over you like a rash or she'd drop you like a ton of hot bricks. She's always been like that – you were either flavour of the month or a nasty disease – there was no in between with Tonia.

She said I slapped her around the face with a hairbrush – I didn't – but I did slap her, just once. I must have just flipped. My father was upstairs, where the dormer room had been converted into his study. I heard Tonia go up the stairs screaming and shouting: 'Either she goes or I go'. My father came down with a wry look on his face which implied, you've done it this time girl. I said: 'No problem, I'm off.'

I must have just turned 17 because I had a little grey Triumph Herald which my father bought for me. I remember packing up my things. It had already been pre-arranged that I was going to work in the Lake District in a few weeks' time, where more friends of my father, Norman and Betty Buckley owned a handful of hotels including the Low Wood and the Wild Boar at Windermere. The hotels are now part of the Lake District Hotels Group.

But even though I wasn't due there for a little while, I was determined to get out of the house there and then. So I got in the car and drove to Leo and Joan Villa's house to confide in them and they arranged for me to stay with Leo's son Tim and his wife and daughter Linda who was around my age, at their home in Derby. When Tim was a young boy they all lived at Headley Grove with my grandfather. By this time I remember he worked for Cherry Blossom shoe polish and he was a drummer in a band.

I headed off up to Derby, thinking it would show Tonia that I could be independent, and stayed with them for a few days. I felt very superior because I thought my father didn't know where I was. I felt I had run away and left them to worry about me. But I'm sure Leo had told my father exactly where I was and deep down I knew what I'd done was wrong. I remember the joy of being with a girl of my age because that was something I missed. I had it at school with friends but with no siblings, I spent a lot of time with adults or on my own. Where we lived in the country, it was not easy for pals to visit and I didn't have the Mum and Dad taxi in those days which seems to always be on tap for children today. It was a whole different world. Whether I stayed there four days, a week or ten days I can't recall but I just remember having a lovely time.

I eventually drove on up to the Lakes to the Buckleys' fabulous house, called Crag Wood, on the shores of Windermere. It had beautiful gardens leading down to the boathouse. I had been there before and I remember Norman taking me out in one of his Albatross speedboats. The house is now a hotel.

Norman was a wealthy man, a solicitor and hotelier who was very involved in the creation of the Windermere Power Boat Records Week in November and an important figure in the Windermere Motor Boat Racing Club. He was a record holder in his own right, breaking the endurance world water speed records half a dozen times in his motor boats called *Miss Windermere III* and then *IV*. He was also a timekeeper and he figured enormously in my father's life – he was so much more to him than a good pal.

I stayed with them and Betty used to take me into work each day. I don't remember being paid as such, just my board and lodgings, so how I survived I don't really know. For all I know my father paid for me to be there.

I was going to spend some months there – another example of my father's 'school of life' philosophy. In some ways we had a privileged life but we didn't have the money to back it up. As soon as money came in, it went straight out. My father lived the showman's life but I don't believe he had a huge pot of money. He was very stylish – he loved Turnbull & Asser shirts and Jermyn Street suits and yet at home he was something totally different. He had two personas. At home, he would slop round in a pair of ill-fitting trousers with oil all down the front, a jumper with a hole in the elbow and yet he was voted as one of Britain's ten best-dressed men. He was a bit of an enigma in that respect.

I worked as a receptionist at The Royal Hotel but used to spend some time at the Low Wood, which was very much a bus tour hotel. And that's where I met Helmut, the head waiter, a blond-haired, blue-eyed German – gorgeous. He had a little VW Beetle which we used to drive around in. I thought I was the Queen Bee. Inevitably I slowly detached myself from the Buckleys to spend more time with him, whenever we could get time off together.

During that summer season, my father came up to the Lake District a couple of times, once in August 1966. His mother, Lady C, kept a letter he wrote to her inviting her to the Wild Boar for dinner the following weekend. Another time he turned up at the Low Wood with Lady Aitken, wife of the newspaper baron Sir Max Aitken, his paramour at the time. Everybody knew about their friendship but no-one referred to it openly. I had the sense that my father's marriage to Tonia was deteriorating and I believe he was very much in love with Lady A - and vice versa. They were good together. She was very sporty and countrified and probably very good fun and yet he was still married to Tonia. You could not have two women who were more opposites – on the one hand a lady with a title, breeding and all the social graces and on the other, the glamorous showgirl. Today some might describe Tonia as a bimbo – all costume jewellery, makeup and clothes. What is it they say a man likes? A whore in the bedroom, a cordon bleu chef in the kitchen and a lady in the drawing room. You can't get all three, but my father certainly tried his hand!

At the Low Wood, there was a bar coincidentally called Lady A's, but named after Lady Arran who held water speed records in her own right – she became the first woman to break the 100 mph speed limit on water. She was a character and was still racing in cruisers when I started racing. That's where I sat and talked to my father and Lady Aitken, which must have been September or October in 1966. They left, all smiles and hugs and kisses, and I just assumed my father was going on to Coniston. What I didn't know was that was to be the very last time I would ever see him alive.

It sounds such a shattering statement now but neither of us could see into the future. And it wasn't at all unusual for me to go for long periods without seeing my father and not to know exactly where he was and what he was doing. I often wouldn't speak to him from one month to the next. At the time that didn't seem at all strange to me – I rarely used the telephone and anyway he was rarely in one place for long, at least not on the end of a telephone. It only strikes me now when I think about kids today heading off on their big OE (overseas experience) or Gap Year that my time in the Lakes and then in Switzerland was probably my equivalent. But the difference today is that kids can stay in touch constantly and when the year's over, they often head back to live in the hotel of Mum and Dad, even if they are at university, until they are 25 or so.

Not long after that last meeting with my father, Helmut and I drove to Germany in his VW, which was a huge adventure. I can't remember what happened to my car. His parents lived in West Berlin but to get there, we had to drive through Potsdam, which was then in Communist East Germany. When we crossed the border, I remember the guards peering at my passport photograph which was taken when I was a child – can you imagine what I looked like – and looking back at me, now aged 17. We drove through parts of East Germany where the huge autobahns were all virtually deserted and Helmut kept telling me not to look at the security cameras, which was all a bit scary. I was amazed at the contrast between East and West.

We finally arrived at his parents' home, which was on the sixth floor of an old apartment block virtually on the Berlin Wall near Checkpoint Charlie. It had huge wooden doors and I couldn't believe that there were bullet holes in the outside walls.

One day I thought I would go through the Checkpoint which was only 200 yards away – it was an American crossing. I walked through and probably on for half a mile or so across this barren, desolate, no-man's-land between the two countries. It was known as the 'death strip' because it's where people were killed trying to escape. I suddenly panicked and thought 'what the hell am I doing here?' so quickly turned round and hightailed it back again. But from their apartment windows you could see over the wall and while we were there Helmut told me that a family had made a dash for freedom in a mechanical digger. The man had reinforced the cab with steel plating and at a given moment he and his family just drove through. Helmut's parents told me they actually managed to escape.

There were Alsatian dogs on long, long leads – I used to watch them walking up and down, up and down over about 200 yards. I spent a lot of time looking over the wall, something very brown and barren.

Helmut's parents were tailors who made clothes for the fashion houses and they were absolutely delightful, very friendly towards me but didn't speak a word of English. They even taught me some sewing and with the little bit I learned at school, I'm now actually a very proficient needlewoman and all my friends bring their clothes to me to be altered. They had a workroom in the apartment and the old man was the cutter, which is a real skill. I remember going with his mother, a stout, matronly woman with her hair in a roll, to a client and watching the client inspect every little seam. They even helped me to make my own dress while I was there.

Helmut and I had always planned to find jobs in a ski resort for the season and we both headed off to Arosa in Switzerland in late November to work in the Park Hotel. My job was in the basement laundry room, ironing the guests' clothes on big tables – they didn't use ironing boards.

The housekeeper was French and all the other women were Italian and it was like a sauna down there. I was always opening the windows which were at ceiling-level – ground level outside – only for the Italian women to close them soon after. We had enormous cardboard boxes lined with tissue paper in which you had to lay out all the ironed clothes – you couldn't leave the slightest crease. Then you had to take the box to the right guest's room and occasionally you would get a couple of francs as a tip. I was always very shy about that.

And that's where I was when my father was killed. He knew I was there because I got a letter from him just a few days before he died. He told me he was going for the record, that *Bluebird* would then go to the Boat Show in a blaze of glory and then we'd all meet up in Courchevel, me included, for some ski. I never kept that letter. Tragic. I wrote back to him, saying it all sounded great, fabulous and I remember Leo giving me back that letter unopened because my father never received it. He died between my posting it and the letter arriving. I didn't keep that letter either. Isn't that strange?

The morning of my father's accident, I was called upstairs to take a phone call about nine o'clock. I don't remember what day it was. It was my mother and I knew straight away that the very fact she was calling at that time meant something was wrong. The phone was in a little wooden booth with small windows – like a confessional box – in the reception area. She was trying to be nice and trying to avoid actually saying that he'd been killed, just that he'd had a terrible accident. But I knew what she meant and I went sobbing my way back down all the flights of stairs to the laundry.

The housekeeper was immediately told what had happened and was very sympathetic. She took the day off and spent it with me because I couldn't get a flight that day. My mother arranged my flight home and the next day the housekeeper took me to Geneva airport which was about 200 miles away - it's still all a bit of a haze. It was strange, surreal. I have vivid memories of sitting in the departure hall opposite a news stand where every single British paper and even the French ones had the picture of *Bluebird* going up in to the air. I looked at them with a total sense of disbelief. It's such a very poignant picture. It's like when there's a crash in Formula 1, your eyes are drawn to it – I think it's because you just want to see some signs of life – and when you do, you think: 'Thank God for that'. I didn't buy one.

I was escorted off the plane in London and into the airport through a discreet entrance. My mother and her husband Tony met me and took me back to their place. I look back now and wonder how I coped. I remember spending a lot of time watching the television – I saw the film of his accident the day I got home. It was shown on the news which in those days was your only medium other than newspapers. In a strange way, I couldn't take my eyes off it, it was surreal, and although I couldn't quite accept that my father was in there, it wasn't long before it was obvious they were not going to find him. The argument was that his body must be fairly intact otherwise the divers said they would have found pieces of him.

I believe that within about four or five days, it dawned on my mother that there wasn't going to be a funeral. It was then that Lord Mischon, the family solicitor, called me and asked me to go to London to see him. That's when he explained to me about the family trust that my grandfather, Sir Malcolm Campbell, had set up. The terms of the trust were that my father had the use of the interest on the capital but that on my father's death, I inherited the capital of £22,000, a lot of money in those days. But Lord Mischon said: 'There's a problem. Your father has broken the trust and spent the money and we cannot do anything until you release your claim on the estate.' My immediate reaction was to say I'd sign and agree to it but he advised me to seek the help of a different solicitor, as he was acting on my father's behalf. I had known nothing about the trust but I remember leaving his office and deciding to go to see Tonia, whom I hadn't spoken to since the accident.

She was staying in Dolphin Square, in the flat which my father had leased, and she was laid out on a sofa, people mopping her brow with a cold flannel. I don't remember who was there with her but I couldn't get any sense out of her. She was laying there in Greta Garbo mode, like the drama queen that she could be, while I tried to explain what Lord Mischon had told me.

Then I went back to my mother who then lived in the hamlet of Capel, between Dorking and Horsham in Surrey. And it can't have been too long after that when she announced, quite calmly: 'Well, you can't stay here for ever.' That was my mother. All my life she had put herself first, popping up now and then but never wanting to take responsibility or even show me any love. So there I was, effectively homeless and penniless.

I decided to go back to Switzerland. Helmut was still there but we obviously weren't in a position to live together and I had given up my job so I took a room as a lodger in a house owned by a really nice lady, who was so kind to me. I spent my days skiing – it's funny I should do that, bit I had been skiing with my father so many times. We both loved it. How long I stayed – a week, 10 days, two weeks, I don't remember. Eventually Tonia called me and we patched up and she invited me to go back to England to stay with her.

I flew back to England where Tonia divided her time between Dolphin Square and Prior's Ford. Then my father's memorial service was organised pretty quickly at St-Martin-in-the-Fields church in Trafalgar Square. Tonia took me shopping to buy something suitable to wear – a pale blue coat, I think.

It was held on February 23, 1967 and it was attended by the Duke of Edinburgh and Prime Minister Harold Wilson. Victor Mischon gave the address in which he said 'Britain and the world have such need of the indomitable spirit, the sheer dedication, the unconquerable determination, he (Donald) had.'

I believe Tonia specifically said my mother was not to be there, but afterwards we saw her name on the list of people who had been in the church. I went through it all in a bit of a haze and it still seems that way to me now. I just remember coming out of the church to be greeted by lots of journalists and photographers.

Tonia soon decided she was going to go back to the States and, to be fair to her, she said I could go with her but I didn't want to go. She put Prior's Ford up to let, Dolphin Square was on a lease so what the hell was I going to do? I needed somewhere to live and a way to earn some money and it suddenly struck me that I could use my experience with horses. So I picked up a copy of *Horse and Hound* magazine and looked for jobs as a girl groom.

I had also discovered that my father had left me £500 in his will. I went into Reigate with Leo and immediately bought myself a car, a Triumph Spitfire, navy blue with a soft top, for £485. I had £15 left.

Chapter 5

BUT WAS I IN LOVE
WITH HIM?

There was a job advertised in *Horse and Hound* magazine for a girl groom in Canada, so I went along to the agency which was handling it, explained what I could do and they were happy to offer me the job. But then they explained that there were strings attached, that if I was to leave within a year, I would have to pay my own fare back to England. Although at first I'd loved the idea of a new country, I couldn't be certain that I wouldn't want to come back in that time and so I decided against it. Instead the agency steered me towards another ad, which on reflection was a major turning point in my life.

A couple who lived in Droxford in Hampshire wanted a girl groom to live in and look after their own horses. The agency fixed me up with an interview and I drove down there to meet Donald and Poppy Muirhead, who were just the most lovely elderly couple. He was an ex-military type and just like something out of Jorrocks, the character from the comic papers and novels. He wore breeches and a jacket, carried a whip and was steeped in horses. Probably if you looked in his breeches there'd be mushrooms growing! Poppy was his second wife, a real horsewoman who loved hunting. They seemed to like me too and they gave me the job there and then. So I drove home – wherever that was – packed my things, mainly clothes and a few bits and pieces, and two days later I started work.

The Muirheads ran a stud farm, the Mayhill Stud, which was at the end of an unmade road, through the trees. It was just idyllic. They had a couple of stallions and brood mares at the stud and around the corner was their home and half a dozen private stables down the garden path. I lived in their cottage, in my own downstairs room with its own entry, and my job was with their private horses. I had always worked since I left school, I was pretty resilient so it never struck me as odd that I was now living and working there.

They knew the Campbell name – probably on reflection it was what got me the job and there was even a little piece in a newspaper, I think in William Hickey's column in the *Daily Express*, that I'd started working there. It gave Donald's age and he was indignant because they made him a year older than he was!

I look back now and wonder whether I was still grieving for my father and how did I grieve? What was it like? What is grieving – is it a sense of loneliness, is it a sense of get on with life, of self-preservation, do you tell yourself not to be a silly bitch, to pick yourself up and get on? I think I was working on instinct, automatic pilot, the practicalities of life stepped into the way. I don't remember one person asking me how I was feeling. But then, at the time my father died, there were so many people hardened by the war, who had suffered terrible losses, that his death must have seemed desperately insignificant.

I hadn't ridden a horse or done any physical work for many months, so I remember getting up early on the first day, mucking out, grooming, riding, exercising, cleaning tack and going to bed absolutely shattered out of my brains. The next morning I could hardly move I was so stiff because I'd used muscles I hadn't used for ages. I went through sheer physical torture for four or five days with muscular pain. But I am a very disciplined person and if I have to be there at 6am, I'll be there at quarter to six and if I have to work till 6pm, I'll still be there at 7pm. That's the way I was brought up by my father. I'm a 'go for it' person and they really liked me, they appreciated my work ethic and I know I earned their respect.

The Muirheads also really mothered and fathered me and I thought I'd landed in heaven. How lucky was I to have found the Muirheads from an advertisement, a couple who could step in and prop me up emotionally, give me a home, a job.

They had dogs of all shapes and sizes and suggested that I should get a dog of my own which could live with me there. They hinted it would be something to love – maybe they sensed my loneliness. So I drove to a place in Berkshire that I'd seen advertised and fell in love with a yellow Labrador called Lisa. She was quite small and very nervous and she and I drove back in my little Triumph Spitfire. But she could be a little bugger! I used to like those sherbet fountains and one day she found them in my glove box, so when I came back, my lovely navy blue car was covered in white sherbet powder which was frothing all over the place. She lived with me and slept in my room but if she had the chance, she would run off, so if I was outside working I had to tether her.

I'd work all day, go to bed exhausted and up early again next morning. I had one day off a week when I would probably drive up and see Leo and Joan or I would just go for a drive with the hood down if the weather was half decent. I loved that.

I didn't have any friends there but I wouldn't have missed that. I'm a very self-contained person in that respect. Even today my friends are my immediate contemporaries. There must be so many people out there who remember Gina – I met her here, here and here – and to say I don't remember them is not to be insulting. I've lost touch with so many people from the past. But because everybody knew my dad's name, they all felt they knew me by association. It's one part of my life which is very sad.

One day when I had been with the Muirheads for a few months, around September time, they told me we were taking the horses over to the Percys, a family who lived nearby. Jim Percy was a man with no social airs and graces but who had pulled himself up by his bootstraps and had done very well. He had a car dealership in the city and was a director of Portsmouth Football Club. His wife Olive was a kind woman.

They had three children and one of their sons, Clifford, was a good horseman. It was coming up to the hunting season, Poppy was joint Master of the Hambledon Hunt, and Cliffy was going to prepare them, give them a pop over the jumps and some schooling. So off we went, the three of us, leading a couple more horses as well. And up we rode to Walton Farm, the Percys' home, which to me looked like a mansion, new and immaculate.

Ironically, when I had been looking for the Muirheads' place to go for my interview, I had driven past the house set up on the hill. It was a little bit out of character because it was a very smart, red-brick house, all neat and tidy and I remember wishing the job was there. It all looked in apple pie order and I'm a bit of an apple pie person. The Muirheads' place in comparison was a bit more ramshackle, with bits added on and everything a little bit Heath Robinson.

We were introduced and I stood there with the horses while the Muirheads chatted with old man Percy. Cliffy duly gave the horses their schooling and afterwards I got to chat with him. He was a smallish man, dark hair, nice, kind and a damn good horseman. He offered to ride one of the horses back with me and on the way he asked if I'd like to go the cinema or for a drink or whatever the courting words were in those days. I said yes and there we go, we started a friendship, a romance which developed over the next year.

But was I in love him? I don't know. He was probably the first man who had ever said to me he loved me. I fell over backwards with delight when he asked me to marry him. That's one big mistake I've made in my life – I've said yes to everybody who has asked me to marry them, I've just done it and never stopped to think about it. To anybody who wanted me, I said please.

I can look back now and be a bit of a sage and realise I probably didn't appreciate my own self-worth, I just wanted to be loved. I didn't have brothers and sisters, no father, I hadn't had my mother through my life. And of course there was a physical relationship. It just seemed the right thing to do.

I was still aware that my father's lawyer Victor Mishcon had told me I must see a separate solicitor to sort out my father's estate and as Jim Percy seemed to know everyone in Portsmouth, he put me in touch with a solicitor called Mr Sotnick. I duly explained the whole thing about my father's will to him.

He asked whether I just wanted to give my stepmother Tonia, who was the main beneficiary of my father's will, the money that remained in trust from my grandfather, or attempt to claim it. It was about £22,000 and although my first instinct was to write it off, I soon decided it was probably better off in my pocket. It was a lot of money in those days.

He wrote to Mishcon, who was an executor of my father's will and therefore looking after Tonia's interests, obtained all the details, and told me that our counsel said I had a very strong case. Letters went back and forth and we finally learned that my real mother had been instrumental in helping my father to break the Trust. She had to sign as one of the trustees. His argument was that he needed the money for my upbringing but I suspect the reality was that it paid for spare parts for *Bluebird*. I remember my mother ringing me to say that if I made a claim, I would denigrate my father's name and would have the press camping on my lawn. At that point I decided I could not proceed. I still have a copy of the will. My father had also stated that as far as his family heirlooms and trophies were concerned, his wife Antoinette, Tonia's real name, could have any one she wished and the rest should go to his daughter Georgina.

However my lawyers now said the will was ambiguous, not clear whether it meant Tonia could choose *only* one item and the rest were left to me, or that she could choose which she wanted. By now two or three years had passed and I was asked to list everything, from memory, that I would like. It wasn't easy but because some years earlier my father asked me to write an inventory of the most important items at Roundwood, probably when he was about to sell, I remembered quite a lot. I was to receive my booty at Leo's house, seen as neutral ground. I drove there and met Tonia who had arrived earlier and laid the whole lot out. She had obviously had it all cleaned because that was Tonia's way – she was going to do this with some style and panache.

There was everything from salt cellars, cutlery, trophies, trinkets, the whole thing was most extraordinary on reflection. I was such a trusting person that I accepted this was everything. She produced a couple of old suitcases, I packed the lot in there and took them away. Who got the better deal? I don't know.

It was months later when a hawker came to the door, asking if I had any unwanted bits of gold and silver. I knew I had all this stuff, some useful, some not, some which might have been inscribed. I thought I could do with some 'cash in the attic' and I sold some, not for a massive amount. There were some lovely things which on reflection I should have kept.

As the years went by and I rekindled a relationship with Tonia, I would visit her and notice all these pieces that had been my father's and realise that although she had given me everything I had listed, she had clearly kept a good percentage. And when I lived in Lymington in the early 1990s, Tonia auctioned quite a few pieces of Campbell family memorabilia – I still have the catalogue. The first I knew of it was when the auction house rang me to see whether I wanted to buy any of them!

But I did inherit some money from my mother's stepfather Andrew Harvey who was a very wealthy man from his business in the cotton trade in India. My grandmother Ethel Calvert married him after her first husband died and he left £20,000 to me for when I was 18, which was such a lot of money then.

I had been visiting my mother occasionally on my day off. She was still married to Tony and living at the stud. When I told her that Cliffy had asked me to marry him, you could almost see her thinking, thank you Lord. After my father died she'd probably thought, oh my God, now I'm lumbered with this bloody child. She knew Tonia had gone back to America by then – the house at Prior's Ford was let.

I remember her glee and she literally took over. She set the date in June 1968 – people don't believe me but I honestly cannot remember the exact date – and she set the place, at my grandmother's estate, the house called Lock in Partridge Green, off the main A24 London to Worthing road. It was a very grand place, Grade II listed, standing in 25 acres and it later became the Convent of the Visitation, when it was bought by a silent order of nuns. And early in 2012 I couldn't believe it when I read that the singer Adele, who won six Grammy Awards and then the Brits, was renting the place for around £15,000 a month. There were stories in all the papers after she showed an American TV show host around the place with its ten bedrooms, tennis court and apparently it now has two swimming pools and a helipad. Apparently she didn't stay there for long because she thought the place was haunted!

My mother wanted the wedding reception there for her benefit, to show off to all the people she knew. By then my grandmother was nutty as a fruitcake. She'd often say: 'How's Daddy, dear?' She was a rich old bag but looked like a charlady. Every door in the house was locked and she had this massive bunch of keys, like a jailer, and if she wanted to move about she had to fumble for 20 minutes to find the right key. It was a massive place, with something like 3,000 acres of prime Sussex land where she lived alone with staff. That's why my mother decided it would be the ideal place to marry off her daughter.

The wedding all happened in a bit of a blur. I wore a beautiful white dress, hired from Moss Bros, but because I was so tiny, nobody had worn it before. The wedding photographs were taken by Madame Yevonde who was a society photographer of the time and a first cousin of my grandfather, Sir Malcolm. She was famous in society circles as a portrait photographer and an archive of her pictures still exists in the Mary Evans Picture Library in Blackheath, in London. Strangely the only picture I still have of me in my wedding dress is with a bull mastiff, this massive guard dog owned by my grandmother. I don't have any showing Cliffy and me because once the marriage was over I tore them all up along with my marriage certificate and threw away the pieces.

I remember getting dressed upstairs and having a few pre-wedding nerves and my mother telling me to have a gin, which I think was the cure for everything in those days. Being a non-drinker it probably worked pretty quickly.

We were married in the village church. I was 18 and I became Mrs Percy. There was a marquee on the lawn and in the old-fashioned style, the presents were laid out on a table and there was lots of handshaking. Jim Percy gave us £400 as a wedding present. I recall my grandma, who was in a wheelchair by then, trying to stand up after a couple of Mother's gins and toppling out.

My other grandma, Lady Campbell, was alive but I'm not sure she came, nor my aunt Jean, my father's sister. There were two separate parts of the family and loathing between them, and because my mother arranged the whole thing, I doubt whether any of the Campbells were invited. Leo and Joan must have been there as he was neutral and my mother knew him from her time with my father. I think Tony gave me away – we must have looked ridiculous because he was 6ft 8ins and I'm 5ft 2ins. I don't remember any of my friends being there. My life with the Muirheads had been all-absorbing, I lived and worked there and I didn't think to keep in touch with people. Our honeymoon was a weekend in a hotel in Hayward's Heath.

But before the wedding, I discovered I was pregnant for the one and only time in my life. When I missed a period, I suspected straight away – let's face it, it happens. I told Cliffy as we were walking across one of his father's fields and he was physically sick. Well, it is a scary moment – although we'd decided to get married, the last thing we needed was a baby. I was all of 18, he was 21 – what did we know, or want to know, about parenting. We wanted the fun, if you like, but none of the complications.

I didn't want to tell the Muirheads and Tonia would have been in the US, but I remembered what she'd told me after my spell in France – that if ever I needed this kind of help, to go to my father's secretary Rosie. For all her faults, Tonia was quite wise on some issues and she must have thought 'God, if anything happens to this kid, she's on her own'.

There were no easy over-the-counter testing kits back in 1967 so I had to take a sample to a local laboratory which did pregnancy tests to have it confirmed. When they came out and said it was positive, my heart sank. Fortunately, Rosie lived in Redhill so I went to see her and she gave me the name and number of a London clinic who she said would arrange a termination.

It was an overnight stay and I went to London on the train on my own. I don't believe we told anybody else. It was a put-you-to-sleep job and when you wake up next morning, it's all over. It was very early in the pregnancy and I don't have any strong moral feelings about the termination of unwanted pregnancies. I was relieved of course, but it's something I never dwell on, I've almost forgotten it happened. It was pretty expensive but we had enough money between us – I earned a wage and Cliffy had some money. After that I had a coil fitted because I never believed in the pill. My dad had almost asked me to say I would never take it because he didn't believe in mucking around with nature.

Chapter 6

HELLO OWEN, HOW NICE TO SEE YOU

Before Cliffy and I got married, we'd seen this little farm advertised in a glorious setting in a village called Owlesbury. There was a cottage on a T-junction with 55 acres of prime Hampshire land. I had the £20,000, inherited from my mother's stepfather and I bought it for us for around £15,000 which gave me a few quid change as well. I think the Percys thought I was a good catch because I had a few quid.

We put up new stables and established quite a large business with livery, hunter livery and breaking in horses. Cliffy and I became professional horseman and woman and I started competing seriously. The horse community was a fairly small one and when I competed at the weekends we'd meet the same people, the Harvey Smiths and the David Broomes in those days. We never had horses as good as theirs but ours were good enough to compete, although we never had a prayer of winning like they did.

We grafted hard ourselves and had the help of girl grooms from the village. It was very much the farming life. I still had my dog Lisa and we added a string of other dogs and cats over the time we lived there. I sold my Triumph Spitfire just before I got married and with the proceeds we bought a Morris 1000 pick-up, a brand new one. Moving to a farm, it was more practical. But looking back, I was so gullible – we needed, so Gina bought.

The idea was to make money out of horses but horses being horses and our being a little wet behind the ears, it did not always work out. Cliffy tried extremely hard but he was always seeking the approval of his father who was much more worldly and astute in business than his son.

But I was happy, working hard, living with horses – I always call horses shit machines, you stuff it in one end and pick it up at the other. My dad used to say horses were dangerous at both ends and bloody uncomfortable in the middle! And it's quite true. The routine was to get up at six every morning, muck out, feed the horses, exercise, schooling, tack cleaning, mucking out, grooming, going to bed. I learned so much from Cliffy about horses.

Each day is different when you are dealing with live creatures and I relished it. I was in demand as a rider from a couple of trainers including Bill Wightman who was not far away at Upham. I remember riding out on Cathy Jane, a chestnut mare, which was owned by Mick Channon, the footballer who played for Southampton and England. He was tall, dark, good-looking, every girl's dreamboat at the time. He had always had an interest in horses and later became a successful trainer himself. He still is. But this was the first horse he bought and he sent it to Bill. Toby Balding, the National Hunt trainer, used to send young horses to us to break. He is the uncle of Clare Balding, the BBC sports presenter, and he went on to train two Grand National winners. Horses were my life at that time, I lived and breathed horses, but they gave me a real sense of achievement, of fulfilment.

But we never really made much money and if we did, we blew it. I remember when Triumph Stags first appeared – we bought one for £300. What did we do that for? It was flashy. We were never flush with money but maybe a bit flash.

We spent a lot of money on the place, extended the cottage, decorated it – I love decorating to this day. Looking back the taste was probably awful, gaudy wallpaper on two walls and the others painted, and wall to wall carpeting. We were really posh. I love being a homemaker.

But I had some awful accidents with horses. We once bought a young good-looking horse cheap at auction, which was listed in the brochure as being unbroken. So we went through all the breaking procedures, the training with saddle, girth, long reins, which I enjoyed because I'm a person who likes detail, until it came to the day when I had to get on the horse's back. The normal procedure was to lay across it first so it could get used to my weight but just as Cliffy got me into that position, this horse exploded and sent me flying through the air, right against a bloody wall. I had a total dislocation of my shoulder, the collarbone came out, I split the back of my head open, blood everywhere, and I was three quarters of the way out for the count. Cliffy drove me as fast as he could to Winchester Hospital and then came this wonderful feeling when they gave me the morphine. I stayed in hospital overnight and was patched up and then was allowed home the next day.

Mondays were always a quiet day so I often used to go to see my grandmother, Lady C, in Yateley, near Camberley, where she was in an old people's home. Her skin was the colour of paper, milk white. It was sad to see her like that when once she had featured in society magazines – she was reputedly the socialite of Surrey and strikingly attractive. She was Sir Malcolm's second wife and the only one who bore him children – my father and his sister Jean.

She was very frivolous – Sir Malcolm, the old man, gave her money to pay the household bills, and then after six months she got rude letters from the milkman, the butcher and the baker to say they hadn't been paid, but in the meantime my grandma had bought 25 new hats. She had no sense of perspective, probably she'd had such a sheltered life in that elite circle that she had no common sense.

When I lived with my father and Dorothy, we went to visit her somewhere in Kent, where she bred poodles and showed them at Crufts. I always loved animals but I was not allowed to touch them – the child was not allowed to touch the dogs. She once gave one of Sir Malcolm's trophies to The Kennel Club as a prize and years later, they found it in their cellars. In 1984, they decided to present it to the RAC Club, where my grandfather had been a member and they invited me to hand it over. Prince Michael of Kent was the patron of both clubs. When I went into The Kennel Club to arrange it, they told me I was the first woman to be allowed into one particular room.

Sometimes she would come to stay with us but you had to be really careful, otherwise she would stay for months. If my father saw her coming up the drive, he'd say: 'Here comes trouble.'

She once went to the South of France as a lady companion but everything went pear-shaped. I'm not sure exactly what happened but she said she was ill and my father had to find an 'ambulance' to bring her home. He was very harassed. The Flowers had to organise it from that end.

She always had quite an affinity with Dorothy and when she finally decided to leave my father and go back to New Zealand, Lady C offered to ' look after' her mink coat and diamonds. She said she would have them cleaned and sent on to Dorothy – but they never arrived. Dorothy told me that years later she watched a newsreel featuring my grandmother wearing the mink coat!

She had loads of suitors after Sir Malcolm left her but she never remarried – my father said she did not want to lose her title. When the old man died, in his will he left his estate to be split three ways – father, Jean and her. He had made provisions for her but not his third wife.

She always used to wear a gold bracelet that was my grandfather's identity bracelet with an oval plaque set in it with the Cross of Lorraine on one side and the reverse his regiment The Queen's Own Royal West Kents and the white horse with the motto *Invicta*. I once commented that it was a beautiful bracelet and she left it to me but my aunt was furious because she said Grandmother had always promised it to her. I used to wear it all the time but the links and plaque are so thin now, that I hardly do. It's a lovely piece.

In the early days of my marriage to Cliffy I'd bring her back to the farm, stick her in the chair with a cup of tea, she'd fall asleep and I'd take her back in the evening. I would have been the last member of the family to see her alive.

It was while we were at Elm Farm that my mother rang me out of the blue to say that she had left Tony and their home at the stud and was currently living in a hotel in Silchester, between Reading and Newbury. She was with a man called Owen Shaw, who had been the chief stud groom at the National Stud in Newmarket where she used to send her mares to big-name stallions like Mill Reef. My mother had bred some half decent racehorses in her time. She sold one for a record amount of money at the time to Freddie Laker, who pioneered cheap air travel in the 70s with his Skytrain and had a stud at Epsom.

She and Owen had decided to split up with their respective partners – Owen was married with two adopted sons – and run off together. They had taken a long-term booking at the hotel and were living as Mr and Mrs Whatever. She said she'd like me to meet him but that when I arrived, I was to just walk up and give him a kiss and say, 'Hello Owen, how nice to see you,' as though I knew him. She was convinced everybody would be watching. The wonderful subterfuge of happy families!

Owen was a nice enough little 'fella' but a bit of a country yokel. My mother had gone from being married to my father, to Tony, who was a diplomat, to Owen. There was even a piece in the paper, again the William Hickey column I think, which said something like 'never have a filly and a colt turned so many heads at the Newmarket sales as the former Mrs Daphne Turner and the former stud groom Owen Shaw as they breezed in to buy a couple of horses.'

My mother had always said that Owen was impotent but then she came up with this wonderful fallacy that she was pregnant – God knows how old she was at this stage. I remember thinking, 'Fuck me, after all these bloody years I'm going to have a sister or brother, albeit a half one'. But this was her clever cunning to make him feel good, that he wasn't firing blanks, so of course this pregnancy never materialised. And I wasn't bright enough at the time to twig it must have been a complete fantasy.

They decided to get married and invited me. But it was on the day of an important competition, the regional final of the Foxhunter Championship, which ran from March through the summer, for qualification for the Horse of the Year Show. In those days it was one of the most prestigious competitions and this was the day I could qualify to go to Wembley. My mother just announced her wedding date was on the same day, never asking me if it would be convenient. She put me in that awful position of having to make a choice, so I made it and I didn't go to the wedding because horses were my life and my mother hadn't been part of my life for years. I made it to Wembley, where I jumped in the morning and qualified for the evening session where I think I finished sixth or seventh.

It was a time when property prices were rocketing and our home, Elm Farm, was suddenly worth nearly £100,000. We spotted we could make a hefty profit and we decided to sell up. We soon had a buyer, a man called Olaf Lambert, who became the director general of the AA (Automobile Association) who was based in Basingstoke. The M3 had opened by then so our place was an easy commute for Olaf, who also liked his hunting at the weekend. He was very proper, another ex-military man and one day after we had agreed the deal, he arranged to come down and measure for the curtains. I was hacking out up through the woods not far away when I spotted him. He had obviously come from his office and he'd stopped in the woods to get out of his office jacket and tie and as I came round the corner I caught him peeing against a tree. He was frightfully proper and to suddenly see him in his underpants made it very difficult when I had to face him back at the house a few minutes later.

We decided to move to Devon where property prices were much lower and found a brand new house with a big, new empty shell of a barn at Pinhoe, near Exeter. It was a bigger house than Elm Farm but had no character whatsoever. We converted the barn to house integral stables and set about building a livery business. We used to buy and sell a lot of horses, too – we'd try to buy for £100 and sell for £150, but we never went out of our way to buy a top-class horse, more someone else's cast-offs. Cliffy had this vision that just because somebody else could not cope with a horse, that didn't mean he couldn't. But in our time there we had some good, bad and indifferent horses.

It was there that I had another awful accident when I was nearly killed by an electric grooming machine, which was a piece of kit with a long arm and a brush, really quite good, although some of the horses didn't like it. It was a bit like a strimmer with an on/off switch near your hand and a long cable. We'd had a problem with the wiring and we had an old boy who had tried to repair it, but when I switched it on it turned out the wire was live. It threw me and tossed me all around and I couldn't let go, the motor was so powerful. The horse was going ballistic. I was so lucky that there was a builder in there with me, standing right by the mains switch, and he was intelligent enough to realise what was happening and turn it off. I burned all my hands but he actually saved my life.

In the winter of 1977, I know it was then because it was the year Elvis Presley died, we had a tremendous snowstorm that left parts of Devon virtually cut off. The snow reached our upstairs windows and when we opened the back door inwards, we were faced with a white wall. We had to have food air-dropped for the horses. The farmer across the valley had milking cows and he told me he had to let the milk run away on the floor because the tankers couldn't reach him to collect it. It was unbelievable, you couldn't even see the road and it seemed to last for weeks. It really reminds you how vulnerable you are and that nature is so powerful. We think we're so clever but it brings it home to you that we're not. We may be able to survive on bread and water for a while but when you have animals, they have to be fed and watered.

After we went to live there, and by sheer coincidence I'm sure, my mother and Owen also moved to Devon, to a village called Colyford, not far from Axminster. I remember her giving me a dining table. She bought a pretty little black and white house with a river at the bottom of the garden and she managed to get a stream diverted through her land. She created a duck pond and bought ducks from all around the world. Then she bought a piece of land adjoining the garden, put up some stables and decided to keep miniature ponies and the ducks all disappeared. Next she sold that house to a doctor and moved literally next door to a bungalow. She lived there until her death in December 1998.

Probably within about a year Cliffy and I began to feel a little isolated in Devon and we weren't making much money so we decided to sell up again. We sold the place to an Australian and made a profit. Then we moved to Newbury and rented a nasty little red-brick flat and some stables at Snelsmore Farm, owned by a Swiss man. The main property was a lovely manor house off the A34, close to junction 13 of the M4 motorway. The farm is still there. We rented the top floor of what once would have been a farm worker's cottage. It was all we could afford because we knew very well by then that we had been living beyond our means.

By then Cliffy and I had become more like brother and sister than husband and wife. I was still only in my late 20s and I had started to exchange letters with Tonia, establishing a bit of a rapport with her again. I told her that Cliffy and I hadn't had any physical contact for ages and, typical Tonia, she said he must be getting it somewhere else. But I said I'd cut my right arm off before believing that...although later it turned out to be true. Tonia was booked for a summer season in the casino in Estoril in Portugal, she was living in a little flat there and asked if I fancied going for a week or two for a holiday. What was a holiday? I'd never had once since I got married so she didn't need to ask me twice and off I went.

I thought it was wonderful. The casino was in the square and Tonia's rented flat was almost opposite across a piece of greenery. Today people take photographs of everything but I didn't have a camera so I have no record of these places. Tonia was singing every night; she was the cabaret and I'd sit and watch. Going to Estoril probably made me realise there was more to life than I was having...I wanted to be more of a lady. I didn't have too much of a misspent youth, apart from a little bit in the south of France, and I was locked into this life of monotony – get up, do the horses, go to bed, get up, do the horses, go to bed. It just suddenly flipped me. And it wasn't too long before I met this nice looking Portuguese boy and I enjoyed a brief relationship with him for the rest of my holiday. When I got back home I realised I would have to tell Cliffy, I knew I couldn't carry on as if nothing had happened. So I said, 'I've been a naughty girl and I'm going to have to divorce you.'

It turned out he'd been screwing one of these girls who kept a horse with us, so it just sort of fitted in. Like a fool, I agreed to split everything 50/50. I've always been one for a bit of fair play and I think we just agreed that's how it would be. We shared the horses we owned, it was most extraordinary. His mother was desperately upset because by then all three of her kids had got divorced.

Cliffy left the house, he probably went back to his father's place for a while, and I stayed there and paid the rent. I don't remember my emotions – fear, trepidation? Probably I was relieved.

Chapter 7

A SHOTGUN THROUGH MY WINDOW

Leo Villa died on January 18, 1979, just eight months after his lovely wife Joan. He was 79 and had spent almost his entire career with my grandfather and then my father – he was my father's chief engineer, the lynchpin of his team. His real name was Leopoldo Alfonso Villa – his father was Italian – but he was always Unc, both to me and my father. A more loyal man to my family you could not find.

Leo was diagnosed with lung cancer, he was never without a cigarette in his mouth. But, blow me down, Joan died before him, also with cancer, but it had not been diagnosed. Leo and Joan were always joined at the hip, such a devoted couple. Their son Tim died of a heart attack and their lovely daughter committed suicide – they had been such a cohesive family at one time.

I knew Leo for so much longer than I knew my father and he and Joan were always very kind to me. I didn't notice it then but I look back now and realise that quite a lot of adults felt sorry for me, including Leo and Joan. They knew only too well that my father was with this woman and that woman and then divorced again.

My aunty Jean used to say that how I grew up sane, she'd never know. I didn't quite understand what she meant then but as you go through life you reflect on those thoughts. My father would have been locked up now for the beatings he gave me, smacking me and frightening me so much. I was terrified but I don't blame him. It has made me very opinionated about the behaviour of children – I don't tolerate bad behaviour because it was never tolerated in my life. I believe children should be seen and not heard. And maybe it was because of the way I was brought up that I believe the world doesn't owe you anything.

At Leo's funeral I met his nephew Philip again. I'd first come across him when he used to help Leo, working with my dad. I knew him a little and before you knew what, he was my boyfriend.

Philip worked in the petro-chemical industry, designing gas and oil rigs, and used to divide his time between his office in London and working abroad, often in Abu Dhabi, which at the time was a pretty bleak place, mostly desert and oil rigs, nothing like it is today. He was a clever man with his hands and years after my father's death, he set up Project Q which stood for Quest for Speed, to build a hydroplane capable of breaking the world water speed record. He had to raise funds but tried to keep the whole idea pretty secret. He had some help from students at Imperial College, London, where they named a wind tunnel after my father, and he reached the stage of building models and testing them on water. But sadly the early 80s was a difficult time financially and there simply wasn't enough money around to build a full-scale hydroplane. The tests showed that it should have been capable of over 400 miles per hour. If that had happened, it would have smashed the record of 317 miles per hour set by the Australian Ken Warby in 1978, which still stands today, and returned that record once held by my father to Britain. But sadly, we'll never know.

Philip owned a house in Effingham, a village near East Horsley in Kent, and I moved in with him before we got married. Originally it was a very old cottage which he had rebuilt to create a beautiful house. But because I still owned two horses, and there was not enough space to keep them at home, I rented some land and two stables at a big house not far away. It was called White Hill House and had been the home in the 1930s of Sir Barnes Wallis, who invented the 'bouncing bomb' that was used in the Dam Busters raid. I used to chat to an older lady at the house who had been in service to Lord Louis Mountbatten and she used to tell me some real stories of life there!

I used to spend most of every day with the horses – mucking out, grooming, exercising – and it was one summer day in the early 1980s when I was driving back home that I was caught up in an armed robbery. My route took me across a railway bridge, on an S-bend near Effingham Junction station. As I came round the corner, I thought there must have been an accident, because a car seemed to have cut across the front of a security van coming in the opposite direction. I braked and within seconds there was a shotgun through my driver's window and a masked man demanding my keys. I had my two little Dachsis on the seat beside me, barking their heads off. He said: 'Shut those little fuckers up,' grabbed my keys and flung them over the railway embankment.

From nowhere more men in masks appeared and one jumped up over the bonnet of the yellow and green Securicor van, on to the roof and whipped the aerial off so they lost radio communication. I was just sitting there watching, it was like a film playing out, while they used a chain saw to cut a hole in the side of the van. It looked like there was a kind of foam between the metal panels which kept jamming up their chainsaw.

They managed to hack a hole in the side of the van and open it a little way, like an envelope, and pulled out a canvas bag of money. But I found out later it was only loose change. I saw one of the drivers being dragged out and taken round the back of the van and the next thing, he was on the floor and there was blood. While it was all going on, one or two more cars came up behind me and the same guy took their keys, but some at the back of the queue must have thought it was an accident and turned round.

Suddenly the gang obviously decided it was time to leave and they disappeared in their cars through the railway yard. I had a camera with me and I took some photographs of the van but I only dared to do that once they left. I gave them to the police and I still have one or two which they returned to me. The whole thing seemed to last about 20 minutes.

It was quite scary but my biggest fear was for my dogs – Susie and Smartie. Although they'd taken my keys I never really felt threatened. I think I actually walked home, it was only a quarter of a mile or so, and Philip was already there. He didn't know anything about it but he'd wondered why I hadn't picked him up at the station.

When the police came to the house, one officer was hobbling up the path. He said he had run down the stairs at the police station so quickly that he fell and twisted his ankle! I made a statement and they said it was most likely to have been the same gang who had carried out a few security van robberies around that time. The story was all over the local news. I know they found the cars abandoned – they had been stolen – but I don't think anyone was ever caught. I was never asked to look at any photographs of possible suspects. I eventually recovered my own car with the spare key.

It was later that summer when we finally decided to get married and this time Tonia agreed to organise a reception at Prior's Ford, which she still owned. In fact she did rather well out of it. She let the main house for a long time before finally selling it – she once gave me £100 to redecorate some rooms for her between tenants. But she also cleverly obtained planning permission to convert a huge workshop building, which had been big enough to house both the *Bluebird* car and the boat, into another house, a cute, little open-plan place. She called it The Lodge at Prior's Ford. It overlooked the river and it's still there to this day. Tonia lived there for a while when she was in the UK but then later let it to an American couple.

The wedding was very much smaller than my first, with only about 15 people there. We were married at Epsom Register Office in July 1980 – again I'm not sure of the exact date and what does it matter? – and we all went back to The Lodge where Tonia put on a buffet. My mother didn't come because she and Tonia hated one another. Philip's parents were there of course – his mother was something of a battleaxe. Once, after I divorced Philip, she spotted me walking on the opposite side of a road in Leatherhead and started screaming obscenities, calling me a whore. The whole street was looking and she didn't stop until I was out of sight.

I was living a rather domestic life for the first time, driving Philip to the station in the morning, picking him up in the evening, looking after my horses in between. After a while he sold the house at Effingham because there was a chance to make a good profit and we moved to a bungalow up towards The Downs. It had a flagpole in the garden, which was a fair size, and I think that's where my interest in gardening began. We had a sit-on lawn mower and I'd spend hours on it, until there wasn't a blade of grass left.

Philip was always full of ideas and he once came up with a scheme to go into business with an Australian fella he knew, who lived in

Kingswood, coincidentally in the same road where I was born. His scheme was to sell caravans in Spain but needed cash to invest in it. Philip's own money was overseas for tax reasons and after a while I fell for it and gave him around £20,000. We went to an exhibition of caravans in Spain and there were endless meetings about how this business was going to make money, but it never came to anything and I had to write off my investment.

Philip and I were together for three or four years, with him going away for weeks or even months at a time. We had one or two holidays together, one skiing in Courchevel, where Philip crashed my Lancia driving too fast. That's when he gave me a car which had been Leo's and which Philip had bought from his estate – a bright red Triumph GT6. It later became a huge issue during our very bitter divorce.

I soon became thoroughly bored and I guess that's partly why I got involved with Michael Standring. I met him through Philip because Michael was a good mechanic and often used to look after his cars. Once when Philip was going away he told me Michael would be coming round to collect a car. I was there on my own, we probably had a coffee and started talking. We didn't just leap into bed but we started a friendship which developed into something else. Michael was a bit younger than me, a good-looking guy who was very vain about his appearance, particularly his hair. He was married to Christine, a hairdresser, but they had no children and they lived in a modern terraced house in Ashstead, just a few miles away.

I was happy with Michael, so much so that one weekend when Philip was away, I stupidly took him down to meet my mother in Devon. She was all sweetness and light while we were there, but after we left, the old cow rang Philip and told him I was having an affair. Extraordinary behaviour, she was so spiteful. The next thing I know, Philip rings to say he's flying back the next day. I went to Heathrow to collect him, I'll always remember it. I was in the arrivals hall in the old Terminal One, feeling dreadful, and who should be standing next to me but the boxer Henry Cooper. He was enormous.

It was awful when Philip arrived and we almost parted there and then. We sat in the car for a while, there were tears and recriminations and when we arrived home, I was keen to pack up and leave as soon as I could. Once something like that is spoiled, there's no going back for me. And the idea of sharing my body with two men at the same time is just abhorrent.

Michael said he would leave his wife and Tonia told me that Prior's Ford was empty and that we could stay there. So that's what we did. Although I had lived there before, it didn't really feel the same and anyway my old bedroom had been turned into a bathroom. We didn't have much money between us but Michael had a job in an automotive business and I got a job with an American company called Snapdrape, who sold tablecloths and napkins to hotels. I worked for a couple who ran a Snapdrape office from their garage in Cheam and I had a company car so I could visit hotels to try to sell their products.

My divorce was pretty bitter and took a while to settle. I went to Lord Mishcon again and I seem to remember that at first they expected me to receive half of more or less everything, but as time went on it was whittled down to pretty much zilch. That's when my resentment of solicitors really took hold and I'm afraid I have little respect for them even now.

Even Tonia would not let me keep one of my father's models of *Bluebird* which she had given to both of us as a present. She liked Philip and the association with Leo's family and at that point she thought I was being foolish so she said Philip must have it. Eventually the dispute came down to the car which had belonged to Leo. Philip wanted it back but in the end I was allowed to keep it, although soon after I sold it to a buyer in Guernsey. And that closed that chapter. Surprisingly it was sold by a classic car company as recently as 2011 for almost £12,000, with the provenance of once being owned by Leo Villa and Gina Campbell.

Chapter 8

I NAME THIS BOAT BLUEBIRD

From Prior's Ford, my father's last beautiful home overlooking the river, we moved to number 12, Aquila Close in Ashstead, a small terraced house where Michael had lived with his wife, Christine. For once, my mother came up trumps and gave me the £11,000 Michael needed to buy Christine's share of the house so we could live there. Aquila Close was a 'going nowhere' road and behind the house was the Goblin Teasmade factory, which eventually became huge offices for Esso. The house was small – you could hear the neighbours going to the bathroom – but I didn't mind. I have never had high expectations since the time I lived in my first home, Little Abbots, even though my father later lived in some lovely houses. Michael and I were both still working, we made friends with people around, particularly Michael Meech, who worked for the BBC, and his girlfriend June Fish.

It was then that we started to get interested in boats, although I wonder how we ever afforded it. Michael loved speed and had driven in Mini Clubman races and he had a pal in the automotive industry who raced boats. We had spent the odd weekend on the south coast watching people with boats and decided we wanted to join them. We checked out various boats and just a week or so later we became the proud owners of a 16-foot Phantom, with a Suzuki outboard engine, which we kept in the garage and which of course we christened *Bluebird*. It was the summer of 1983 and every weekend and some long evenings after work we would go down to Littlehampton on the South coast and bomb about in this boat. I used to waterski – my father taught me when we were in Canandaigua in America all those years before. But it was the first time I'd actually spent time in boats, it's not as though I felt it was in my blood.

We spent as much time as we could with the boat and soon began to watch people racing. Michael's pal Tim Grimshaw invited us to his workshop to look at his race boat and we immediately thought: 'We'd love a piece of that.' Tim raced off Brighton Marina and asked us to go down to the next race. We launched our little boat down there and bombed around. Then we followed him to Fowey in Cornwall to watch him in the next race, trailing our little boat down there, too. We went to three or four races and just knew it was something we'd like to do.

Our first race boat was a 25-foot Phantom which cost £6,500 for the hull alone. We had enough money for a deposit but we needed a marine mortgage. We had it built at the Barnet Marine Centre in Hertfordshire, who manufacture and sell all types of boats and engines, and where we'd bought our little boat. By the time she was fitted out with two engines, a pair of fuel tanks, gauges, instruments, a floor, two seats, the cost was nearer £25,000.

All the boats that raced had sponsorship and we were pretty confident we could find a sponsor. We had some brochures printed to advertise ourselves, inviting companies to have their name on our boat, driven by Gina Campbell, daughter of Donald Campbell, and Michael Standring. We said we would be competing in the 1984 Round Britain Race, which had not been held since 1969, and that we would be taking part in Records Week, which was staged on Lake Windermere at the end of the year. It is still held today. But remember, neither of us had ever raced boats.

I was still working for Snapdrape and borrowed a reference book which listed all companies above a certain size. I was in bed with flu, and spent the day writing covering letters to send out with the brochures. We had a few responses from Bluebird Toffees and Bluebird Caravans but the only company who said they wanted to see us was Agfa, which I remember had been number 69 on my list. They asked us to present ourselves to their reprographic division at the offices in Brentford.

It turned out that the boss of Agfa's Repro Division, Tony Burton, had met my father and our letter struck a chord. They had a budget and we did a deal there and then for the 1984 boating season. It was probably worth about £55,000 to us in our first year of racing, £15,000 towards the cost of the boat and the rest for a full season of racing and competing in the 1984 Round Britain Race. The boat immediately became *Agfa*

Bluebird. And their sponsorship meant that at every race, their huge PR machine would go into action with a marquee, hospitality for their clients, photographs of Michael and me, the works.

The first event they organised was a massive launch for the new boat at St Katherine Docks on the Thames in April 1984. Michael and I had been given the use of a slipway at Lambeth Palace and then we sailed into the dock, hooters blaring, the Agfa publicity machine in full flow. They decided to ask my mother to launch the boat and even sent a taxi for her to Devon. She was not my choice. Initially Agfa had talked about asking a big name and Terry Wogan was mentioned. But the PR company rightly said that this was a big enough story in its own right and didn't need a name to muscle in and so they decided on my mother. Agfa treated her like the Queen of Sheba and she said the obligatory: 'I name this boat *Bluebird*, God bless her and all who sail in her'. There were floating pontoons in the dock, one of them full of press photographers, so many of them that the whole craft nearly went over. You know how they all dive to get the best shot as if we were only going to be there for 30 seconds when in fact we were there for almost the whole day.

But just two or three nights before, a strange thing had happened which almost made me late for the launch. Michael and I had gone for a meal to our local curry restaurant in Ashstead. Three guys came in and sat next to us and then when Michael had to leave quickly at the end of the meal, they started a bit of banter about leaving me to pay the bill. It was all good-humoured. I paid with my Snapdrape American Express card and went home.

The next day Surrey Police rang Snapdrape and said they were coming round to see me. They checked it was me who had used the credit card at the restaurant and asked whether I'd noticed three men at the next table. It transpired that after the meal, the three had committed an armed robbery at a big house in Ashstead Park, terrifying the family and driving off in a car laden with all kinds of valuables. When they were in the house, one of them had made a comment about having a curry so the police had checked the local restaurant and found my name because I'd paid with a card. They took me to Guildford police station to see whether I could identify the men from photographs and all the time I knew I was pushed for time because I needed to be away to go to London to get organised for the launch. I did not recognise any faces and I never heard whether anybody was arrested for the robbery.

Anyway, after the launch came the first race, which was something else. The Agfa razzmatazz meant there had been masses of pre-publicity in the national and the boating press – talk about all eyes being on us.

From May to October the Royal Yachting Association ran a series of weekend offshore powerboat races for the UK Offshore National Championship. Everyone had to belong to a club and we joined the UK Offshore Boating Association, known as UKOBA, which is Europe's longest running powerboat club. Even so, they had never seen anything like the attention surrounding us. We knew the other race boat owners were thinking: 'All this money and a scrap of a girl who thinks she's something special because she is Donald Campbell's daughter.' There were some wealthy owners but there were others who had scrimped and saved and they resented our massive sponsorship. There was a hell of a lot of bad feeling. People pretended they liked it but really they hated it. The sport had never attracted much publicity but suddenly Agfa transformed all that.

Our first race in May started from Portsmouth harbour and we were there with about 20 minutes to go to the start with the world and his wife watching. And by now we've amassed a crew of engineers, helpers, well-wishers and hangers-on. We still had our first little Phantom speedboat as back-up for our engineer, Doug Ashley. These boats are inherently bad-tempered and as we were coming out of the harbour, one engine conked out.

We called up Doug on the two-way radio and he was bobbing up and down alongside, taking off the engine cowl. Agfa had a huge press boat, everyone waiting to see how we would perform, and there we were struggling to make the start. Thank God, with a stroke of genius, he managed to get it started in time for us to make the two-minute starting gun. We didn't have time to do the pre-parade lap – we just had to gun it.

There would be maybe 50 boats in the race, all shapes and sizes, and the race was about 80 miles long. At speeds of up to 70 miles per hour plus, it would take a good hour or more. Each class of boat completed a different mileage so the one that crossed the line first was not necessarily the winner, which made it very spectator-unfriendly and is probably why it never took off as a major sport.

On board, one of you is steering and the other navigating and crewing, yelling instructions. It was flat calm which suited the catamarans which ran in our class best – our monohull was better in rougher waters. But we came second and you would have thought we'd won the World Cup. There was champagne, lots of lovely food and dozens of journalists and photographers. Being in the cut and thrust of it and with all the adulation was just amazing.

The second race in Fowey was completely different – in contrast to the flat calm at Portsmouth, the sea was as rough as guts and the catamarans were all over the place. I remember being so scared, it was like riding a mechanical bucking bronco, leaping around all over the place. The boat had a long bow which would dip into the wave and you could see two feet of water riding up towards you. There's no windshield and if you're not careful the water smacks you in the face. I was learning as I went along and soon knew to see it coming, duck and then feel the water dripping down my neck. The race was curtailed because it was so rough but because we were so far ahead, we won under the rules which applied to a shortened race. Agfa were thrilled – and so were we.

I've always said that you don't need the skill of a brain surgeon to race boats. Of course you need to learn the rules of the sea, rights of way, navigation and the basic principles which you learn the hard way – if you've got a big wave coming towards you, you want to hit it on the nose, not on the side which sends the boat rocking.

For me, it's all about the feel, the seat of the pants, big balls, a lot of good luck and a dose of bullshit. But it seemed to come very naturally to me and it was something I really wanted to do.

But we had terrible teething problems with the boat and used to spend hours after work and at the weekends at Barnet Marine, where Michael helped our engineer Doug. It was then I realised how diligent and meticulous Michael was – every screw was turned to the same position and there was not a speck of oil or grease when he had finished. You could have put a newborn child down in there. Michael's car wasn't big enough to tow the boat so my mother gave us £2,000 to buy an old transit van which was painted up and our name emblazoned across it. The Agfa sponsorship money meant we could maintain it.

After the second or maybe third race, Agfa asked us to go to their offices. We thought: 'Oh my God, what are they going to say?' But it was good news. Their proposal was for us both to give up our jobs so that we could be 100% available to them and their publicity machine. In return, we were to be self-employed but contracted to them with a salary, expenses, a car. We didn't need asking twice. It meant we were professionals, the only ones at that time. It was the most exciting thing to hit the sport and I felt like the belle of the ball – they were treating me like Princess Diana, unbelievable.

I gave up my job at Snapdrape and Agfa were good enough to invite my old bosses along to some of the races. And Michael gave up his job in the automotive parts business. All of a sudden we were loaded – or so we thought – and still living in our little terraced house.

But we had a bloody exciting time – yes, we were working hard but we were being paid to take part in what had become our sport. I'd be lying if I said I didn't enjoy the flattery and attention, even though I didn't court it. I'd walk into a room of grey-suited men, often Agfa clients, and they'd all clap. Everybody wanted to shake my hand, give me a kiss, sign an autograph, have their picture taken with me, sit in the boat, have me sit on their knee and Agfa treated me like a goddess.

In 1984, Everest Double Glazing decided to sponsor the Round Britain Race, which attracted boats from around the world – Australia, Italy, Norway, Sweden – and some of the big names in powerboat racing. Some stages were going to be around 200 miles so we had to have a massive extra fuel tank put in our boat so that we could make the long distances.

Sadly the race did not have the ideal send off. Prince Michael of Kent was there to start us but although it was July, there was a Force Seven gale blowing which meant that only 15 of the 40 boats reached the first day's destination of Falmouth. We never should have started really but so much organisation was at stake.

It was a logistical nightmare and we had to hire another van for a second back-up crew with spare parts, engines, clothes and money as one van could not have covered every stage in time. We made it to Falmouth and the next day we were due to round Land's End and go on to Fishguard in South Wales. I have never been so frightened in my life. There we were in a 25-foot boat in a 30-foot sea. At one point, I suddenly said to Michael: 'Hell, there's a herd of sheep on the horizon.' But as we got closer, we realised it wasn't a herd of sheep, but so much white water.

You couldn't race, it was all about survival. You become totally disorientated and all you can do is keep the land on your right. We hadn't seen any other boats until we came across one floundering in a bay. It was a yellow catamaran belonging to Ted Toleman, the Richard Branson of his day, who also owned a massive Class 1 boat, which was being raced by his twin sons. All race boats are honour-bound to offer assistance but fortunately they said they could cope.

We limped on and round Land's End but we'd taken in so much water – the bilge pumps couldn't keep up – that everything you touched was live and gave us mild electric shocks. We managed to reach Newquay and pulled into the bay. We were physically and emotionally finished. We must have looked a rare sight plodding up the High Street in our wetsuits, leaving behind a trail of wet footprints. What people don't realise is that when you're racing, there's nowhere to go for a pee and no way to stop for one either. So, you just have to let it happen. By the time you do stop, the results are not much fun!

We had radioed to our back-up to give them our location but before they arrived, we simply had to buy some basics. We had one credit card between us and used it for new underwear, T-shirts, jeans. We booked into a bed and breakfast where I tried to wash out our socks and underwear and dry them on a radiator. That was to be the most disastrous leg of the race and there are penalties for not completing a stage, but next morning we had to refuel and were off again.

Later in the race in Scotland, we chose to miss out another leg, which went through the Caledonian Canal, and take the boat on the trailer and travel overland instead. It was a strategic decision because it would have been a long day with a speed limit through the Canal and we thought it wasn't worth using our engine and our fuel. We had a few days in Inverness, regrouping and licking our wounds before heading off down the East coast.

We pulled in at Whitby where we had the most wonderful fish and chips. Never in my life has food been more welcome. But soon afterwards, we lost our orientation again – satellite navigation systems were just coming in but the organisers decided we could not use them because only those with money could afford them. We saw some guys fishing and cruised up gently and said: 'Excuse me, can you tell me where we are please?' They looked bemused but one replied: 'Scarborough, luv,' in a broad Yorkshire accent. On again to Great Yarmouth where I committed the cardinal sin – putting my foot out to brace us when the boat was on a swell and cracking a bone in my ankle. I had to go to the hospital where they set it and off we went again the next day.

We had to limp in again – literally for me – at Dover because we'd picked up a rope round the propeller. We got permission to go into shallow water, cut off the rope and then wait for the OK to leave again. And finally we reached Portsmouth. Not many others completed the course and we won our class. Before the start, we'd never stopped to think what it might involve and when I look back now, it was just amazing. Powerboat racing is so different from the skills of my grandfather and father. They needed water with a surface like glass to achieve their record skills yet powerboats run in choppy or rough seas.

After the Round Britain, everything else was such an anti-climax, although the racing season went on and we travelled to events in Wales, the West Country, along the South coast, the Thames estuary. However, I was slowly becoming aware that although Michael was loving the racing, he was also pissed off that it always all seemed to be about Gina. And yet, I always included him. When I was asked to go on a lunchtime television show called *Pebble Mill at One*, produced in Birmingham, I said I would only appear with Michael because we were a team. My father was always a team player and I was the same. And Michael was good, he'd put just as much into the boat as me. But he wasn't big enough to see that it wasn't just all about Gina, it was in fact about Donald Campbell.

Record-breakers: Grandfather, Father and I, three generations of the Campbell family at the height of our racing careers, painted by artist Barry Rowe.

Badge of honour: Captain Malcolm Campbell's Royal Kent Regiment identity plaque which I have incorporated into a bracelet that I wear on special occasions.

Sea urchins: At the seaside with cousin Malcolm, my father's sister Jean's youngest son.

A girl's best friend: With Maxie, our labradoodle and my constant companion while we were living at Roundwood, near Reigate in Sussex.

Ho, ho, ho: Meeting Santa on a day trip to Harrod's organised by Dorothy, my stepmother.

Madeira, my dear! Dorothy and I on the holiday island...and our carriage is waiting!

Say cheese! My father and his second wife Dorothy pose for a holiday snap.

This Is Your Life: My father was the seventh person to appear on Eamonn Andrews' programme in 1956.

The book was one of my father's most treasured possessions.

An ocean wave: From my father and I aboard *Bluebird* en route to America on the liner *United States* in June 1957.

Clunk, click: Watched by my father's third wife Tonia Bern (and Mr Whoppit!), I demonstrate the safety harness for the *CN7 Bluebird* car in which he broke the world record in 1964.

Daughter of BLUEBIRD – GINA CAMPBELL

Horse sense: All dressed up with somewhere to go, in this case the local gymkhana.

Home is where the heart is: Of all the family homes of my childhood, Roundwood was my favourite.

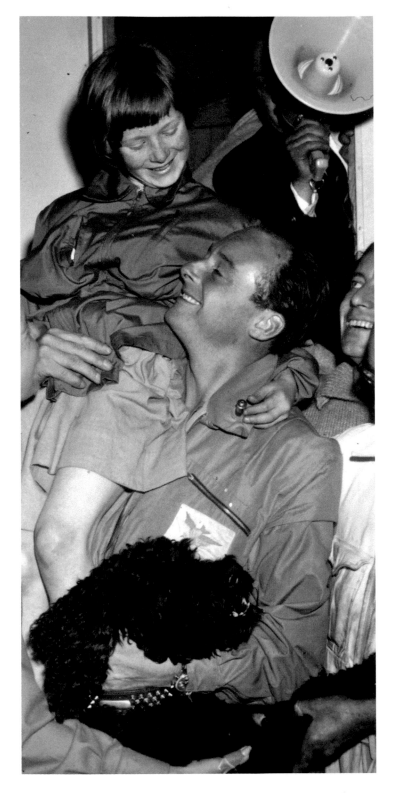

World beater: With my father, and of course Maxie, after his new world water speed record at Coniston in September, 1956.

High-fliers: Tonia and I alongside my father's private plane, at Redhill airfield in Surrey, with his good friends Bill and Betty Coley and their son, Chris.

All systems go: A thumbs up as my father prepares for another run in *Bluebird*.

Weather watch: My father, on his last visit to Coniston, waits for conditions to improve.

Day of destiny: January 4, 1967 and Bluebird's fatal crash at Coniston. My life would never be the same again. (Press Association)

Pedigree chums: A nuzzle from Major, my grandmother's mastiff, on the day of my wedding to my first husband Clifford Percy in June, 1968.

Spick and span: The new stables built for me and my first husband Clifford Percy at Elm Farm, the home we bought after our wedding in 1968.

A Bluebird legend: A word with Leo Villa, my father and grandfather's mechanic, alongside *Bluebird CN7*, father's record-breaking car.

Horse sense: Panache, one of my favourite prize-winning horses, which I took with me after I left my first husband Cliffy.

Marriage Number Two:
With Philip Villa, Leo's
nephew, after our
wedding ceremony at
Epsom Register Office in
July 1980.

Sign language: On the
wrong end of a practical
joker at a trade fair while I
was working for Snapdrape,
a table linenware company,
in the early eighties.

Power game: With Mike Standring, my partner and co-driver, and my mother and her partner Owen at the launch of the *Agfa Bluebird* powerboat in February 1984.

A lotta bottle: Final briefing from Roger Jenkins before my near-fatal crash at Holme Pierrepont in 1984. His head honcho always known as Mr T left the scribble.

In loving memory: At Lake Dumbleyung, Western Australia, alongside the memorial stone dedicated to my father, who broke the world water speed record there in 1964.

On yer bike! Pedal power proves rather more sedate than powerboats on my trip to Perth, Western Australia, in September 1984.

Easy riders: Mike and I take *Agfa Bluebird* for a gentle workout for the benefit of the cameras.

Chapter 9

GET MR WHOPPIT, PLEASE

My first involvement with World Water Speed records happened almost by accident – and ended in the most spectacular way. The last event on the season's racing calendar is Records Week at Windermere at the beginning of November. It's powerboat racing's equivalent of The Horse of the Year Show, the chance to show just how fast your boat can go. It's the time when those who have said all season that their boat will make 85 miles per hour can be found out when it only reaches 69! When Michael and I were asked at our launch whether we would be going to Records Week, of course we said: 'Yes', although at that stage we had no real intention of actually making a record attempt ourselves

However, towards the end of the 1984 season I received a call from a man called Roger Jenkins, a Welshman, who the previous year had become the 1983 World F1 Powerboat Racing Champion. He told me that if we wanted to break any records, there was no way it was going to happen in our boat. He was repeating what a few people had muttered during the season, that our boat was not built for record speeds. He said he had just the boat for me and so I put him in touch with Agfa.

They knew this was yet another cog in the publicity machine so agreed that Roger would supply me with a boat and would mentor me in advance of Records Week to give me a real chance. And again they organised a massive launch, this time on the Serpentine in Hyde Park. We were to go to Holme Pierrepont, the National Water Sports Centre built in 1973 in Nottingham, which has held many international events and was a training centre for the 2012 Olympics. The date was set for October 9.

They hired the water – a two kilometre lake – and brought the boat, which was a totally different animal from anything I'd ever raced. It could do 0-100 miles per hour in four seconds. Michael came with me and Roger was there – he was a musical instrument dealer, a bit bumptious but likeable – along with his engineer sidekick Terry, timekeepers, a few people from Agfa and a television crew who had been following me to make a programme for the QED series of science documentaries on the BBC.

Somewhere at the back of my mind I was aware that four F1 powerboat racers had been killed that summer, Britain's Tom Percival, two Italians and a French racer, but that was never going to stop me. I got in the boat – these things are like sitting on a two-year-old racehorse, so skittish. It was light – two people could lift it – and the only weight was the engine, so the centre of gravity was at the back. It had a drive, but no gearbox, so the moment you start the propeller, it's off. And there's no brake.

The first couple of times I was really slow so then Roger sat on the side, crouched on the flat area, explaining this and that. He must have been a good teacher because within an hour I was flying up and down at 100 miles per hour, loving it but scared. If you asked this boat to go, it went, because it was so light with a massive 4.2 litre engine, fuel injected. It was serious kit. The water had to be flat calm but when you reached a certain speed, about 75 miles per hour, it would vibrate like a car with a serious wheel wobble, which is known as porpoising. Once you drove through that, it increased speed. It was an incredible thrill.

Once you pass the mile marker, you start to slow down, easing off the throttle very gently. If you decelerated too quickly, the nose would drop and it would be dangerous. But you'd be amazed how quickly the boat starts to sink back in the water.

To increase the boat's performance, or 'attitude' as it's called, you can trim the engine: either to bring the propeller closer to the surface of the water, reducing the drag and lifting the nose slightly to achieve more speed, or trim it down for the opposite effect. The top-class drivers who had been racing for years were trimming all the time during races and record attempts but it was out of the question for me because I had no experience. So Roger set the trim and the front wing, designed to keep the boat's nose down, at the points he thought would give the best performance.

So off I went again, this time for a record attempt. And to do that, your speeds must be measured between A and B and B and A, and the average time taken, the same as my grandfather and father had always done. The record stood at around 120 miles per hour and there were great screams of delight when the timekeeper said I had set a new unofficial record of 122.85 miles per hour. Because I had been very quick one way and not so fast the other, Roger decided to take off the front wing to increase the speed. But in the excitement, no-one remembered to realign the trim.

Off I sped. By now I had been in this boat for a couple of hours or more and I was on an adrenalin high when this thing just went up and over, I don't know how high. I didn't realise what was happening, just that one moment my eyeline was straight ahead and the next I was telling myself: 'Don't look up.' But I wasn't looking up, I was going up. And the boat's gone, gone, gone; the moment you've lost contact with the water, you're off. It was a complete copycat of my father's accident, which is what these boats are prone to do. If you trim them out too much, the nose lifts, the wind gets underneath and over you go. I remember wondering who would look after my little dogs Susie and Smartie, and that this could be my very last moment. But the next I knew I could hear that 'glug, glug, glug' noise you hear when you resurface after jumping off a high platform.

I had not been strapped in – the thinking at the time was that you were safer that way, although it has changed now. And fortunately for me, I was thrown out at the top of the curve. I believe I survived because I was so small, no more than seven stone, a little lightweight bundle. Had I been a bigger person and stayed in the craft, I don't think there's any way I could have survived.

As I surfaced, I saw the rescue craft coming towards me, I must have been semi-conscious. They told me afterwards the first thing I said was: 'Can you go and get Mr Whoppit, please?' He was my father's teddy bear mascot which was found after his accident and which had been strapped to the steering column. He went everywhere with us when we raced and became a big star with the press. I'd have to say I didn't really believe in his superhuman powers to keep me safe, but he was a good story.

The front of the rescue craft drops down so you can be floated in but I managed to stand. One of the guys said he was glad to see I was still smiling – but he was standing behind me, not in front. I had split my trousers on impact – I wasn't even wearing a race suit, just a helmet and lifejacket – so the cheeks of my bum were hanging out of my jeans. Probably they were nice and firm and tight in those days! He thought I wasn't wearing any knickers because I only ever wear G-strings. It all became a bit of a joke.

Because I had unofficially beaten the record before that final run, the QED crew had already packed up their equipment, so there are only a few still photographs of the boat flying through the air. We went back to the shore and they went down for the boat which, when you saw what was left of it, made you cry. The superstructure had smashed so it looked a bit like a go-kart, with the steering column all bent and the engine attached at the back.

I walked off the rescue boat – I'm pretty tough and you don't want people to see you in a heap and anyway I still had my dignity, even though my bum was on show. I was soaked, shaken and I had bent the steering column on my exit and had terrible bruises across my thighs. Eventually I was taken to hospital. Roger was in a real state because it dawned on him what he'd done – taken off the front wing but not reset the trim to compensate. I didn't have the knowledge to realise – I was just the stooge who got in and drove it. The whole idea had been for me to know what speed I had done before we went to Windermere for Records Week.

It turned out I had broken both collar bones and fractured my sternum, but I spent just one night in hospital in Nottingham. The accident was front page news everywhere – Gina Campbell almost killed in a copycat accident of her father's. I was a kind of celebrity, whatever that meant, and was being feted as though I was the star of the show. It was surreal. For me, I felt as though I'd had a dismal failure.

The following morning, I remember watching BBC's Breakfast Time where the politician Norman Tebbit, who was then president of the

Board of Trade, was reviewing the morning papers ahead of that year's Conservative Party Conference in Brighton. He said something like: 'This young woman Gina Campbell is in every paper after her great escape – and I knew her father.' He told the story of how he'd met Dad at a pub called The Seven Stars in Leigh, the village pub near our home at Abbots, and after a few drinks, they ended up having a soda siphon fight of all things. Little did anybody know then that less than 48 hours later, in the early hours of the 12th, he and his wife would have to escape from The Grand Hotel after an IRA bomb exploded and tore it apart. It killed five people and injuring over 30 more. The next time I came into contact with him was at Stoke Mandeville Hospital where I was visiting patients as part of Agfa's charity programme and he was visiting his wife Margaret who was badly hurt in the bomb blast and was left permanently disabled.

The severity of my own accident didn't strike me until a few weeks later, when I saw some fast-shutter frame photographs of an Italian in a similar accident, and realised just how close I'd been to death. You could see the point at which his neck was broken and the poor man was killed. I rarely think about it now. I would never say I was a person who had no fear, but I certainly wanted to explore the unknown and the more exciting it seemed, the more I wanted to try whatever it was. If someone had asked me to aim a horse at an eight foot wall and told me he would jump it, I'd do it, as long as they set it all up. But there was one occasion when I ducked out. I was taken to Santa Pod Raceway in Northamptonshire, where they race jet cars and dragsters. I thought I would have a go until they put me in the car, closed the top and I had a panic attack. They had to get me out straight away because I cannot be closed in. It's bad enough being in a helmet and I rarely closed the visor but I cannot bear that trapped feeling. I don't know why, whether it is because of my father's accident, the fact that he couldn't get out, I just don't know.

Despite the accident at Holme Pierrepont, Michael and I agreed we had to honour our commitment to go to Records Week. We knew we were never going to break any records in our offshore boat and it would have been embarrassing to try. Yes, it had a top speed of 85 miles per hour but it was designed for the sea and not built for records. Still, we said we would do some demonstration runs for the press, whizzing up and down the Lake.

We had to drive all the way from Dorking to Windermere in our white Range Rover, pulling a great trailer, at 50 miles per hour. The trailer was specially adapted with a steel frame at the back into which we had to slot a massive board, with electrics for the brake lights, to protect the outboard engines. The whole vehicle was painted with the *Agfa Bluebird* offshore powerboat racing team logo and our names in huge letters. It was quite an outfit and there was no mistaking who we were.

It was a hell of a journey so we stayed overnight on the way and set off again early next morning. Somewhere up the M6 in Lancashire, a car came alongside full of people waving at us. At first we thought they'd recognised our names and were being friendly, so we were waving back until we realised they were furiously pointing behind us. When Michael looked in the mirror, he saw that the board had come adrift and was sitting plumb in the middle of the nearside lane, what looked like about half a mile back. We pulled in straight away and fortunately the road was very quiet because it was early morning.

We had to trudge back and carry this board – me with broken collarbones – along the hard shoulder. By then a police car had arrived and we thought they might help us. But no, instead they drove slowly along the inside lane to shield us from any traffic. Thank God they didn't prosecute us for having a dangerous vehicle.

We were staying at the Low Wood Hotel on Windermere and some of our pals joined us. But the organisers of Records Week were absolutely horrible to me and I've never felt so much hatred from the other boaties. The organisers thought I had stolen all the publicity that should have been around their Week – as if I'd staged the accident deliberately. And is there a strange aspect of human nature that means that even those around you start to resent it when you have had such blanket press coverage? The press saw me as a superhuman superwoman but I just saw the accident as a terrible disgrace – I'd written off the boat and I could have killed myself. I could sense a 'Who do you think you are?' attitude among people there, maybe some jealousy, I don't know.

I even became aware of it again from Michael who loved it all when he was involved, but not when it was just about me and my family. I sensed it created a barrier between us. But we stuck it out for a few days and then went home, totally knackered at the end of a long season.

Agfa loved all the publicity, of course, but could hardly say so. It was around that time that *Marketing Magazine* carried a feature about sponsorship, looking at Agfa's contract with us. The headline said: 'Who says sponsorship doesn't pay?' alongside a picture of me. They wrote that Agfa had gained worldwide publicity worth at least five million pounds from the £50,000 sponsorship of our boat. After all, by then we wore Agfa branded T-shirts, jackets, caps, the lot. I remember doing a BBC Breakfast show interview and the researcher telling me that I must not appear wearing branded clothing. One BBC guy joked that he assumed I wore Agfa underwear.

Because I was often in the news, all kinds of invitations came my way around that time, some for charities, others more commercial. Koo Stark, the American actress and photographer who dated Prince Andrew in the early 1980s, once asked me to pose for pictures – in a bubble bath of all things – for a book she was putting together. I was in the water for so long, I felt as though I'd shrunk by the time I climbed out, a mass of wrinkles. She had taken part in a Cancer Research rally with me, so it was a bit of return favour.

I also did quite a bit of television, which I've always enjoyed. Yes, it can be frustrating if filming doesn't quite go as planned but I usually had a few laughs with the people involved. So when I'm asked, my attitude has always been: 'Why not?'

Although I was not allowed to appear on the BBC when my father was the subject of the *This Is Your Life* programme back in 1956 – children had to be members of Equity then before they could be on television – I was filmed with him for a TV interview when we were in America. I only have very vague memories of it and I never saw the programme, which I think must have been shown live.

By the mid-60s when I was in my teens, my dad and I were invited to appear on a programme called *Whose Baby Am I?* There was a panel of four celebrities and guests were like us – father and daughter, or any parent and child – and it was my first time in front of a live audience. The pancl were blindfolded and they were allowed to ask me 20 questions and I had to answer 'yes' or 'no'. Each time they got one right the audience clapped – probably somebody was holding up a card with the word 'applause.' I remember they guessed right quite quickly. Graham Hill, the F1 World Champion was also on with his son Damon, who was much younger than me, but later became the World Champion too. I wondered why they had chosen two families who were both linked to speed. I'm sure I never saw the programme – it probably went out live too, or very soon after it was recorded and we didn't even have video recorders in those days.

In the mid 80s, I was asked to take part in a programme with the magician Paul Daniels, who was a big name then and had appeared on the *Royal Variety Performance,* and Jeremy Vine, who was probably in the early stages of his TV career then. The idea was to film some kind of escapology trick and I know it was shown over and over again on television because I kept receiving royalties from it.

Anyway, I had to go to Lake Windermere and the stunt involved two race boats, our first *Agfa Bluebird*, which by then had a new name, and our new *Agfa Bluebird*. The idea was that Paul Daniels was supposedly tied on to a cross-like structure and then fastened into this box, almost like a coffin, which was attached to both boats. The boats had to drive in opposite directions at exactly the same moment and he would be torn asunder unless he could escape in time! It was very bizarre. Of course although the cross looked like wood, it was made of some kind of synthetic rubber so he could quickly untie himself and in the coffin was a dummy made to look like him.

Paul's wife Debbie was there – she never left his side – and Paul was charming, absolutely charming even though everything that could go wrong, did go wrong. The weather was terrible and we ended up being there for the best part of a week. I was driving one boat and the buyer of our first boat, the other. They both had to move at exactly the same time but because the boats are sitting idle, ticking over, they're oiling up, so when you put your foot on the gas, they splutter. And one of the engines was direct drive so more prone to oiling up anyway. So we did it time and time again, filming all the time. Lots of frustration but, hey, it was quite good fun too.

I think it was around the same time that I did *Jim'll Fix It*, with Jimmy Savile which amazingly ran for nearly 20 years on the BBC. The programme was about a young boy who wanted to go in our race boat so they arranged for him to come to one of the races and we showed him round the pits and took him out in the boat. Health and safety regulations were just creeping in around that time so we gave him a ride, I think somewhere off the Thames Estuary, but had to be a little bit careful. Frankly I don't think it was that much fun really. When the programme was shown, it looked as though Jimmy Savile was there the whole time, but that wasn't the case – you know how cleverly they film and edit these programmes. I don't remember going to the studio, I think my part was all shot on location. Oddly enough, when I later moved to Leeds in the 1990s, I lived in a flat at Roundhay Park overlooking Jimmy's home. I met him once or twice more at various events but was amazed at the huge turnout for his funeral in Leeds after his death in October 2011.

Then there was a TV series called *Driving Force*, a kind of stunt driving show which involved one 'professional' driver and one celebrity. Apart from my powerboat racing, I'd driven for Renault for a season or two in a series of races at circuits like Brand's Hatch and Donnington Park. I drove a Renault 5 and the only prizes I ever won were for the driver who started the furthest back but made up the highest number of places. I think they liked me because I was careful, never wrote the car off or did any serious damage. *Driving Force* was a bit of fun, filmed over two days, and people like Barry Sheene, the world motorcycling champion, Lenny Henry and the actor Michael Havers all took part. I was teamed with the actress Leslie Ash, who appeared in the TV series *Men Behaving Badly* and then much later, in 2010, in *Holby City*. Leslie was married to the footballer Lee Chapman and later became known for her 'trout pout' after an injection to plump her lips went horribly wrong. Sadly, a few years afterwards, when she was in hospital receiving treatment for two cracked ribs, she contracted an MRSA superbug, which left her unable to walk without sticks for a long time. I read she was paid £5 million in compensation.

I also appeared on *Blue Peter* a few times over the years and I finally did get to play a part in a *This Is Your Life* as a guest. In December 1983, Richard Noble was the subject, just after he broke the land speed record that year. I knew Richard a little then – he was following in my father's footsteps with his land records. He became the project director for ThrustSSC which broke his land speed record in 1997 at Black Rock desert in Nevada and he is now busy developing what he calls BloodhoundSSC, which will be capable of reaching an amazing 1000 mph in 40 seconds, speeds my father could never have even dreamed of. Anyway the BBC asked me if I would appear on the show live and present Richard with his certificate. They're very beautiful – I have my dad's at home – and he was almost more proud of that than anything else. They always have a hand-painted image of your boat or car or whatever it is.

It was quite short notice when they asked me because I was on holiday with Michael and two friends in Lanzarote – in a four star hotel which turned out to be a complete dump. Our room had a bare light bulb hanging from the ceiling – it was awful so I didn't mind being interrupted. The BBC flew me back and sent a car to pick me up at Heathrow. The driver drove me home to Ashford so that I could get changed – the poor man must have had a bad stomach because he had to use my toilet in a hurry – and then took me to the studios.

I had been given some lines to learn which I practised in my head as we drove there. I was to say: 'I know how proud my father was of his record certificate so it gives me great pleasure to present this to you.' But as I walked on to the stage when I was prompted, Richard seized me and he was frightfully exuberant and he was whooping and the crowd was clapping and all the time Eamonn Andrews was holding the certificate behind his back. I was trying to speak and Eamonn was gesturing to me: 'For goodness sake, get your words out' and all the time Richard was whooping and I didn't know whether to speak over him. I kept starting my lines but in the end, Richard quietened down and I was able to finish my sentence. He was thrilled. Then the BBC flew me back so fortunately I didn't have to spend the entire week in that awful place.

Then in 1985, the BBC made the QED programme – it was their crew which was at Holme Pierrepont – which was shown on May 15, 1985 and called *Gina – The Last Campbell.*

Later on, when I travelled to New Zealand and became involved in the Water Safety Campaign, I seemed to be on TV there quite often. And when I competed in the World Powerboat Championships both there and in America, there were always TV film crews around.

Then in the late 1980s I worked with Melvyn Bragg on a documentary about my father and once Bill Smith found Bluebird, I was involved in yet another BBC documentary. Of course since then there have been so many stories about my father's body being found, the funeral, Bill's rebuilding of *Bluebird* – and very often they involve a TV interview for either local television in Cumbria or national TV.

Chapter 10

WHERE THE MURDERS TOOK PLACE

My love affair with New Zealand began in 1984, the same year as my speed record at Holme Pierrepont, when, out of the blue that summer, I had a phone call from someone I had not seen for almost 30 years. I recognised her voice straight away. It was Dorothy, my dad's second wife and the one real mother to me. She was in London and wanted to meet. It turned out that for years, Dorothy had been wary of contacting me because she didn't know how I felt about her – she thought I would feel she had abandoned me when she left my father. Then she was sent a cutting of an interview with me in the *Daily Mail* in which I had said how much I loved and respected Dorothy. I am not a person who looks backwards – I have been treated badly by a lot of people but I am a great forgiver, not that I had anything to forgive Dorothy for.

After she split with my dad in 1958, Dorothy had returned to New Zealand, where she was a very well-known actress with a really impressive CV in the theatre – she was never out of work – and a handful of films including *Middle Age Spread*, a successful comedy drama about a midlife crisis made in 1979. She kept her maiden name Dorothy McKegg as her stage name – she came from a very large family of Scots descent and all her siblings were professionals and generally well-known in the country. She loved London with a passion and came as often as she could to see the shows – she usually rented a small basement bedsit for a month. She had remained friendly with my dad's sister Jean and her husband Buddy Hulme for a long time after she returned to New Zealand but eventually she and Jean fell out and she just stayed in touch with Buddy. Jean and Buddy were divorced by then.

Back home she had married Hans Wenk, an Austrian who was a director of Ciba Geigy, the pharmaceutical company, in New Zealand

and they had three children, two boys of their own, Max and David, and an adopted daughter Lisa. Max and David are complete chips off the old block, peas from the same pod as their father, both with wonderful hearts and heads on them. Lisa was from a part-Pacific Islander background and was so beautiful. But when I first met the family, Lisa was in Australia with her now husband Bobbie and Max was down in Wellington and, at that time, hotly pursuing his now lovely wife Anne.

We met for lunch and it was as though we'd never been apart. By then I had already been invited to Australia for a ceremony on December 31, 1984, to celebrate the 20th anniversary of the day my father broke the water speed record at Lake Dumbleyung in Western Australia. That was in the same year that he'd already broken the land speed record at Lake Eyre, the only man to achieve both in the same year. I had been asked to unveil a memorial. When I told Dorothy, I said: 'I'll come to New Zealand for Christmas then.' And she said: 'That will be nice dear' – I could almost see her thinking that she didn't believe I would because I probably said it almost too flippantly. That comment was so Dorothy. But then she immediately invited Michael and I to Auckland for Christmas.

It was a huge adventure for us. Before disembarking we had to sit on the aircraft while two guys walked up and down the aisles spraying all and everything in sight with insecticide to make sure no-one was bringing anything 'nasty' into the country. There were no air bridges in those days, so it was just a walk from the plane to the terminal building and the very first thing that hit us was the amazing blue sky and the smell of fresh air.

Dorothy and Hans met us at the airport and took us back to their home in Bassett Road, Remuera, the Knightsbridge of Auckland. But it was also famous throughout New Zealand for the Bassett Road gangland murders of two men back in 1963 so when you told people where you were living, immediately they said: 'Oh, where the murders took place!'

Their Christmas tree was already trimmed and there were presents underneath, including lots for Michael and me. There was such a feeling of extreme kindness towards me, even from her children who could have hated me. They called me their half-sister even though I am no relation to them at all – Dorothy's influence meant they felt no malice towards me, even though my father at times had treated her very badly. I still receive birthday cards from her children 'to a loving sister', which is how they see me yet my family had caused nothing but heartache to their mother. It was overwhelming really because I've never had those same feelings, that same unconditional warmth and love, from my own family.

She told me that after Max was born, she desperately wanted more children but when she didn't get pregnant, they decided to adopt Lisa as a baby. No sooner had they done so than she found she was expecting David. And it was when she was eight or nine months pregnant with David, in bed with a streaming cold, that she heard the news that my father had been killed. She said she was heartbroken and soon she had the world's press banging on her door which upset her so much because despite Dorothy's life and career, she was a very private person and had always avoided any press contact as much as she could.

It was clear that Dorothy had an extremely stressful life. Hans was a man of routine who, when he came home from the office, put on his slippers, had dinner and watched TV. It struck me as so strange that the whole family sat down to watch every episode of *Coronation Street* even though they were some six months behind the storyline in England! I had to try so hard not to interject and give away what happened next.

Dorothy held her family together with the daily routine of shopping, cooking, washing and all the other jobs that a regular 'housewife' would do. Then she had a mad rush to the theatre for the daily rehearsals or a matinee performance, back home again in the late afternoon to prepare the dinner, clean up and back to the theatre for the evening's performance. She'd climb into bed at midnight or 1am and then start again next morning. She revealed to me that she had reached the point where she started drinking – gin or vodka was her way of coping – until she knew she was in danger of becoming an alcoholic. But she took herself off to Alcoholics Anonymous and by the time we were there in '84 she did not touch a drop, ever.

Dorothy also told me about an experience she had late one night when she was driving back from the show in the pouring rain and her car went into a violent skid. She was about to hit something when she saw and felt my father's hands on top of hers, pulling her out of the skid! Anyone who knew Dorothy would totally believe that this must have happened, for sure, as you could never meet a person more sceptical about these surreal kind of experiences. She for ever said that my dad saved her life that night.

We had a fabulous time with them all and after Christmas, Michael and I flew to Perth as arranged for the trip to Lake Dumbleyung. We were met by a big burly, sandy-haired man, whose business card told us he was Mr A.A. Lewis, a Member of the Legislative Council of the Upper House of the Parliament of Western Australia. He was known to everyone as 'Sandy'. He took us to our hotel and then showed us around the city, which I thought was just fantastic with the magnificent Swan River its main feature. The whole place was just so beautiful, clean, tended and modern. Sandy showed me where my father had triumphantly driven the *Bluebird* at very fast speeds down the Swan River after his successful record until some idiot in a speedboat crossed right ahead of him, very nearly causing a catastrophe.

Then the next day he and his wife drove us to Dumbleyung, which is about 170 miles from Perth – a fabulous drive through wild, barren countryside but with lots of wildlife, including brightly-coloured parakeets, kangaroos, possums and the whole big nature thing. I loved it.

Dumbleyung itself looked like a bit of a one-horse town, a dusty street with a pub with a wooden balustrade outside, like you see in the Western movies. It was really the sort of place I had never been privileged enough to see before and everyone was so hospitable and friendly. The actual event was amazing because although the community was only a few hundred people, thousands turned up to this place in the middle of nowhere on New Year's Eve. They'd organised a jamboree with so much going on: live music, jazz bands, country and western music, just so full-on for the whole day. There was waterskiing and boat racing, balloons, barbecues and lots of booze. And of course the weather was so fabulous, so strange to experience the boiling hot sun in December. The whole thing happened in a bit of a haze for me, with so many people coming up and shaking my hand, kissing me, telling me how wonderful my father had been. It blew me away that they felt so proud that my father had put their place on the map of Australia. Michael and I felt so privileged.

The monument is an enormous piece of granite, over 20 feet high by some eight feet wide and eight inches thick. It is roughly hewn into the shape of Western Australia, with a tiny hole, the width of my finger, drilled through it at the exact geographical point of Lake Dumbleyung. On the ground below is a concrete slab with a brass plaque in the shape of the Lake with all its features and in the middle a brightly polished model of *Bluebird*, measuring about three inches long. At the exact time my father started *Bluebird* on its record breaking run – 3.14pm – a beam of sunlight shone through the tiny hole on to the Bluebird. I didn't realise then that until that moment the dignitaries had been holding their breath to see whether the local blacksmith's mathematical calculations and hard work were 100% accurate and would achieve the result they wanted. Because the shaft of sunlight only rested on the model for some 60 seconds, and this would only happen at this exact time on this day of the year, just shows how precise his calculations had to be. When it worked, there was one huge collective sigh of relief.

I made a speech – I don't remember a word of what I said – and I was just overwhelmed by the whole occasion. It's a bit like your wedding day: you come away afterwards knowing it's been wonderful but all too much.

Years later, when my father's body was finally recovered from Coniston, all that time after his death, I received an email from a man called Ian McCormack on behalf of the people of Dumbleyung. They knew the date of his funeral and Ian wrote: 'I would like to advise you that the people of Dumbleyung will be joining with you on this day in a remembrance and tribute to a great man, your father, Donald Campbell. Many members of the community, and other people from across Western Australia, will be travelling to Dumbleyung for this memorial service. He will forever be regarded by this community with admiration and respect.' It was very moving and proved that what I saw there in 1984 was something genuine and lasting.

Although Michael and I were booked on a flight back to Auckland, we asked if we could extend our stay for two or three days because we loved Perth so much. It's a lovely city and to me then, it seemed like England in a big, wide open way and America without the crass. And of course there was the sun – I'm a sun-lover which I shouldn't be with my fair colouring.

We eventually flew back to New Zealand, rented a car for a few days and drove around Auckland and all the waters' edges because in New Zealand water is everywhere. We crossed over the hugely impressive Auckland Harbour Bridge and drove around all the little bays and inlets until we arrived in Takapoona, which is now so chi-chi, where we got talking to some boys with boats. They nearly fell over when they realised who my family were and even knew of my own powerboat racing achievements. They took us out on their boat, round the islands, and without doubt, right then, Auckland harbour and its surroundings blew my mind. It was so wild and rugged, so beautiful, so blue. I did fall in love with it.

What I didn't know then was that two years later I'd be part of a team competing in the World Powerboat Championships held in Auckland. But a lot happened in between.

Michael and I probably spent about three weeks there altogether and crammed so much into that time. I still have photos of the day we flew out of Auckland — I look so funny because in those days, people used to travel in their best clothes and I am wearing one of my best Mondi skirts. Today it would be a pair of joggers, anything to be comfortable. I think the organisers of the Dumbleyung ceremony flew us business class so we definitely felt we had arrived on the international jet scene.

Back in England, Michael and I continued racing and we were really at the height of our success. It was in 1985 that we changed the boat for a carbon fibre, more high-tech version but which somehow never felt to perform as well as our original. Agfa changed everything: the livery was a bit more arty with go-faster stripes, the colouring slightly different and everything was redesigned, the logo, the notepaper, the shirts and clothing. It's commonplace today but then it was a very big deal and must have cost them a fortune. Again they organised a massive launch which took place at a waterski facility at Bedfont Lakes, close to

Heathrow Airport which I believe received the surface drainage water from the runways.

The boat was lighter which in theory meant it would go faster. But it also meant it would twist about and be very lively. To add insult to injury, we sometimes had to watch our old boat, the original *Agfa Bluebird*, go sailing past us during races. But it didn't stop us winning the European Championship, decided over a series of races for which we amassed the most points. We raced in Class 3, which was the most fiercely contested but also because it was in some ways affordable. We could still tow our boat to the races behind a suitable vehicle without needing an enormous low loader and lifting gear.

It was still a dangerous sport, no mistake. Didier Pironi, the Formula 1 driver who turned to powerboats, was killed with his two crew in a race called the Needles Trophy off the Isle of Wight in 1987. I was in that race but you're not aware of what's happened unless you are right behind. We saw Didier's boat spin out but because there are so many spectator boats and rescue craft in the vicinity, you don't stop. Agfa had hired a hospitality boat for that race and were asked to tow in the stricken craft. It's only afterwards that you discover and then it's a terrible shiver down the spine and a 'there but for the grace of God' feeling. And in 1990 I was in Monaco when Stefano Casharagi, Princess Caroline's husband, was killed in an offshore powerboat race off Cap Ferrat.

To be involved in the rolling start of an offshore powerboat race is something to experience as you may have up to 50 or 60 boats from all classes, sizes and power thundering down to the start line behind a fast-moving boat. When the green flag drops it's every man for himself, jockeying for position in the spray and the noise and trying to avoid all the wash from the other boats. After a few minutes you start to slot into position, the fast boats moving ahead and thereby getting some clear water and vision.

Nobody ever talked about my going for a record again and we never went back to Records Week, partly because they had received me so badly. People had tried to make me feel I was just a publicity-seeking little bit of nothing. But when Agfa were sending out press releases nearly every damn day, I was completely at their mercy.

I was still having to treat Michael with kid gloves so he didn't feel second rate. I was constantly saying to the press: 'This is my partner Michael, he is more important than me.' I don't think he ever appreciated how much I pushed him, brought him to the fore. If I'd been a boy, even then, I wouldn't have received so much attention and now it wouldn't matter at all. But then I was a little waif, an only child, the last of the Campbells, prepared to put my life on the line in a sport I didn't really know much about.

Chapter 11

THIS IS MY LAKE, F... OFF!

Michael and I parted suddenly at the end of 1985. I knew he was running around with a girl who was a hanger-on with another offshore powerboat team. She and some friends had also been out with us on our ski boat off the south coast. I remember her whipping her top off, leaving her boobies leaping all over the place as we went over the waves. Michael was a full-blooded male and of course wanted a bit of that. He went off to Devon on a holiday and I knew it was obviously with her. It was always going to happen some time – Michael was at least five years younger than me. In fact his nickname for me was Old Cam. While it was supposed to be a bit of fun, it always touched a raw nerve in me because I believe that many a true word is really said in jest. I was still working for Agfa whenever they wanted me and one evening I went back to the house and everything of his had gone. What a horrible, sick feeling – it had never been discussed, he'd never said he wanted to leave.

I was knocked sideways because we had been so intertwined and my pride was hurt. When you're in the public eye, you feel a bit stupid, you cannot lick your wounds on your own. I am a sensitive soul and I do hurt inside, terribly, although I try not to show it, even though it may be written across my forehead. It comes from being rejected, discarded, kicked around all through my life.

You could say I've had an awful lot of pluses in my life – a very famous father, a fabulous man. Was he a good father? Who knows. He rejected me as a baby. He used to say he didn't know I was at High Trees but I have to question that. I certainly respected my father but as for loving him, what is love, how do you love your parents, what do you love them for? I see kids today who love their parents because they get everything they want out of them. Is that love, or gratitude, or just greed on their part?

I suppose in my teenage years I started to realise that other girls of my age had different lives. Then, at 17, I lost my father and my mother was barely a part of my life at all. I could be very self-pitying but in the end you have to pull yourself out of it. Maybe because I don't have siblings or that protective shield of a family around me, I always feel I have to carry this on my own. Friends are great and they help for five minutes, five days, five weeks, but you cannot burden your friends with your problems for ever. I'm a great believer that a friend in need is a pain in the arse! So in the end, it's down to you and eventually I had to get over Michael.

I did race again with him once or twice, even though we were no longer a couple. And there was just one more time that we really got together. It was the day Prince Andrew married Sarah Ferguson, July 23, 1986. We'd been parted for a while but he came round for something or other while I was watching the wedding on television. I opened a bottle of champagne and we must have got a bit tiddly and started flirting – after all we had been together virtually 24 hours a day for over 18 months and even though it hurt me when he left, it wasn't difficult to relight the spark. So after a few glasses, we both ran upstairs .... but then that really was it between us.

My mother actually gave me a few quid to eventually buy him out of the house so that I became the sole owner. My friends Michael Meech and June were really good to me and they helped me through that period enormously. Michael was married and lived the proverbial double life. One Hallowe'en night, I was at June's house for dinner and Michael had the rubber gloves on washing up after our lovely meal, when there's a knock at the door. Michael answered it, still wearing the gloves, expecting it to be trick-or-treaters, but it was his wife. 'Michael, what do you think you are doing?' she said. 'Washing up, of course,' he replied, without batting an eyelid. She knew about June yet she never left Michael and he never left his wife. But I had a lot of fun with those two.

It helped that I picked up a brief romance with a fellow called Dick Sutton, an absolute playboy who raced boats. He was so good for my ego! He was a powerful man, good-looking, lots of money. He was madly attractive to me at the time and my ego popped up when it was clear he was interested in me.

We met through a friend of his, Colin Curran, who raced a boat called *Red Rum*. He found out that I owned a parascender, like a parachute which is towed behind a boat. I bought it when I was with Michael and we took it down to Sandbanks in Dorset with our little ski boat. You strap yourself into a harness and straighten out all the lines and ropes and then as the boat moves off, you take one, two, three running steps on the water until you take off. The faster the boat goes, the higher you go. The first time, I was absolutely terrified – there must be 100 feet of rope and it's quite cold up there. The second time was good fun although there's all the performance of getting disentangled between each run and if the boat slows, you slowly drop until you're paddling on the water. The party piece is when they then put their foot down and whoosh, you're off again. But if they slow too much it means you're dragging your legs in the water. Today, in the south of France, they winch you on to a deck on the back of the boat so you don't get wet. We used it about three times, but somehow it was one of those novelties whose appeal didn't last. Dick Sutton wanted to buy it and Colin knew I had one, so that's how he got the two of us together in the first place. I think I got my £400 back, or whatever it cost.

Dick and I had a ball for the time we were together. I thought I'd fallen on my bottom and landed in heaven. But it doesn't take long to realise that before too long he'd be saying bye-bye and asking another woman. But he took me on a couple of trips. He rang one day to say he was off on a business trip to Puerto Banus, close to Marbella, which at that time was *the* place to be on the Costa del Sol. He picked me up, whisked me off to Heathrow, threw £1,000 into my hands to change into pesetas, and on into the first class lounge. I thought my ship had come in. Then it was a room in some fancy hotel where I was on my own by the pool most days while he was working, then back in the evening for dinner.

At one point he was even threatening to take his boat out to the World Powerboat Racing Championships in New Zealand that winter, with me as crew, but in the end the cost of transporting the boat, crew and spares and everything else was just too much. I would have loved Dick Sutton to go to New Zealand – I could have been his pit floosie or whatever you call them, although actually he wanted me as crew. But it was immensely good for me while it lasted because I did take a knock when Michael left. It's that sense of abandonment which as I've said goes back to my childhood and maybe I take it worse than others. I suddenly think my whole world has collapsed whereas in the scheme of things it's probably not that serious. But it knocks the absolute stuffing out of me. It must be like someone who has a serious illness – they wake up in the morning and, for two seconds, it's a bright new day and then the reality is straight into your brain again and you cannot block it out.

It was around then too that I had a rare moment of passion, totally out of the blue, from a man whom I'd worked with at Agfa since our sponsorship started. Tim Light was in Agfa's PR team, a man with beautiful, thick, glossy, shoulder length hair. He was artistic, maybe even fey, but masculine for all that. We had met so many times in their offices and at functions but it had never been more than a working relationship and a friendship between us, but it turned out that we did hold a torch for one another. Then one evening when we met he walked up to me and gave me the most passionate kiss, which felt like the proverbial electric shock. It's not often in my life, if ever, that anyone who has never hinted at a romantic interest in me, has kissed me like that. I've never forgotten it. He rang me a couple of times afterwards and we spoke affectionately, but he knew that nothing more could happen between us. It had changed our relationship. It left a massive mark on me. I am quite romantic, I love kisses and cuddles and I'm a nurturer. I'm a Virgo, an earth sign, a homemaker, it's my raison d'etre.

I knew I was going back to New Zealand for the winter, so I took a lodger who could stay in the house. His name was Philip Rowley, a nice man who worked for Canon, which was ironic as they were competitors of Agfa. When we were there together, there was not much privacy – it was only a small terraced house – but it was fine when I was away. He was keen on rowing and used to coach a ladies' rowing team.

A well-known Kiwi racer John Garrity had asked if I would crew in his boat for the World Powerboat Championships in Auckland in 1986 but before I went out there, I had a call from Dorothy to say that her husband Hans had died suddenly. He had a ruptured spleen. She was booked on a tour of New Zealand with *The Pirates of Penzance* and didn't want to pull out, but nor did she want to leave David, her younger son, alone at home. Her elder son Max was working in Wellington and her daughter Lisa was still in Australia. She asked if I could go out earlier than planned.

So I flew out and moved into the house with David – he was in his late teens then. He was stable enough and we became very close friends, spending a lot of time together. We'd go to the beach and if Dorothy was appearing not too far away, we'd drive there and surprise her after the show.

I competed in the World Championships with John Garrity in a boat called *Harris Cat*. He had a small engineering firm and I think he hoped I could be his girlfriend as well as his driver, but there was never a chance of that happening. There were just the two of us in his boat – in some there are three to include a throttle man – so I was the steerer, the driver, the team principal, because accreditation is given to the driver. It means that navigation is a joint responsibility which can be tricky. We spent endless hours of practice out in the Hauraki Gulf, day after day, before the Championships proper started and it felt like almost every time, the boat broke down. It was a bit of a Heath Robinson affair to be honest. But it is such a beautiful part of the world to hold any boating spectacular and there was so much excitement around the championships, that I had lots of fun. And after all Dick Sutton didn't turn up! So even if I ended up with second best, I was just thrilled to be involved.

The Championships were a huge event with all the top teams from America and Italy taking part. We were totally outclassed – a joke really – but he just wanted to participate. There was a lot of publicity about my racing with him but on many of the legs the boat broke down again and we'd have to be towed in. When it happened once too often, I decided it was so bad for my reputation that I went down to the pits, told him he was wasting my time and I was quitting. As I turned my back and walked away, a photographer from the *New Zealand Herald* snapped me and the paper ran the picture on the sports pages, painting me as a petulant prima donna. So after rejecting John first when he tried to woo me and then because his boat was useless, he really started to bad-mouth me something chronic. But hey, I suppose I was a mini celebrity then and I enjoyed that status, so it didn't cause me too many sleepless nights.

While I was in New Zealand, I had a call from the UK. It was from Melvyn Bragg, asking me to co-operate on his remake of a documentary film that was first made in 1968, the year after my father was killed. It was called *The Price of a Record* and was scheduled to be shown on the 20th anniversary of my father's accident.

I flew back from New Zealand specially and spent three days with Melvyn at Coniston. I hadn't been there for ages – it used to make me feel positively ill, so much so that I'd have to rush behind a bush to be sick. I'd always said I would never go on the lake, so when they asked me if I would drive a boat up the measured mile, I said a very definite, 'No'. To me that was like walking on my dad's grave.

There was a full production team there and Melvyn was very persuasive and smooth and managed to schmooze me enough by saying it would really add to the poignancy of the film. They must have all been particularly persuasive because eventually I agreed, but reluctantly. I wasn't even dressed for it – I was wearing a lovely black leather jacket.

It was freezing cold, the middle of winter, and we all trooped down to where the Bluebird Café is now – then it was just a wooden shack. And after I finally agreed, a powerboat came backing down towards the slipway, all written up with artwork very similar to my *Agfa Bluebird*. There was me saying there was no way I would go on the lake but they had obviously anticipated that I would eventually agree.

It was bitterly cold, but still and calm. Then suddenly, as we stood watching the boat back down, the weather just turned – black skies, fierce winds, rain, almost hailstones – and the lake turned into mountainous waves. The guy pulled the boat out of the water, it almost looked as though it was going to sink. We all dived into this little wooden shack, which then only opened in the summer for ice creams but now is a beautiful modern glass and timber chalet, to let this squall blow through. Eventually it passed and they managed to put the boat back in the water when it happened again – the weather went from being still and calm to a huge squall blowing up the lake.

This had happened three times in the space of three or four hours before Melvyn said to me: 'Somebody doesn't want us on this lake and is telling us to bugger off.' So I never drove that boat - whose boat it was, where it had come from, to this day I don't know. The whole thing was spooky. We went up to the Sun Hotel for soup and sandwiches and I finished the interview there with shafts of sunlight coming through the windows.

It sounds melodramatic to say but I think that weather was warning me off. In my mind's eye I could see my father's face, like one of those caricatures of God with bulging cheeks, breathing down on the world, with a speech bubble coming out of his mouth saying: 'This is my lake, fuck off.' Isn't that extraordinary?

I never wanted to go on the lake in the first place, among other things I didn't want to make a complete fool of myself. But the film was finished and shown on television and Melvyn wrote about that experience of the weather on the lake in one of his columns in *The Observer*. He was so complimentary about me, flowery beyond words, I wondered if I was reading about the same person. He had been so charming, it's no wonder women find him attractive in that craggy sort of way and with that accent which you cannot quite pinpoint.

I was in England for such a short time that I flew back to New Zealand with the same air crew I had flown out with. They were so impressed that they'd had the same first class passenger on the flight out and back, that the captain invited me in to the cockpit for take-off at Heathrow and landing at Auckland. I remember sitting behind him coming in to land in the enormity of this Air New Zealand jumbo jet and seeing the runway in the distance. It looked just like a pencil, so small and yet you have the feeling of this enormous aircraft behind you.

Flying is not my favourite means of transport – in fact I'm quite a scared flyer and on one of the journeys it was extremely bumpy. I sat next to a man who introduced himself as one of the training pilots for Air New Zealand and I always remember him telling me to relax, that the aircraft had several back-up systems and was much more able to cope with the turbulence than I was.

His words came back to me in 2011 when I was on a boat heading back from Corsica to Antibes. It was so rough around Cap Corse, water coming over the top, chairs flying, everything on the top deck soaking wet and pretty uncomfortable for about two hours. It felt very scary but I knew that, like the plane, the boat could hack it. It's the people who struggle.

Back in New Zealand there was still quite a lot of publicity about my competing there and a few days before I was due to fly home, I had a call from a girl called Joanne Ruscoe, on behalf of a PR company, Findlay Kitchen. She told me New Zealand was struggling with some of the highest death rates by drowning per head of population in the Western world because most places are pretty close to water and lots of people go swimming and boating, not racing necessarily, just for fun. A lot of their problems arose because the Kiwis are known for their gung-ho attitude and they used to load up the boat with a chilly bin of stubbies – as they call a cool box of beers – and head off with scant regard for safety. There would be kids, grannies and grandpas, maybe eight or ten in a boat designed for four, off for a day's swimming and fishing. Joanne told me they had been commissioned to come up with ways of reducing them, to educate people that it was great to go out there but they must have communication, take flares, have lifejackets for everybody on board, the basic safety equipment. There were also some incidents where people had driven off the road into a river and drowned, others where people who'd had a can of beer or two decided to cool off by jumping off a bridge into a river below. But because they were wearing big, heavy jeans, soon got into difficulties and sometimes drowned.

She asked whether I'd be prepared to talk to some schoolchildren about water safety and introduce them to Mr Whoppit. I had talked a lot about water safety after I survived my speed record attempt at Holme Pierrepont and although I always thought it was down to my small size, whenever I was asked, I made a point of saying it was helped by my preparation, my lifejacket, helmet, the rescue craft. Of course all the guys who had sadly been killed in such accidents had the same back-up. And I could have said I was just bloody lucky or that it was down to Mr Whoppit or my father was looking down on me, but I always wanted to highlight the safety factors.

So I went to the school, which had a swimming pool – most have in

New Zealand – with Mr Whoppit under my arm. Then, I was asked if I could give a short lecture on water safety to what looked like hundreds of the most smiley, bonny, happy-looking kids I'd ever seen. Talk about winging it! I had no training in talking to schoolchildren. But at the end I said that Mr Whoppit had survived after my father's accident because he was buoyant – and I threw him into the pool. I knew he would float and sure enough, there he lay on his back in the water with his little snout in the air.

The kids loved it. We pulled him out and dried him and they all wanted to hold him. It struck a chord, the local TV and radio covered it and what had started out as a bit of community spirit, really took off. Before we left New Zealand, Joanne rang to ask whether, if they could attract sponsorship for a Government Water Safety Council initiative, I would be interested in fronting a safety campaign. It would run for about three months during their spring, from October or November. I jumped at it – I didn't even need a reason to go back to New Zealand on a regular basis but this would be a great one.

Sure enough, the Safety Council found a sponsor in the ANZ Bank and for three years from 1987, from October to January, I travelled everywhere in New Zealand promoting water safety. In total it was a $300,000 campaign so you can imagine it was full-on. I had to make TV commercials, give interviews to television, radio and newspapers, visit schools, travel to every branch of the ANZ Bank, often having lunch with the staff, everything you could think of. I loved it but it was hard work.

I was there not just to promote boating safety – with lifejackets and buoyancy aids – but all water safety. I was told that between January 1 and November 30 in 1987, 129 people drowned in all kinds of accidents and so I tried to feature all dangers, included those of drinking before swimming or going out in a boat. The Safety Council were very pleased with the response and the ANZ Bank said it had been their most successful sponsorship of any campaign up to then.

And it was in the middle of this first year's campaign that I flew to Key West in Florida to navigate for two Kiwi racers, Graeme Sutherland and Kevin Green, in the World Championships again. Graeme was a big name on the racing scene in New Zealand and had commissioned a 41-

foot Apache, which he named *Warlord*, and then shipped it out to the US for the Championships.

It was held in America every other year but the joke was that although it was called the World Championships, very few other countries competed due to the cost of transporting the boats out there. But Key West was razzmatazz and attracted all kinds of celebrities.

Because I had started my work with the Water Safety Council, they had asked me to make a daily radio update for broadcast in New Zealand. I had a little transmitter which I learned to operate and I had to plug myself in and give a live broadcast, as if I was hot and panting straight off the race boat. On one broadcast I said the greatest excitement was that the actor Don Johnson, who was in the TV series *Miami Vice*, had blown me a kiss.

The reigning world powerboat racing champion was a guy called George Morales who had won the title three times. Then he really hit the headlines when he was arrested for conspiracy to smuggle cocaine. He pleaded guilty to drugs and tax evasion charges in January 1987 and was jailed for 16 years. The story was that he would race out to the furthest point, maybe 15 or 20 miles off shore and fake some kind of breakdown, so that a support boat would pull alongside while they remedied the problem. But in fact what they were doing, so the rumours were, was transferring drugs from one boat to another.

Unfortunately for us, our boat *Warlord* had massive reliability problems and we didn't achieve very much. But it was just great to be there and be part of it. Then it was back to New Zealand to complete my first year of the Safety Campaign.

Back in the UK, I had still been doing my bit for Agfa but I was racing as a freelance, with anybody who asked me. During the last race of the 1987 season I broke my nose when a wave smashed into my visor. I was starting to get fed up of the same old places, same old people, same old bullshit – it became incredibly repetitive. There were new brooms at Agfa, management changes and inevitably my deal with them fizzled out.

Chapter 12

I THOUGHT I HAD MY DAD BACK BESIDE ME

Early in 1988, the BBC made the film *Across the Lake,* in which the amazingly fabulous actor Anthony Hopkins portrayed my father. It was set in the final months of my father's life, up to and including his time up in Coniston and the Lake District, an area that was so dear to my father and my grandfather, Sir Malcolm, and which played such a big part in their lives. My entire family has had an enormous affinity with the Lakes, this most beautiful part of the British Isles, and a real love, respect and admiration for its people and families, built up over many years, leading up to the time when my father was killed on January 4th 1967. I went along to the filming of one or two scenes, including one at Lake Coniston, and the nightclub scene in which my father so smart in his dinner jacket is sitting in the audience watching Tonia singing and he then goes backstage to see her. It was shot in a rather seedy looking nightclub in Windermere, filmed that way because not all of the places Tonia performed in were 'The Talk of the Town'. It was a big budget dramatisation specifically made for the BBC, with the same writer and producer of a previous BBC production nine years earlier about my grandfather. It was called *Speed King* in which Robert Hardy played the lead role. Both productions received outstanding reviews and coverage.

For me, watching the filming of these episodes was just surreal. It is quite extraordinary to watch your father and stepmother being portrayed as they were in life, being played out before your eyes, and yet with all the associated paraphernalia of extras, crew and film-making stuff. But nonetheless, it was very exciting and emotional. I only wish I had had the presence of mind to have taken more of it in…but I was mesmerised and so almost detached.

The morning of the transmission on the BBC, I was interviewed on

Breakfast TV with Anthony – now Sir Anthony – and as we sat in the 'Green Room' prior to our bit, he just suddenly transformed himself into my father. He not only looked like him but he had captured the voice intonation, his mannerisms, the whole thing. I found this very unnerving as Anthony was so charming, sexy and desirable that I had to pull myself away and realise that I couldn't fancy this man, for goodness sake... .he's my father! It did make me realise though why both men had so many women just fall at their feet, and hoped to make it into their beds! As we sat next to one another on the sofa my one desire was to hug him to bits because for one moment I thought I had my dad back beside me. The same piercing blue eyes, the hair, the build, and he was the same sort of age that I remembered my father. It was amazing how he could just suddenly become him but, of course, reality dawned, in some ways very sadly, that this was just an act. I had to ask him to stop the 'act' as I was overcome with emotion and the whole event has left a lasting impression on me. Some months later, when I was spending a weekend at a health hydro in Surrey, lo and behold who should be there but Anthony? We spent some time talking, reminisced, and he told me that after the film was shown, he kept receiving Donald Campbell fan mail and was sent all sorts of photos and items that people had collected over the years, relating to any meeting or interest they had had with my father, as they too had thought he was 'Donald Campbell'. I wish I'd had the presence of mind to ask him to pass these things on to me as they would have been wonderful for my own collection and memories. I think Anthony was quite overwhelmed by this experience too and probably, later in life, only thankful that he was not so closely linked with his other alter ego which made him so famous...namely Hannibal Lecter!

Soon after this I returned to New Zealand to take up my duties with the Water Safety Council where the initial process involved making lots of promotional material for the oncoming tour of New Zealand – all the TV ads, radio commercials, posters, the fliers and the brochures for the ANZ Bank who were the main sponsors of this campaign. It involved an enormous amount of work, patience and some very long days as many of the outdoor shots were weather dependent. In charge of all the advertising material was a charming guy called Denis Robinson – he owned the ad agency. He was really nice, friendly and put me at ease in front of the camera and the TV crews, and over the weeks we became very friendly. The third member of our 'team' was the gorgeous Joanne Ruscoe, who was to be my guardian and travelling companion, and for weeks the three of us had a wonderful time together – we laughed, we talked, we worked and we played - well not all at the same time! During this time Denis and I unwittingly built up a very good relationship, which somehow turned into something a lot stronger and we became a couple when he invited me to spend a couple of nights at his weekend beach house in Waikanae. This is a very fashionable little spot about 40 miles north of Wellington, where it seemed everyone who was anyone went for R & R. Denis was divorced and had two lovely teenage daughters – one called Bianca, the other name escapes me – and we would all spend wonderful weekends on the beach, in the sea, walking, eating, just doing what people do in such a magnificent setting. In those days it was nothing posh but nowadays it's very upmarket and chic by New Zealand standards. I loved it there, and felt on top of the world, although in fact it was the opposite, Down Under!

My previous book had been published that summer and Michael Meech, who had co-written it with me, and June, his very long-term 'lady friend', decided to come over to New Zealand and Australia to join in the various book signing engagements that had been arranged by the publishers. They had set up quite an extensive tour, covering the major cities in the North and South Islands, so this was an ideal time for us all to have some touring and fun together. We went everywhere in my car, a super little Mazda 'something' in electric blue, with all the bells and whistles and go-faster-everything. I really thought I was the bee's bollocks behind the wheel.

Although the three of us were always very close friends, we were just about to become a whole lot closer. Denis had organised his office Christmas party and boy do the New Zealanders know how to party – I guess the country that produces some of the finest wines in the world should certainly know how to consume them! Naturally June, Michael and I were invited to join all the merriment and it was all going superbly until a gatecrasher arrived. By then the wine stocks had gone down considerably and, before you could blink an eye, a minor skirmish had turned very ugly. There was Denis and the gatecrasher wrestling on the floor, a broken glass and an awful lot of blood spurting from Denis's hand. I stood transfixed until Denis looked up and said: 'Don't stand there with your mouth wide open looking like the bloody Queen of England.' I was gobsmacked. But as we were all staying in Denis's lovely apartment overlooking Wellington waterfront, the prospect of clearing the air quickly was pretty slim. We all at least tried to go off to sleep, but I was so uncomfortable that I crept into Mike and June's room and asked if I could sleep with them! There were only two bedrooms in the flat. It gave us a lot of laughs and Mike couldn't resist commenting that he'd always dreamt of having two blondes in bed at the same time. Unfortunately, but not surprisingly, this incident brought my close relationship with Denis to an abrupt end. That was a shame because we once spent a fabulous weekend together in France of all places when I was invited by Moet et Chandon to spend a weekend at a private villa owned by them, near Epernay in the heart of champagne country. Moet were one of my side sponsors when I was with Agfa – I used to carry their logo on my race suit – and I asked Denis to join me. We flew to England, drove over there in my red Porsche and had a wonderful time – more champagne than you could ever drink.

Many years later I heard from Denis after one of his daughters married an Englishman and moved to Saltburn-by-the-Sea, which is not so many miles from my home by that time in West Yorkshire. We renewed our friendship and now get together for lunch each time he visits this part of the world, but never has the past been discussed.

Michael had to return to the UK but June stayed on with me for the publicity trails and signings. Michael is a kindly man, very sensual and lived this double life with his wife at home and June as his lady friend. June is a lovely woman – we're still friends – she is almost identical to the actress June Whitfield: blonde, bosomy, her blouse buttons always straining at the leash, immaculate in every way, beautifully groomed, jolly, active, never stops talking.

June and I went on to Auckland but we couldn't stay with Dorothy for some reason – I think her daughter Lisa was home, so we stayed in a motel round the corner. That's where I had this strange dream that someone had found my father's body. In the dream, he is lying on a table and I'm standing by his head when he leans up on one elbow, pats the back of his head, looks at me and asks: 'Tell me Gina, is there any blood in my hair because I don't want anybody to see blood?' I said: 'No Daddy, you look just fine and anyway you don't have that much hair.' And that was the end of the dream. Isn't that amazing? I hardly ever dream anyway but what happened next made it even more incredible.

Of course I told June the details in the morning and when we went round to Dorothy's for breakfast, I repeated it to her. In typical Dorothy fashion – she'd never use 12 words where four would do – she said: 'Oh dear, that's a bit upsetting.' Nothing more was made of this and the conversation moved on.

June and I flew to Sydney for the book launch two or three days later but soon afterwards, Dorothy rang to say that the press were at her door because a body had been found in Coniston which they thought could be my father's. The body had been found by two amateur divers near the bottom of the lake and they told the police it was decapitated. At first they thought it was dressed in a boilersuit, which was what my dad was wearing when he was killed. Apparently within hours dozens of journalists descended on Coniston and the Australian papers and TV channels were calling local police to find out if the story was true.

If I hadn't told June and Dorothy about the dream straight away I'm sure people wouldn't have believed me. That dream is as clear to me now as it was then. In it my father was all in one piece and ironically the divers who completed the initial search for his body straight after his accident said they believed he would be fairly intact , otherwise they would have found a bit of this and a bit of that. And in fact, he was all in one piece when the diver Bill Smith found him all those years later in 2001.

The publishers had to hurriedly arrange a big press conference on the top floor of this posh hotel in Sydney – we were staying in a far less salubrious lodging, at the expense of the publishers! The room was absolutely packed but I spotted the rock star Sting, who was about to give a concert at the Sydney Entertainment Centre, at the back, obviously quite puzzled as to what was going on. I had never been to quite such an enormous gathering of the press before, with flash bulbs popping everywhere and everyone firing questions at me. It was quite frightening. It was a few days before the body was identified because at first the police underwater search team could not relocate it. And in the meantime the press had a field day. There were headlines in the *Sydney Morning Herald* and all the big daily papers in Australia and New Zealand, with journalists suggesting I might cut short my book signing tour to fly home. But I never planned that, at least not until we knew if it was my dad. After a day or two, the cynics among the press surfaced and suggested the whole thing was a hoax dreamed up to generate more publicity. But finally, they were proved wrong when we got the news that in fact the body was clothed in a T-shirt, jeans and shoes and they believed it was that of a young man, who had been missing for years after a boating accident. And, like all these sensational stories, it quickly died in the press.

I was still working for the New Zealand Water Safety Council, visiting schools, swimming pools, the ANZ bank branches, all pre-arranged for me, anywhere and everywhere across virtually the full length and breadth of the country. But they were happy for me to fly back to the UK in December for Agfa's Christmas party, which coincided with the 50th birthday of Tony Burton, the head of Agfa's Repro division. He had been my main contact at Agfa and the man who really embraced the whole involvement with powerboat racing and spotted the potential of my sponsorship. He was always crazy on boating and still potters up and down the Thames in his own boat. We still exchange Christmas cards.

Agfa's parties were always very lavish affairs full of gaiety, fun and laughter. At the dinner I was seated, of course, next to Tony Burton, who was a real pocket rocket, full of life and verve, and on my other side was Tonni Jensen, good-looking, blond, blue eyed, Dane, typically Scandinavian, who was the export manager for Helioprint. It was a company who used to make massive reprographic cameras and did enormous business with Agfa. He was very charming and we laughed and flirted through the evening.

The wine flowed, although I've never been much of a drinker, and there was obviously a mutual attraction. So when the party ended, I guess around 3am, we both went to the same bedroom. I was a free agent but it wasn't obvious he was a married man – it was never discussed but I suppose under these circumstances it rarely is! You wonder how these things happen but I was a bit wild in those days, I felt a wonderful carefree spirit. I had never really had a misspent youth, never been clubbing; instead, one minute I was a child and the next I was married. Maybe I was making up for lost time and I had become a bit of a star through the powerboat racing, although I like to think I never behaved like one because I took what I did very seriously.

We parted the next morning and I roared off in my lovely red Porsche because I was heading back to New Zealand a few days later. But Tonni told me that he was going to be coming to New Zealand and then on to Australia on a work-related trip in March and would get in touch. I gave him Dorothy's number. She had moved house by then to Epsom, a suburb of Auckland, and her younger son David was still at home with her. We were all very happy there and I had slotted into my work and almost a proper home life with 'family' where they all treated me as the older sister.

I found plenty of other work also came my way through my name and the connections I had already made. I had a stint as a TV presenter for a motoring programme that was shown weekly on TV, a sort of latter day Top Gear, but not with the same panache as Jeremy Clarkson! But New Zealanders are passionate about their cars and all things related, so I met some fascinating people and covered some interesting topics. In between I was busy doing all sorts of different things, getting involved with boats, boat showrooms, dealerships and manufacturers, and there were still Agfa dealers to visit on a commercial basis. I was keeping myself employed and so keeping the wolf from the door and living at home with Dorothy. I had a wonderful group of friends who all went to the beach waterskiing, barbeques, a real outdoor life of fun and fresh air, just like every Aucklander, surrounded by water, blue skies and healthy sports.

Then, blow me down, Tonni rang, unfortunately in the middle of the night because of the time difference from Denmark. I was surprised when he told me he was flying to Auckland the following week and asked me to meet up with him. He duly arrived on a work-related visit and set up in one of the downtown hotels. His days were taken up with work, visiting clients, making sales and later we would meet up for romantic evenings and so to bed. I would head back to Dorothy's in the early hours and I seem to remember this routine went on for a few days. Then Tonni was to move on to Sydney and, at his suggestion, I agreed to go too. I had a very good friend in Sydney called Rosemary Fitzgerald, her married name, who had been my father's secretary for many years during our years living at Roundwood. I was and still am very close to her, so I arranged that I would go and stay with her, but of course in reality I was going to spend the evenings and nights with Tonni. By now some of his colleagues were very well aware of what was going on between us and, of course, I had discovered that he was married with two young children. We said goodbye at Sydney airport – he was flying back to Denmark and me to New Zealand – and he seemed very melancholy. I went back to Dorothy, who knew I had been seeing this guy because I never had any secrets from her, and who had realised that this was more than just a few one night stands, but had now developed into something much deeper. Then 48 hours later, Tonni rang and told me his wife had met him at the airport back in Copenhagen and knew immediately something was wrong. So he told her about me and she threw him out – understandably. Almost immediately he said he thought there was a life for the two of us together in Denmark.

I look back now and wonder how I could have been so naïve, but equally, here was someone who wanted me. I was on my own and I had the mentality that if someone said they loved me, they had to be the best person in the world and I must love them, too. Tonni continued to ring me at Dorothy's, usually in the middle of the night so I'd have the phone on silent. He asked me if I'd go and take a look at Denmark once I was back in the UK. And that's what I decided to do. Of course I had an enormous amount of guilt running through my head and heart because I had been sleeping with a married man with two young children and, because of this I had broken up, albeit unintentionally, a complete family.

I was filled with remorse and I suppose I felt the only proper and right thing to do was to try and help him to pick up his life. After all I was the other woman, although I wasn't proud of it, and I discussed it with Dorothy at great length. But as she always pointed out it took two to tango! Ever the pragmatist.

I owned my own home in Ashstead and still drove my Porsche, so I must have earned some money somewhere. So as soon as I was back in the UK, I booked myself on the ferry from Harwich to Esbjerg, which ironically was close to the sands where my grandfather Sir Malcolm had attempted a land speed record many moons earlier. Unfortunately a wheel had flown off the car at high speed and careered into the crowd and killed a small boy even though my grandfather had warned the officials that the crowd watching were much too close for comfort and this was an accident waiting to happen. I headed off in the Porsche, wearing my Ray-Ban sunglasses and thinking I was pretty smart, pretty damn clever. I had nobody to advise or caution me – my mother was still living in Devon with Owen and we were barely in touch and Tonia was in the States. And I was nearly 40 years old after all, although that didn't make me any wiser!

Once off the ferry, I was driving to Copenhagen on roads which were so quiet, passing houses which all seemed to fly the Danish flag in various different shapes – some long, banner-type ones and others that traditional size and shape. They looked wonderful and fresh and patriotic. It seemed like mine was the only car on the road until this guy drove up, overtook me, then slowed down so I had to go past. It happened so many times that I realised this was no accident and eventually he gestured to me to mean did I want a drink. So we pulled in at the next place. It was exciting, why turn down any opportunities? All my options were open and I still had this wonderful carefree spirit. We had a coffee and a chat, exchanged ten details about each other and that was it. I cannot even remember his name and I never saw him again.

Tonni had booked me into one of the city centre hotels in Copenhagen. I know it was the Sheraton because I still have one of their big white towels – they took one of mine to their laundry by mistake and gave me a hotel towel in return. Tonni had taken a few days off from work to show me round. We visited the Tivoli Gardens, which I loved – like Disney with style and with a European flavour – and we drove up the coast here and there. We visited all the sites, the little Mermaid, who really is very little and seemingly very insignificant, and I did warm to the Danish way of life. There were carefree, wonderful streets with excellent sausage stalls on every corner, a beautiful waterfront and harbour, everything and everyone so clean, organised and liberal in every way. I was very impressed.

Then suddenly he suggested again that I should go to live in Denmark, that we should buy a house and move in together. It was May time and it all happened in a flash. I knew so very little about him and yet before I knew it we were looking at a house. In Denmark then, home owners who were selling held an open house and negotiations were completed very quickly. Once you agreed to buy, you put down a deposit and you were committed. If you changed your mind, you lost the deposit.

So we went to look at number 5, Johann Ottersons Vie in Frederiksberg, west of the capital but part of the municipality of Copenhagen. It was a single storey, open-plan house with a basement, which was a proper room with windows at ground level.

We looked round one Sunday afternoon and, if I remember rightly, we put down a deposit there and then. At least I did, Tonni never put a penny into the house although to be fair he warned me he had no money but could afford to pay the outgoings on the house. It suddenly felt right, and so romantic, a bit à la Barbara Taylor Bradford, almost as if it was meant to be.

But then the misgivings kicked in and I drove back to England with a very heavy heart. I returned to Ashstead, and had sudden pangs that something was wrong. I asked my friend June to come with me to see a solicitor to explain what I had done. I showed him the documents and he told me what I suspected: that if I didn't buy the house I would lose my deposit, which was a considerable amount of money. I cannot remember how much it was but I know it was too much to lose. So I put Aquila Close on the market, sold it quickly and fortunately made a not inconsiderable profit, and then completed on the house in Denmark. I arranged for all my furniture to be shipped out to a country I didn't know, where they spoke a language I couldn't speak. But then I probably thought, nothing ventured, nothing gained. Tonni was a good-looking man, he had a job, he wanted me but had been rejected by his family and all the garbage that goes with that. But if some of that was my fault, I had to bear the consequences and try to make a life with this man. The only way I can explain my thinking process is that I must have believed that we could make a real go of this – that if he was willing to do that, he must think I was very special. If so, I must be special and it must be the right thing to do.

We moved in, the furniture all arrived, the house suddenly became a new home and his kids would come at the weekend. He had a son David, blond, a typical Dane and his younger sister, Katya, a beautiful, innocent child. They were maybe ten and eight. Naturally the little boy was a bit surly, stand-offish and would throw tantrums. At the time I thought he was a snotty little so-and-so but on reflection, I was this woman who had turned his life upside down and I was not very proud of that, although I hadn't driven the split between his parents. When I met Tonni, I can honestly say I never wanted anything more than a quick fling in the sheets. But he wanted more and I was enormously flattered by that.

Tonni was duly divorced and after some months we decided to marry. Our wedding was a civil ceremony in the Town Hall at Frederiksberg, the equivalent of our register office, in February 1990. They conducted the service in English for my benefit and I became Mrs Campbell-Jensen. I wore a lovely dress I bought in New Zealand, strapless, white with brightly coloured yellow flowers and a bright yellow jacket. Much later I had it remodelled and wore it to my Investiture at Buckingham Palace, when I was decorated for my work with the New Zealand Water Safety Council, and to lots of other social engagements. I still wear it to this day because amazingly, I am still exactly the same size.

There were only about eight or ten of Tonni's friends there and we went back to our house for a small reception. TV New Zealand were making a fly-on-the-wall programme about me called *Gina The Spirit of Bluebird*, covering an entire year up to my world water speed record attempt which was planned for the following month. They included some footage of the wedding, of us coming out of the town hall, guests throwing rice and Tonni and I driving off in my Porsche.

Of course it felt strange this all happening in Denmark, a country I'd never visited until a few months before. But I just seemed to be swept along with the euphoria of it all. At that stage it was an adventure, exciting – and I thrived on excitement – and the reality of it didn't hit home. It was almost as though I was playing a part. When I look back now, it's like I'm not looking at myself, but at a different person. It all seemed so right at the time.

I could always turn to my friend June if I needed advice but June is the nicest person in the world who had seen my break-up with Michael and just wanted me to be happy. She was probably swept along with the whole thing too and told me what I wanted to hear. She came out to stay with me in Denmark one time and so did Dorothy, all the way from New Zealand, with her new partner Desmond. She had known him for years and he was her boyfriend when she first came to England and met my father. They got together again after Hans died.

Our life fell into a regular routine. Tonni would go off to work in the morning rush hour because he had a good hour's drive north up to Helioprint's head office and I stayed at home. It was a lovely house with a nice garden with a fish pond at the bottom and an area with big rocks. I spent most days remodelling the garden. I even brought my gardening equipment and Flymo from England. The house was near to a little community with all local amenities, including shops and a supermarket and everything you needed. Because I was blonde, some people assumed I was Danish and luckily most young people spoke English, although the older people did not. I learned a few words of Danish but TV was non-existent for me because of the language and I did start to get a little lonesome during these days, although because it was summer, I was happy in the garden.

When Tonni came home from work, we would either stay home or he'd take me to the Tivoli Gardens or some little taverna for dinner, although he also liked to cook. I did notice how much the Danes in general drank alcohol and Tonni was no exception. You would see many poor souls, old and young, sitting on the park benches, seven sheets to the wind. As export director for Helioprint, Tonni travelled quite often and I'd go with him when I could. For the price of a flight I could go along and stay in his hotel room and in this way I had a wonderful time visiting some of the most fabulous countries and cities that form this part of the world. I just loved them all: Sweden, where we stayed in Stockholm which is just gorgeous, Finland – or Souimi as it's known locally – from where you can look across to Russia, and Norway to view the Northern Lights. It was all very exciting and interesting and I really enjoyed those trips. And there were also visits to Spain, Italy and many others countries so life was very varied and exciting.

However, it was back in our home in Frederiksberg where I picked up a habit that I rue to this day – it's where I learned to smoke. Tonni was a very heavy smoker, which was not unusual in Denmark then. All Tonni's friends smoked too and every time you visited a bar or restaurant you had to force your way through a fog of smoke, mainly caused by smokers in our particular age group. Tonni left the odd packet of cigarettes lying around the house but I never had any interest in trying one.

In fact, I'd never smoked in my life…until one fateful day! The first time I thought about having a little try, I had a massive coughing fit after two or three puffs and I had to rush to the bathroom, not too sure whether to sit on or look down the loo, dropping the cigarette on the stone floor. I think I ended up both sitting and looking…bit too much information. Once I had got over this rather unattractive moment, I picked up the ciggy from the floor and continued to puff away! What a sad day, one that I shall regret forever as I have been a smoker ever since. It is an unpleasant habit, now so socially unacceptable, it's bad for your health, makes your clothes smell, keeps you poor, and really has no good points at all except it can become your little friend. It's maybe one that will kill you, but when the going gets a bit uneasy, reaching for your 'friend', albeit your deadly one, gives you a comfortable feeling. But I definitely do not recommend anyone to become friends with my little 'friend'!

Chapter 13

SO I JUST WENT AND I DID IT

My world water speed record attempt was planned for early 1990, the year New Zealand staged the Commonwealth Games. I think the organisers thought it would add a bit of extra excitement in that same year.

I had not attempted speed records since my somersault at Holme Pierrepont back in 1984 when there was no official women's world water speed record. But by 1990 the sport's governing body, the Union Internationale Motonautique (UIM), had established an official Women's 'Outright' World Water Speed Record and a separate one for the Women's Unlimited Hydroplane. In April 1989 both of them were broken by an English girl called Heather Spurle, whose family had emigrated to New Zealand in the early 1970s. She had started out in various types of motor sport and then moved on to the water – she broke the records on Lake Karapiro with a speed of 132 miles per hour.

So there were one or two people keen to back me to have another go, to see whether I could take the records. But as with so many events in my life, it came about after various chance meetings, including one with John Mayes, a boss of Woolworths, which is a supermarket chain in New Zealand, not like the shops we had in the UK. We met in the first class lounge on an Air New Zealand flight, we started chatting and it was obvious he knew all about my father and my own powerboating career. So he came up with the idea of sponsorship from Woolworths and Bluebird Potato Chips, which were New Zealand's equivalent of our Walkers crisps of today.

I had bought my own boat from a guy in New Zealand, this time a three point hydroplane, which originally was red. I had it painted white with pale blue streamlining, similar to the design on my *Agfa Bluebird*, but once the deal with Woolworths and Bluebird Potato Chips was signed, they changed the livery. So when it arrived at Lake Taupo for the attempt, it had all been painted a darker blue which was a bit of a surprise.

Lake Taupo is in the centre of North Island, an enormous lake of more than 230 square miles, which now has lots of holiday resorts around it. I had spent a lot of money having the course measured and arranging timekeepers and was lucky to have a man called Maher Derry, but who was known by everyone as Blue, a jet boat champion who knew everyone in the boating scene in New Zealand, as my sort of team manager.

Blue introduced me to the guy who used to own the boat, a good engineer, who tried to educate me about the boat, because, believe me, the difference between an offshore boat and this was like moving from a steady hunter to a highly trained racehorse. I'd had a bit of experience on my first attempt six years before but this meant going from a catamaran to a hydroplane, a boat with a massive inboard Chevrolet engine and enormous power. I must admit it scared me to death and I think the two of them wondered whether I could pull it off.

I planned the record attempt for March 23, my father's birthday, not long after my wedding in Denmark. Tonni flew over, at my expense, to be with me. When the day arrived, everyone was ready and the sponsors had hired a boat for the day. But, as the gods would have it, everything that could go wrong on that day, did go wrong. The lake was freshwater and the wind was horrendous, making the surface impossible. It was bitterly cold, high above sea level, and if New Zealand gets a southerly coming up from the Antarctic, it's criminal up there.

I was encountering the problems my father had faced many times – if the lake was right, there was something wrong with the boat. I had terrible self doubts. I went out a few times because Blue said he had to see me drive the boat but I knew the world was watching too. I had dreadful nerves, I honestly didn't know whether I could do it. In the end, I'm lucky I didn't kill myself in the attempt.

It was all well chronicled in the press and all the time we were hoping that when the next day dawned, everything would be perfect for the attempt. But it never was. I was paying for the timekeepers, for accommodation for Blue and the engineers, for Tonni and me. The days went by, time was running out and we all knew it had to be done. So after a week of disappointments, I think on the morning of March 30, we decided to move the whole event to Lake Karapiro, not too far away, where there was already a measured mile. The boat was taken there and we all trekked after it.

We did some test runs on the first day and can you believe we blew a part in the engine. Just my luck. Blue and his team stayed up all night and rebuilt it because they knew I had to go out the next morning and attempt it. The timekeepers were impatient, they had to go home – people don't hang around failure for too long, they become bored hearing the sob stories, the excuses.

The next day the weather was perfect. At crack of dawn, as I waited for them to put the boat on the water, I had my first real experience of the most terrible nervous stomach. It was a real physical pain. Thank God Tonni recognised what was happening and produced a Zantac, which is used to treat ulcers and sometimes heartburn because it reduces the amount of acid your stomach produces. I've had a nervous tummy from that day till this – if anything goes awry in my life, that's where I feel it first.

Although it was April Fool's Day, by then I just wanted to do it. Safety equipment had improved a lot, and I remember I wore a BMW sponsored helmet. I didn't take Mr Whoppit – by then I thought maybe he wasn't so lucky after all. My dad died with him in the boat and I nearly did at Holme Pierrepont. So Tonni kept him in the support boat. The boat was a direct drive, no gear box, so the moment I turned on the engine, I was off. So I just went and I did it!

I knew I was going fast, but it's not like driving fast in a car on a road where you're constantly passing other things. There is nothing in close proximity until you see the orange markers where you enter the measured mile and then the second set at the end of it, that's your focus. I'm sitting up there like a little old lady in the open cockpit – the pressure on your neck is huge, so I'm lucky I'm only small.

I knew I was going at full tilt and I was talking to myself all the way through. When you get through the markers, you have to ease off gently. The worst thing you can do is back off too quickly because the boat would just flip. You turn round and come straight back again because it is your average speed over the two runs that counts.

My biggest fear was to blow the engine again, so everything had to be smooth, smooth, smooth. When I came back to where we'd launched the boat, Blue already had a radio message that I'd done it, but they didn't know what speed. My knees were a bit weak when I climbed out but I was on a massive adrenaline high, mainly relief more than anything. I'd said I would do it, although I didn't know whether I could, and I had. Then the official timekeeper showed me the piece of paper which said I'd set a new world record at 166 miles per hour.

Of course everyone was thrilled, it had been worth the wait and all the frustrations of the previous days. The press were keen to paint me as the third generation of what people call the Campbell Dynasty – my wonderful grandfather Sir Malcolm, whom I never knew, who broke four world records on water and an amazing nine on land and my father who broke seven world records on water and just one on land. And now, here was I, with my one official world record on water.

Did I think of any of this at the time? Absolutely not. My only thoughts during the attempt were of self-preservation and to get the job done. There was so much hanging on that second run and I was so aware of the frailty of the craft, especially after the engine was blown just the day before. But I have always believed that if you possibly can, you have to fulfil what you have set out to do, if you talk the talk, you have to walk the walk.

Of course I was on a high, but do you know, it doesn't last anything like as long as people think. Everything you have worked for is suddenly done and dusted and equally there's suddenly a huge sense of anti-climax. My father used to say the same. You have been so absorbed in the whole thing and now it's over. There's a terrible emptiness, an awful sense of anti-climax. What is there to get up for the next day?

But even before those feelings kicked in, I was brought right back down to earth by Tonni about an hour after climbing out of the boat. That's when he chose to tell me we had been burgled at our house in Denmark and everything of value stolen. A few days earlier, I had heard him talking on the phone to his friend Nils in Denmark – he and his wife were among the few friends we had there – but they spoke in Danish so I didn't understand and I had other things on my mind. It turned out that Tonni had forgotten to lock a gate at the back of the house and that's how they got in. All my videos and some memorabilia were taken. It completely ruined what should have been a fantastic celebration although of course I did the huge round of interviews which followed because there was massive publicity about the record. Tonni flew back almost straight away to sort out the mess.

And as if to prove that there's no point trying to build your life on record-breaking, the same girl Heather Spurle broke my records again just a month later, this time on Lake Ruataniwha at a place called Twizel in New Zealand with a speed of 169 miles per hour. So you see, the sense of anti-climax was not misplaced.

Eventually I returned to Frederiksberg and spent the summer there. My life was nothing. Tonni went to work every morning, I played house. But as autumn came along and the winter loomed, I began to feel isolated and lonely. I would go back to England to see June – I enjoyed the journey on my own, driving to Esjberg for the ferry to Harwich. But it wasn't long before Tonni started to annoy me. He wanted it all to be happy families when his children came to stay, which I can understand, but it obviously wasn't going to work. They viewed me like a piece of dog poo. They were at an age when they understood what had happened but they were not old enough to appreciate why.

I also realised I was running out of money. The deal had been that Tonni would pay the outgoings on the house but that just didn't work. Tonni and his money were easily parted. He was paying money to his wife for her and the children, but he was also a big smoker, a heavy drinker. I had no means of earning, I didn't speak the language so I couldn't get a job and the only option left was to sell the house. Fortunately it sold quickly – we held an open house like the one we went to when we first bought it, and we found a buyer prepared to pay what I had given for it. We moved up the coast to Hornbaek, a beautiful little place backed by pine forests, where we rented a lovely beach house. It was still not far for Tonni to go to his office so it was a good move.

But by then I knew I had to get back to England, to find a way of earning some money. I asked June to send me copies of *Dalton's Weekly*, which lists thousands of businesses for sale, the only way to discover what was available before the days of the internet. I looked at post offices, pubs, restaurants because even if I'm not the most intellectual person on the planet, I've got something between the ears and two hands that work. I've never been afraid of manual work. Even though people viewed me as having had a glamorous childhood, I was always brought up never to think that I was better than anyone else. There was no room in our house for prissy little girls. I was a tomboy, which helped, and I'd looked after horses, which is hard work. Even when I was given my first pony, it was my job to take care of it, not like the people down the road who employed grooms so that all the kids had to do was to sit on their backs.

When you scour *Dalton's Weekly* for long enough, you get to read between the lines about the type of businesses for sale. I had a clear vision of what I wanted – it had to be in the south, somewhere pretty and a bit different and that's how I came to settle on a coffee shop in Lymington, Hampshire. I went over to England on my own to see it, along with a few others on the books of a husband and wife team who acted as agents. I stayed with June for four or five days and drove round a few places. Some I would drive straight past, I'd know straight away they were not right for me because of the location or just the way they looked.

Then I went to view The Lentune – which is the Domesday Book name for Lymington – a coffee shop in cobbled Quay Street. It was almost dusk and they had just closed the doors but I could see the two owners inside tidying up at the end of the day. It looked very atmospheric, cosy and I knew straight away that I liked it. So I arranged to go back the next day and when I went inside, I loved it. It felt to me like an old smuggler's type cottage – you had to duck your head to get in – and it had heaps of charm. I soon found out that it seated 32, mainly at little round tables with a couple of bench tables. There was a kitchen and two floors of living space upstairs so the restaurant felt almost like opening up your dining room. I just knew it felt right for me.

It was run by two gay men, John Spillane, who was maybe in his 60s then, who had worked in catering all his life, the mothering sort, and Mike Willis, a real sportsman who loved windsurfing, skiing, even bungee jumping. John did all the cooking and Mike was front of house. I warmed to them straight away and they to me and they became two of my best friends. Sadly John died a few years ago.

Inside was a doorway to the stairs leading up to the living space, hidden behind a wall panelling. The cake trolley was always parked in front of it so if you wanted to nip upstairs, you had to move the trolley to open the door, usually with customers watching, wondering what on earth you were doing because it just looked like panelling.

Directly above the restaurant was a little sitting room/lounge with a flat roof outside so I could climb out of the window and sit sunning myself on my day off. There was a bedroom and bathroom on that floor, then another flight of steps led into the eaves and the most lovely bedroom with loads of cupboards, a little study and shower room and toilet.

John and Mike showed me round and promised to educate me about how to run the place, because what did I know about turnover, gross and net profits? But I knew that I didn't have to be a brain surgeon to operate this coffee shop. I asked Tonni to come over and have a look because he knew full well by then that I couldn't carry on just sitting in Denmark, dipping into my savings to put food on the table but not earning a penny. And anyway I knew he'd like the idea of playing mine host - it was bang up his street because he was such a good talker. There was no issue about leaving his kids because they lived with their mother and if they wanted to come to see Tonni, we were not far from Gatwick or Heathrow or they could sail to Harwich like I had done.

I agreed to buy the place, which was on the market at £250,000 for the business and the freehold of the property. I obviously had to have a mortgage but when I realised I didn't have enough for the deposit, John and Mike agreed to take my Porsche, which they loved, as part of it. I went to a mortgage broker's to discuss it and when they came back with an offer, typed in capitals on the top was one serious condition: "This woman must never take part in powerboat racing again." That's how dangerous the sport was viewed. Interest rates were flying through the roof then – I think 12 or 14%, they were crippling. But I knew the business had supported John and Mike so I believed it could do the same for us.

Chapter 14

GONE TO LONDON TO SEE THE QUEEN

Once I agreed to buy The Lentune, there was so much to do before Tonni and I finally moved to England. Like any house move, it was hectic but even more so because we were living in another country. We had to pack up our stuff in the rental house in Hornbaek, give notice to the agent, tie up all the dates and make sure everything slotted in. I had to drive over in the Porsche so it could be transferred into Mike and John's names and our furniture came on the ferry and had to go into storage for about a week until we actually moved in. I think Tonni flew over.

Even then we had to stay in a hotel in Southampton for a week until everything was finalised. I'll always remember it was called The Polygon, because the local police rang me there to arrange for me to go to court for the transfer of the restaurant licence for The Lentune. The copper said to me: 'Oh you're staying at the dead parrot hotel.' And I said: 'No, The Polygon.' And of course he said: 'Same thing, madam.' There was a deadly hush for a few seconds while my brain ticked round and the penny dropped. Ha, ha, I thought.

It wasn't the only time we had a laugh there either. We always had the window open in our hotel room – we were probably both smoking – and all of a sudden, on our first day, a pigeon flew in and obviously knew exactly what it wanted to do. It cooed around for a bit, landed on the floor and headed under the bed where it laid an egg and then flew out again. It was absolutely hilarious. I even put the egg on the windowsill in case it came back, but of course the egg rolled off and smashed. But the next day, the bird flew in and did exactly the same again and laid another egg under the bed. It became a bit of a comedy show but in the end we had to close the window because unfortunately each time it laid, it also left a rather large poo behind.

Daughter of BLUEBIRD – GINA CAMPBELL

Each morning, we'd drive to Lymington to watch how they opened up and for Mike to introduce us to their clientele who included both locals and, in the season, lots of tourists. But even among the locals, there was a big mix. There were well-heeled ladies, the twin set and pearls brigade, who often came in with their daughters, rather genteel folk. And then some London girls who had opened shops there, the Sloane Ranger types who had moved to Lymington because of all the handsome sailors, the boat racing and the Royal Lymington Yacht Club which is pretty special. Princess Anne used to come down to the Club occasionally.

Lymington is an amazing little town with its old picturesque area of cobbled streets and no through traffic, then the harbour with the fishing boats where massive container lorries would drive down in the evenings to pick up all the best shell fish heading for Portugal and Spain and Italy on international trucks. So it had a local industry but also this massive tourist influx from Easter through to October half-term: some quite smart boating people, lots of caravanners staying in the New Forest, walkers and hikers, a real cosmopolitan mix of people. They all had their own charm. At the start we also had a few people who were just intrigued to see who we were and what we were like.

It was a cute little place, with a lovely bay window at the front and a kitchen at the back, which was small but had everything you needed and outside were a couple of sheds where we stored dry goods. But the unisex loo was only the size of an airline toilet, so when a 25-stone fellow asked to use it, I'd think: 'Oh my God.'

The first day I turned up in red jeans and red high-heeled boots – so inappropriate, by the end of the day my feet were killing me. I worked with John in the kitchen and it was like doing the tango in that small space. He gave me all his recipes plus lots of patience and love and kindness, teaching me how to prepare, how to do five things at once. You've got the grill going, you're baking cakes, icing others, preparing other dishes, spreading the toast and all the time taking care over the presentation of food to the customers. Then the phone would ring in the middle. I had never done it before – I know it's not rocket science – but John gave me the confidence to take it on. He saw that I had the feel, the enthusiasm and I could do it. At that stage I never thought: 'My God what have we done?'

On top of that there was so much paperwork: the mortgage, health insurance, the environmental health rules and regulations, signing over the Porsche, so that we could buy a cheap, second-hand car instead. John had worked out a gross profit on every single item – we could make a nice scone for four or five pence and sell it for 75 pence, albeit there were our overhead costs and that included VAT. It was no good baking lots of food, putting loads of money in the till but not making a profit.

There was so much to take in and such a short time in which to do it that it even seeped into my dreams and during those few days I had a terrible nightmare that I collapsed on the floor of the kitchen and John was standing over me, beating me with a stick, saying: 'You can't die here, you can't die here.' We had hysterics the next day when I told them, but maybe, somewhere in there, was a bit of a warning.

John and Mike only moved up the road to Barton on Sea and I became very good friends with them, I'd go to their house for dinner, they'd come to me. They were hugely supportive, always on the end of the phone, if anything broke or didn't work, they'd tell me exactly who to go to. It's incredible to buy a house from someone and stay friends, let alone buy a business from someone and do the same, so I think it says a lot for both parties. Ironically it turned out that Mike had gone to school with my cousin PJ – he's Peter John but always known as PJ – somewhere in the south of England.

We finally moved in just before Easter, the busiest time of the year when everything started in the New Forest. So the earlier Easter was in the calendar, the better it was for business because we had a longer season.

We changed the name straight away to The Bluebird at Lentune because it reflected the way we wanted it to be viewed and to give it the family name association. I decorated it with a few bits of Bluebird memorabilia and used to sell postcards which I'd sign. We had a deep window sill where I used to put trinkets and bits and pieces, including some model cars. I even put Mr Whoppit in a porthole window, which was at eye height between the kitchen and the restaurant, and had some replica Mr Whoppits for sale. People would ask if they could talk to me about my dad, so I'd wash my hands so I could pop out and do the whole front of house bit. I didn't wear whites because they're not very glamorous – instead I'd wear jazzy clothes and a bright apron.

Every morning I was up between five and six to make the cakes, the scones, the Danish pastries, the croissants, the baker would come with the bread. We opened at 9.30-ish for coffee and scones and cakes. We had lots of local customers and in the summer tourists would flock in. On Saturdays it was particularly fantastic because there is a street market in Lymington. It was full-on. With only nine tables and 32 seats, I had to double people up if they were in twos as I needed to optimise every seat.

The place had a good reputation and we had an Egon Ronay recommendation for our cream teas – and was well-known for its scones, so I made sure I kept up the standard. We served light lunches but there was probably nothing much over £5.00 on the menu.

In the kitchen I had a six-ring gas cooker and a big grill. I knew how to make good soups, shepherd's pie, chilli, chicken casserole and I liked to stick to what I knew rather than experiment, so I'd pre-make them where I could and stick them in the chiller. One of our main specialities was Welsh rarebit, but not just plain cheese on toast. I used to make a proper roux with beer, Worcester sauce, mustard and cheese. To do it properly could take a long time and I'd make a big tub of it and keep it in the chiller to serve it either plain or with sardines, tomatoes, smoked salmon or ham on top. I'd stick it under the grill and send it out with a nice salad garnish. But all the time I'd be juggling ten things. Fortunately the kitchen was small enough for everything to be within reach. I'm not sexist but I really believe that most women can do 10 things at once whereas most men...let's just say, they struggle.

I'd bake five or six big cakes every single day for the trolley – Bakewell tarts, almond slices, chocolate and coffee gateaux – although the difficulty was knowing what was going to go when. Some of them keep very well in tight containers because there's so much sugar in them. I used to make something called Tiffin, some people called it chocolate biscuit fridge cake, for which you break up Rich Tea biscuits and then melt a goo of butter, margarine, sugar, cocoa powder and golden syrup, add the biscuits and pack into a baking tray really tightly, cover it with thick, dark chocolate and put it in the fridge. One slice really meant calories in a mouthful, but it was popular. I remember staying up late to bake my first gateaux which looked fantastic when I first pulled them out of the oven, but then all of a sudden would collapse in the middle. I couldn't understand why and I'd ring John who'd say you've put too much baking powder in, or not enough, or you've opened the oven door at the wrong moment, or this and that. It took me ages to get it right but I persevered. I've hardly baked since I left The Lentune and I don't enjoy eating cakes. I love sweets, wine gums, chocolate but not cakes or sweet puddings. I don't even make many soups any more, because it just became a chore.

At weekends, in good weather, the place would be heaving, with people queueing out of the door. You didn't have time to think. Tonni was out front and at weekends we had a girl waitress and a boy to wash up. But I was on my legs all day, absolutely exhausted at night.

At the start, I must have been pretty naïve because I couldn't believe the stuff that got nicked – salt and pepper pots, cutlery, toilet rolls, towels from the loo. I had fitted small teddy bears round a stack pipe that ran upstairs – I've always been a teddy person – and one by one they just disappeared. One day my waitress saw a woman walk in off the street, straight into the toilet and walk out with some toilet rolls which was sheer opportunism. People are incredible, but I soon learned. John and Mike told me only to put the cruet sets out when people ordered food which required them and then to collect them again when we cleared the table. It seemed to be the caravanners who'd come in for a cup of tea and nick whatever they'd forgotten to bring. Then occasionally you'd get a nice surprise – someone would send back a cheap knife with an apologetic note saying it must have fallen off the table into their handbag. Two utter extremes of the human race.

Most customers were pleasant and we had very few 'runners', people who leave without paying, or complaints. John and Mike warned me that there would always be the odd one who would eat three-quarters of their food and then complain. You'd make it again and then they'd refuse to pay. It's not nice but there are professionals at it out there. I'm not sure whether the law is still the same, but the police told me then that as long as you can prove you can pay but refuse to because you say the food was not up to scratch, you are entitled to walk out. When you order something, it is a contract between you and the restaurant and if you believe they have not fulfilled their part of it, you are entitled to withhold payment. We had a little old lass who'd come in, order and then didn't have the money to pay for it. It was sad really because she became known to the police for doing the same in various places.

The following spring, March 10, 1992 I had a great excuse for closing for the day when I put a notice on the door, 'Gone to London to see the Queen!' which would make most people laugh but it is exactly what I did. It was the day of my Investiture, the day I was to receive my Queen's Service Order. The first I knew of it was when I took a call in Denmark from the British Embassy which of course came as a bit of a shock. But when they explained that I was to be awarded a QSO for my water safety work in New Zealand in the Queen's Birthday Honours List of June 1990, I felt so excited and honoured. Most people are informed by post I believe but there was some urgency for me to formally accept the honour – maybe it had taken them a time to track me down in Denmark. He explained that, at some future date to be arranged, I would be invited to an Investiture. To be honest I'd never heard of a QSO – I knew all about CBEs and OBEs and MBEs, after all my father was awarded a CBE and my grandfather was knighted. When I received the official citation it explained that the QSO was established by Queen Elizabeth II in 1975 and is 'awarded by the government of New Zealand for valuable voluntary service to the community or meritorious and faithful service to the Crown or similar service within the public sector, whether in elected or appointed office.' I was supposed to keep the whole thing a secret, except for telling Tonni, until the date when I could attend an Investiture.

Anyway I was finally given the date to be at Buckingham Palace to receive the medal, with my two guests. I took Tonni and my great pal June. What an experience going to the Palace! What seems like a lot of people to the Picture Gallery to be given a detailed briefing on what exactly will happen and what you're expected to do. Each group – the knights, the OBEs, the CBEs and everyone with the same award – go in to the Queen together, and each group is led in by a member of the Queen's Life Guards, the ones who wear long boots and shiny helmets with plumes like a horse's tail coming out the top. I wore the dress I wore for my wedding in Denmark.

The actual presentation takes place in the Gold Ballroom where the band is playing on the balcony and everyone's guests are already seated. What hits you is the gold, just shining and glistening everywhere. Each group walks in, takes a right angle turn to a holding station, until it's the moment for them to go forward. It's pretty damn nerve-racking walking out there, desperately hoping you won't trip up, hearing your heels click-clacking across the floor, trying to remember to do everything in the right order, not forgetting any of the protocol. Then you turn right and there is the Queen. Well, when it came to my turn, there was only me in the QSO group. So there's this Life Guard, seven foot plenty in his plumed helmet, clanking sword and little me, five foot two, walking behind. I must have looked ridiculous.

The Queen has a few words with each person and I'll never forget that she said to me that it was such an honour to have had three generations of one family come to the Palace to receive such awards. It was not the Queen who knighted my grandfather but she did present my father with his CBE. She also said: 'This award comes from New Zealand which is a country very close to my heart.' Here is the Queen of England, in her little paisley dress, the sort your mother would wear to go out to tea, talking to me and making me feel so very special. It was amazing.

Then we had been told that when the Queen has finished talking to you, she will extend her hand and as she shakes hands, she kind of pushes you away and that's you, done. I walked three steps backwards, curtseyed and that was me finished. I then sat with Tonni and June until the whole ceremony was over.

Everyone is given a piece of paper with a number on and details of the company that has the sole right to film the Investiture and take photographs inside the Palace – what a little creamer that is for them. I bought the cheapest set of four little pictures of me with the Queen. But once outside there are lots of press photographers picking and choosing the people they want and I know they took some photos of me.

And then it was back to Lymington and back down to earth. And from then on I was slaving my guts out 16, 17, 18 hours a day making shepherd's pies and baking cakes to keep the business afloat. I employed four staff at weekends and we had a good routine – the person waiting on the tables also made the coffees and teas and there'd be someone else washing up. I'd have to bake more scones in the middle of the day, hundreds more on busy days, which I baked in batches of 32, which is still only 16 cream teas with two to a plate. But there's nothing like the smell of fresh baking wafting out from the kitchen which is why we never did any fried food. We wanted to maintain a genteel atmosphere, a very English feel, and definitely not a 'greasy spoon.' We had a snooty diamond merchants next door who used to refer to me as 'Gina in the caff.' I used to go ballistic and tell them it was a coffee shop not a caff, but I'm sure they did it on purpose.

You'd hear people sitting in there, looking at the cakes, and one would say to another: 'Ooh love, wouldn't my Victoria sponge do well in here?' They literally thought that's all it took, bake a little Victoria sponge, stick it on display, take out a slice and serve it. 'Grand little business this, lass,' they'd say. They hadn't a clue. I thought to myself if only you knew, my love, how much hard work it involved. The food had to be good and fresh, we had regular inspections from the environmental health, checking fridge temperatures, records, everything, and I had my restaurant licence to keep together.

Having always grown up with animals and surrounded by pets, I decided I'd like to have one there. I love all animals, creatures, nature but I was limited to what I could have. I must have seen something on TV which sparked my imagination and after doing a bit of research to check out whether it would be suitable, I decided a bird would be good and a bit of fun. So I treated myself to a parrot, harking back to The Polygon maybe! I went to a pet shop in Barton on Sea, where John and Mike had moved, and the shop rang me back about a week later to say they had made enquiries and could offer me a choice of three. They had some photographs and a bit of history of each bird which included an African Grey.

One of them was a blue and gold macaw, hand-reared, and I fell in love with him straight away. How can you fall in love with a bird? But he was a chirpy little character and I paid £1,350 for him. To start with I kept him upstairs – he wasn't chained because he was perch-trained although his wings were not clipped. So I had to buy the perch and the tray and a huge metal cage for when we were going out, all of which was more expense. I called him Cream Tea because I'd bought him with the profit from just that – cream teas. He soon learned to say a few phrases: 'Hello, hello' and, 'What's the matter, what's the matter?' It only takes 20 dedicated minutes talking to them before they learn to repeat the phrases so be very careful what you say. Some people teach their birds to swear and although it might be funny the first few times, after that it wears thin.

Soon I built him a little outside aviary in the garden at the back, which was a private paved area with borders around it. It was an area where he could fly and climb around, drop to the floor, climb up the netting and he was much happier. I put strips of towelling across his doorway and in the morning he'd pop his head out, stretch one wing and then the other, then each leg, just like us humans when we get out of bed. And then he'd do the biggest poo you've seen in your life, followed by one of the funniest movements I'd seen when he looked over his shoulder to see his success, watching it from home to base. He was so funny and I loved him to bits.

During the first winter he came back inside – he could walk up the stairs using his beak as a third leg – but then I put a little heater in his outside home, one without wires, and he could stay there happily. I'd bring him in to the restaurant sometimes when the customers had gone and let him walk around. He'd climb on to the back of my hand. He had a great hook beak with 250 lbs of pressure per square inch – he could take your finger off, or strip a table in five minutes, no problem. But instead he'd sit on my shoulder and the point of his beak would play with my ear, travelling through it so gently.

He could screech now and again, rather loudly, and one day the lady next door looked over and asked if she could see the parrot. She said he was very beautiful and would he be here long? 'Yes,' I said, 'about 65 years' because that's their lifespan. She said that he made the most awful noise and I apologised, but said it was only occasionally when he wanted attention or had spotted something he wanted. I must admit he did make a bit of a racket and it echoed around the small garden area.

The parrot actually escaped once but fortunately only flew to the railings of a balcony on some apartments about 200 or 300 yards away. He just sat there and luckily I guessed what floor, went up, knocked on the door and he was still on the rail when I got there. I put my arm out and he flew on and I breathed a huge sigh of relief.

For a few weeks one summer, I had a young French boy staying with me, Jean Claude, the nephew of the owners of a hotel in Courchevel where I stayed when I went skiing. They'd asked if he could come to England for the summer, work in the restaurant and learn some English. During that time, I went away for a couple of days and closed the restaurant and when I came back, he was standing there, his face in his boots – the parrot had escaped. I was distraught, he was distraught. We went everywhere, driving around looking for this blooming parrot. We had phone calls saying he'd been seen here, he'd been seen there and we'd rush off – and all the time I'm trying to run a business. Once he'd been spotted at the local boys' school, so I rushed up there with the cat basket I kept for Cream Tea, only to find he'd flown off. A week went by and every hour that I wasn't working I was driving the lanes of Lymington, looking for him, asking people, calling him, listening for him, but no joy.

One of my customers told me that the local radio station had a regular lost pet SOS slot, so one Monday afternoon, I rang and asked them to include that a blue and gold macaw had been lost. Blow me down, within no time I received a call from a man who said he thought he knew where it was. The day before he'd seen a man walking on the beach at Milford on Sea, five or six miles away, with a parrot on his arm. The man said it had turned up on the roof of his house and was being dive-bombed by the seagulls, who, like any species, don't like any different creature invading their territory; they wouldn't necessarily hurt him but they would harass him.

This chap had managed to tempt him down because he was a hand-reared bird and he only really knew human contact. And there he was parading him on the beach front. My informant told me where he lived and I was in my car so fast, found the house and knocked on the door which was ajar. When a lady came, I said I understood she had a parrot and she offered to show him to me. Well, when I walked in, I saw that they'd turned their living room into an aviary – there were branches, bits of trees, pieces of canvas, twigs, food, water. And there was the bird sitting on a branch.

I walked up to him, put my arm out and said: 'Hello, Cream Tea.' He immediately jumped on and started nibbling my ear. I told her I was sorry to say that he was my bird, that I could prove it if we went to a vet because he was microchipped, but that she had to believe me. She was upset, but I bundled him into the basket I'd taken and into the car. Luckily for me, the guy was out because I sensed there would have been trouble. I wrote a note giving my address and inviting them to the coffee shop for a free meal and said I was grateful to them for keeping him safe. Jean Claude was pretty damn relieved to see him when I got home. I never really found out how he had escaped, I think he would only have flown off out of panic not a desire to escape. Maybe Jean Claude had tried to quieten him if he was squawking and probably left open the main door to the garden. Whatever it was, we got him back. The man rang later and was harping on – I think he wanted money from me for rescuing the bird.

The only other awful time for Cream Tea was when I'd been away for a few days and left Tim, a man who worked for me, in charge. When I got back, Tim said he'd noticed Cream Tea acting strangely and when he looked closely, he found a family of bloomin' rats had moved in with him, even though his house was about five feet off the ground. Obviously they were after his food but what a horrible thought. It might never have happened if I'd not been away because I would have become suspicious straight away of his food disappearing quickly or his odd behaviour. The poor bird, having to share his home with a family of rats. Anyway we brought him in, deinfested the place of rats and cleaned the whole place out thoroughly.

When I eventually moved up to Leeds, I brought him with me and gave him to the Tropical House at Roundhay Park. He's still there although when I go along now and again and call Cream Tea, he turns his beak up at me!

Chapter 15

GOODBYE, I'M GOING TO DIE

It was around Christmas 1992 that I decided to end it all, I'd had enough. Tonni had become best friends with everybody in the town and was more than happy to spend his days talking and drinking. I was getting peed off with him because at the end of the day, I would be cleaning the restaurant, cleaning the toilet, stocking up from the cash & carry in Christchurch, which stayed open till late, while he was usually down the pub.

It was too easy for Tonni to drink there: we were surrounded by pubs, he was a very sociable character and within a few days he was best mates with everybody, all the drop-outs and deadheads and locals. So when we closed at 5pm in winter, he'd nip up the pub and meanwhile I'm working my nuts off.

The place ticked over, although the mortgage was a crippler. Then Tonni would come in saying he owed the pub £150 on my tab and the kids were coming over for the summer hols. In fact one of their visits was in 1992, the year Denmark's footballers won the European Championship. The kids had gone out with Tonni and I was ironing, watching the football on the television. But they were not there, not at all interested.

Then one day a solicitor turned up at the restaurant with an envelope for Tonni. He was out so I had to sign for it and when he came back and opened it, he found a summons for a debt he'd left in Denmark, which I knew absolutely nothing about. It was for £20,000 and it hit me like a brick. It was a loan he had taken out in Denmark. All the time he was living and working there, he probably made the repayments, but once he moved to England he clearly didn't continue to pay and probably hoped they wouldn't come chasing him. But they came looking for him all right, took him to county court in Southampton and declared him bankrupt. That was scary. Fortunately my solicitors drew up legal documents stating what was mine, because the worry was the mortgage lender would foreclose on the debt and the business and my money would go out the window. My respect for him after that plummeted to absolute zero.

After 18 months to two years, things had become really rocky between us. Our physical relationship suffered, he was verbally abusive, always putting me down. I felt at such a low ebb, no self-esteem, working so hard in the restaurant, and still a home to keep, washing and ironing to be done, meals to make. When I think back, I realise it became absolutely horrible, like a ball and chain round my neck and no way I could get rid of it. It was horrendous. It became a treadmill, six days a week and on Tuesdays, when we closed, not lying in bed, but in the kitchen baking and cooking on the only day when I knew I wouldn't be interrupted. Some nights Tonni went to bed so drunk he couldn't get up in the morning and I'd lost so much respect for him that I wouldn't even wake him.

I'm not a person who can hide my feelings and I'm sure it was stamped across my forehead that he was pissing me off. I'd realised by then that he was a loser – he'd take money out of the till, money I'd worked hard to earn, to pay the bar tab. I told him he'd have to find a job. The dear Lord must have been shining on me just then because Tonni found another Danish guy who had opened a small import/export business not a quarter of a mile away up the road. The chances of that happening must be minute. But it didn't make much difference because by then the whole thing had fallen apart between us. There's nothing I hate more than a lazy person, and not just lazy but prepared to sit there and watch me do all the work. And if he did offer to help, it was more trouble than it was worth. He'd offer to clean up in the restaurant but then he'd leave a tablecloth with a tea stain.

That Christmas, we were really starting to bitch at each other. He kept pulling me down, belittling me and yet I was doing all the graft. I brought a bottle of wine up from the restaurant to the flat – and I didn't even drink – poured it down, glug, glug, glug with a load of painkillers and then rang Dorothy in New Zealand. I was crying down the phone, telling her I'd rung to say goodbye because I was going to die. Such melodrama! And then I must have gone out cold.

The next thing I knew, ambulance men were slapping me round the face, trying to bring me round. I was on the bedroom floor and as soon as I spotted Tonni, I started screaming: 'Get him away from me.' There was a certain amount of hysteria in there, a cross between crying and screaming, all my emotions pouring out in one great cacophony of noise.

The paramedics took me downstairs and because we were on a narrow cobbled street, the ambulance was parked at the top and they half carried me, half walked me down the street with me shouting obscenities at Tonni all the way. I'm sure the odd light went on and faces peered out to see what the noise was, but I was oblivious to it then.

They drove me to hospital where nurses pumped my stomach – they put some kind of charcoal-based stuff inside you to soak up the alcohol and to make you throw up. I'll never forget the contempt on the nurses' faces – and who can blame them? They are there to save lives not to deal with a perfectly healthy person who has tried to take away the most precious thing of all. Was mine justified? Was I so tired, worn out, living with a man who didn't give me any support, a man who had debts, was bankrupt, that I couldn't cope any more? He was subjecting me to emotional blackmail because I wouldn't give him the money. I knew then we couldn't stay together: I was a grafter, he was a lazy bastard. You can only take that for so long.

But my attempted suicide – that's what it was – was totally spontaneous, not planned at all. I woke up in hospital at around four in the morning, feeling like shit. Everything hurt – my stomach, my head, eyes, everywhere. I buzzed the nurse to say I wanted to go home and saw the same contemptuous look on her face. They phoned Tonni – it was dark still, around five o'clock – and he came to take me back home. It was not far away, Lymington had its own hospital. I felt so awful and so ashamed. And the nurses so talked down to me, made me feel like pond life and really that's what you are. You have no right to take away the most valuable commodity, the only basic commodity you have, which is life itself.

Hitching a lift: Photographer Koo Stark, former girlfriend of Prince Andrew, joins me in *Agfa Bluebird* for a cancer charity event.

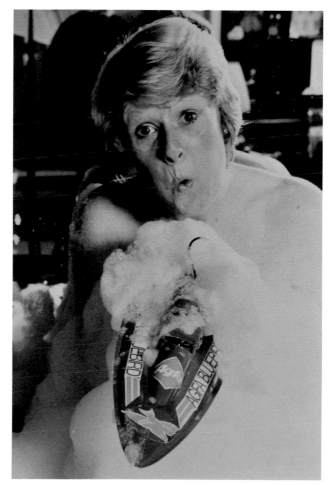

Blowing bubbles: In return for her spin in *Agfa Bluebird*, I agreed to pose for photographs when she was compiling her first book.

That sinking feeling: *Agfa Bluebird* in trouble off Ramsgate during the 1984 Round Britain Race.

Dicing with death: I was so lucky to survive this high-speed crash in a lightweight records boat at Holme Pierrepont in 1984. The similarities to my father's fatal crash at Coniston in 1967 were uncanny.

Back above water: *Agfa Bluebird* at speed in the 1985 British Powerboat Championships.

Winning smile: In the pits during the countdown to another race in the 1985 Championships.

Tanks for the memory: Actress Leslie Ash and I are quizzed by motor racing legend Stirling Moss after driving a tank on the television series *Driving Force*.

Bear necessity: Relaxing, with Mr Whoppit for company, during the build-up to the 1986 World Powerboat Championships in New Zealand.

Cover girl: Mr Whoppit gets in on the act again, this time courtesy of my work for the New Zealand Water Safety Council in the late eighties.

On location: With author and broadcaster Melvyn Bragg (right) in 1986 while filming a remake of his 1968 documentary about my father, *The Price Of A Record*.

Game for a laugh: With Tonia and actor Bill Maynard before their marriage in 1989. I thought they were an unlikely couple…and so it proved.

Bring on the bubbly: Tonni, my third husband, and I hosted our wedding reception at home in Denmark February 1990.

No April fool: Embarking on my world water speed run at Lake Taupo on April 1, 1990 – and setting the record at 166 miles per hour.

Thank you ma'am. Receiving the Queen's Service Order at Buckingham Palace, when I became the third generation of the Campbell family to be honoured.

Cheers! Tonni enjoying the role of 'mine host' in the sunshine outside The Lentune at Lymington.

The Bluebird At Lentune
Coffee House

Gina & Tonni Campbell-Jensen

4, Quay Street
Lymington
Hants. SO41 9AS.

England

Bill of Fayre: The menu at The Bluebird at Lentune, my coffee shop in Lymington.

Who's a pretty boy, then? My lovely parrot Cream Tea enjoying life at The Lentune.

In the frame. I take delivery of a painting from artist John Pittaway, one of his fantastic collection of Bluebirds.

In the swing: Teeing off at Huddersfield Golf Club in my early days as a golfer.

Numbers game. Seven was always a special number for my father and the obvious choice for my personalised number plate.

Unaccustomed as I am: Addressing guests at the inauguration ceremony at Daytona Beach's Motorsports Hall of Fame.

Behind the wheel: In the cockpit of my grandfather's *Bluebird* car, fully restored and a prime attraction at Daytona Beach.

The President's son: Meeting Ronald Reagan Jnr at Daytona Beach when my grandfather's *Bluebird* was inaugurated into the Motorsports Hall of Fame.

Mother's day: Visiting my mother at her home in Devon in the mid 1990s.

My father's Dunhill lighter and the St Christopher, one of my treasured possessions which I sadly lost in July 2012, both recovered from Lake Coniston. The coins, his broken seat belt and *Bluebird*'s Lloyd's Register tonnage plate were also found with his body.

Cuddle up: With Marillion singer Steve Hogarth when he agreed to sing at my father's funeral service.

Final farewell: The Order of Service for the funeral of my father, which I never expected would happen.

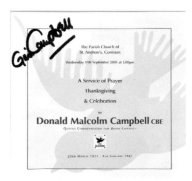

Say it with flowers: My floral tribute to my father.

In loving memory: Some of the tributes left on my father's grave by mourners.

Meet the team: Bill Smith (back row, second left) and the divers who found and recovered *Bluebird* and my father's body.

All hands on deck: With my friend Linda Newman aboard *Bluebird of Happiness* in the harbour at St Tropez.

Country boys: Bill Smith and I visit my father's grave with television's Matt Baker (left) and Marillion's Steve Hogarth (right) for the filming of the BBC's *Countryfile* programme.

Over the rainbow: It appeared from nowhere on a visit to Coniston in September 2011…and fortunately I had my camera handy.

My lucky day: Soon after snapping my Coniston rainbow, this black cat crossed my path as I approached my father's grave, where it had been sitting.

Progress: A visit to Bill Smith's workshop in North Shields in 2012 revealed a recognisable *Bluebird*, compared with the tangled metal which confronted me soon after she was recovered from Coniston. The green coating on the fuselage (above) is merely part of the process - not the finished article!

Cafe culture: A visit to the Bluebird Cafe in Coniston to show off the K7 DAD number plate I finally acquired early in 2012.

Best of friends: Sue Stone (left) and Avril Hamburg who have stayed loyal throughout both the good and the bad times.

Winning smiles: Moor Allerton Ladies 'A' team after winning a Yorkshire County Ladies Golf Association trophy in 2004 with Henry Stone, the men's captain at the time, offering his congratulations.

The whole episode was sad but somehow later, I thought I had been a bit like a comedy of errors because the very next day I opened the restaurant. What I must have looked like I cannot imagine. It was a public holiday and so it was hellish busy and one of my first customers was a very posh mother and daughter, who looked identical, who lived in a house tucked in by the side of Quay Street. They'd obviously heard this terrible caterwauling the night before, and because it was a cobbled street the noise really echoed around there and had come to find out what had happened. I was operating on automatic pilot, sleepwalking my way through it, but I made it through the day, feeling absolutely at rock bottom.

It sounds an obvious conclusion, but I absolutely knew that the relationship with Tonni was finished. A relationship is like a beautiful piece of entwined rope and when you have a row, you are pulling on opposite ends, starting to pull it apart. Slowly you put it back together, knit those few loose threads back in, although they never quite fit again in the same way. Then you have another row and you pull it apart again and this time a few more threads are hanging out the sides and it's not looking quite so pretty round the edges this time. Until one day those threads are so tenuous and thin that they snap. It's a theory I've held for all of my life.

Tonni was the one person I lost my temper with because I found him so unreasonable and in the end I lost all respect for him. He had the gift of the gab and was happy to tell people how wonderful he was, yet the same man could lie in bed, sleeping off a hangover while I was slaving my guts out in the business. And I'd paid for his booze. Respect is the key to any relationship. You have to earn it and once earned, if you then spend it, you will never get it back, it's gone.

Even so I couldn't just throw Tonni out on the streets. And anyway because our front door was the restaurant front door, it was always open and so it was really impossible to keep him out. He'd managed to find work with the Danish guy and eventually he found himself a flat in Lymington. He'd maintained a friendship with a couple of men who worked for Agfa, whom he knew when he was with Helioprint, and he used to spend his weekends up in London with them and with various girlfriends.

But our marriage had one last sting in the tail after I filed for divorce on the grounds of irretrievable breakdown. My lawyer told me that normally more than 90% of those divorce petitions, where both parties agreed, were rubber-stamped but in my case the judge at Southampton County Court decided he wanted to hear this case. We both wondered if it was because of the name or that it was just my bad luck.

So off we all troop to court – I was there with my solicitor, I stood in the witness box, swore the oath on the Bible and the Judge asked me whether the marriage had broken down irretrievably. I said it had and he looked across at Tonni and asked him whether he agreed. I took one look at him, saw that he hesitated for a split second and I realised what was coming. He said, clear as anything: 'No, I don't.' I yelled across at him: 'What do you mean? I can't believe you just said that, what's the matter with you?' The Judge hushed me up, asked ' Mr Jensen' again if he meant it and Tonni obviously realised that he had the power to stop this, power over me. The Judge said he could not grant the divorce on those grounds because Tonni didn't agree, which prompted another tirade from me – what the Judge called an 'unladylike outburst.'

It was pretty clear to me that they'd only asked to hear the case because of my family name. The system didn't have the time or the money to hear every divorce petition where both parties had agreed on the grounds of irretrievable breakdown. So I had to start all over again with my petition and it was probably another 18 months before I finally received my decree nisi. The second time round Tonni agreed. I was still working all hours God gave. I look back and wonder how I found the strength to work 18 or19 hours a day, sleep, start again the next morning and hold my body and soul together. But when you have to do it, you do.

My contact with powerboating was non-existent in those years at Lymington but I was approached to take part in one interesting project, which meant I could close the restaurant for one afternoon. Richard Branson was making a *Welcome to Britain* video to be shown on his Virgin Atlantic flights and wanted to include some shots of Lymington Marina, which is one of the prettiest places in the world, and wanted me to drive a boat round the harbour. You betcha I would. The whole event was organised by Sunseeker boats in Poole, who dealt in top-of-the-range sports cruisers and are now into super yachts, and they met me and got me set up with the boat. I had an absolutely fabulous time, being filmed both from another boat and a helicopter. I enjoyed it so much that I asked if I could take the boat back to Poole and then make my own way home to Lymington. I had such fun that when the production company asked me what my fee would be for my time, I told them it had been such a pleasure and a privilege that I didn't want a payment. That comment must have got back to Richard Branson because I received word from him that if ever I was flying Virgin in the future, I would be well treated. So afterwards, if I was flying to the States, I had a number to call at Virgin and wherever possible, I was upgraded. So sometimes it pays not to be greedy and not just to think of today, for whatever they might have paid me for that afternoon's pleasure could never have matched the value of the upgrades they gave me. For me, it was a small favour at the time, one which gave me so much fun.

I had originally met Richard back in the early 80s, at a luncheon in London organised by the publishers Conde Nast, who each year presented awards for the best hotel, best airline, restaurant, all things travel and hospitality. I was wearing a Rolex watch which I took off in the ladies' in the hotel to wash my hands and left it there. It was only a few minutes before I remembered but when I went back, it had gone – it was my fault. Richard asked me where I was living and I told him Leatherhead because I was with Michael then in Aquila Close. So when Richard came to introduce me – I was presenting the award for best hire car company – he said: 'Here we have the Tina Turner of Leatherhead, Gina Campbell.' I absolutely cringed, it was such an extraordinary thing to say.

That was just one of quite a few invitations I received to attend awards lunches and dinners when I was powerboat racing, including one particular Sportsman of the Year charity lunch at the Grosvenor House Hotel in London. I accepted the invitation and Michael was coming with me. Three or four days before the event, I had a call asking me if I was definitely attending. Of course I said I was and they seemed pleased and reiterated that I wouldn't let them down, would I? There were ten awards to be given and I thought: 'Goody, I'm in for an award.' It was only when I arrived and checked the table plan that I realised why they wanted to be sure – because I was sitting between Prince and Princess Michael of Kent. It was still a bit of an honour with all those sporting personalities there and I'd been chosen to sit next to them.

The world featherweight boxing champion Barry McGuigan was there and Tessa Sanderson, the 1984 Olympic Javelin champion, who seemed enormous next to me when I saw her in the ladies' room. The seating plan meant I spent most of the time talking to the Prince, mainly about horses, although I could hardly hear a word he said. I was a bit surprised at how little effort he put into the conversation as I had been brought up to lead people into a topic that interested them and then let it unravel. And, in the end, I didn't receive an award!

Back at Lymington, there was one more fabulous time still to come – when I closed the place for the whole of January to go skiing. John and Mike had always closed then for a month because the place was dead. So I took myself off to Courchevel, where my father and Tonia had met the most gorgeous, dishy, delightful ski instructor when they were there on honeymoon. His name is Pierre Gruneberg – 'green mountain' in German. His parents were German Jews who fled from the Nazis and he really is a legendary character and the proverbial Peter Pan.

After Dad's honeymoon Pierre came over to stay with us at Roundwood. I was only 12 or 13, a scrappy little girl probably stinking of horse poo but I knew even then he was the most gorgeous man I'd ever seen. Pierre had a fabulous life – he was single and gave ski lessons throughout the winter at Courchevel 1850, the highest and most chic of the four resorts there, and in the winter taught people to swim and overcome their fear of water at the Grand-Hotel du Cap-Ferrat. The names of the people he has taught reads like a Who's Who of celebrities: from Aristotle Onassis to Ralph Lauren, Tina Turner, Andrew Lloyd Webber, the movie star Robin Williams, Bono, the names go on and on. He has all their signatures in his autograph book – and we have **his** signature in my father's visitors' book.

Pierre became a bit of a celebrity in his own right with the method he devised for teaching people to swim, without having to get wet. It became known as The Gruneberg Method. He used an ordinary salad bowl full of water to teach people to breathe properly by putting their face in the water. He was on TV demonstrating his method and was in demand by all kinds of smart hotels, who wanted him to teach their guests.

As I got older I went skiing with my father and we always spent time with Pierre. I suppose I fell head over heels – not exactly in love because what is love at that age? – but boy, did I know he was desirable. He used to sneak into my hotel bedroom some nights, even though I was young, but I was no longer a virgin after my time in the South of France.

I'd kept in touch with Pierre on and off and when I left Lymington to drive to Courchevel it was to meet up with him again. I enjoyed the drive – I love the car, the convenience, the fact that it's your own space, you don't have to rely on anybody else. Pierre lived in an apartment, which had treatment rooms attached where he saw his physio patients, and he had a pal who owned a small hotel underneath, the Hotel des Pins. He gave me preferential rates. In return, the following summer, I agreed that his nephew Jean Claude, a bespectacled 16-year-old who didn't speak any English, could come over to stay with me. He was a big beanstalk of spots and pubescent problems but not a bad lad and he worked in the restaurant, washing up, waiting at tables and learned something of the language.

In Courchevel I spent the days skiing because Pierre was working. And then at night we'd meet up, sometimes go to the cinema, have dinner and then…oh boy, this was one passionate man!

But there was another side to Pierre. Many years before, on the night my father died in January 1967, Pierre rang me in Arosa – how he got hold of my number I don't know. He told me that earlier that night, all the ski instructors from Courchevel 1850 had gone up a slope called La Luz, in the dark, each of them carrying a flame torch, which they arranged in the snow in the shape of my dad's initials, DC. After a while, they collected them and skied back down the mountain in a snake, all out of respect for my father, who was one of the early celebrities in Courchevel and could certainly light up a place.

In those days, it was little more than a village, a tiny, beautiful place which had the feel of a family-run affair, not the ritzy, glitzy, San Tropez-on-the-snow resort that it is today. Like many places that start out as La Little Jewel and then become part of a brash necklace. I know that's not quite fair because now it has become a playground for the rich and famous. However there were not many hotels when my father first went there and it was a place where he was always held dear.

I loved it there too and had my father survived his last record attempt at Coniston, we were going to meet up there again. He had said in that last letter to me: 'I'm going to get this bloody record if it's the last thing I do. Then, come and join me in Courchevel and we'll have a ball.' It was written in his big, extravagant handwriting – all his writing was exactly the same style as his signature, unlike so many people whose signature looks completely different from the rest. I believe my grandfather Sir Malcolm's writing was the same, his signature was just an extension of his normal handwriting. And I'm the same, too. I can't believe I never kept that letter.

Chapter 16

TWO LESSONS AND I WAS HOOKED

Among my regular customers at The Lentune in the summer were dozens of people who owned boats and moored them in Lymington Marina and of course I came to know a good few of them. Many of them lived in other parts of the country but spent weekends and holidays on their boats.

One of them was a businessman from Leeds, who often used to come down to Lymington with a pal – they both owned boats and would come into my coffee shop. I got to know him quite well over a year or two and he finally persuaded me to move to Leeds to be with him.

I spent the next 18 years with him and so much happened in that time which changed the course of my life, they took me back to very many places I had not visited for a long time…to the USA, Australia, New Zealand, South Africa, the south of France and so the list goes on. My father had taken me to some of these countries many years earlier and they're all very lovely places which I was privileged to visit.

But back in 1991, I had never been to Leeds before – I had spent a lot of time in the Lake District and had a friend on the other side of the Pennines but only visited Yorkshire once or twice. However my grandfather had a very unusual connection with Bradford. He once set a challenge to the city's tailors: to break the record for making a suit from scratch in the shortest possible time. The idea was that they had to shear the sheep, spin and weave the wool, make the cloth and turn it into a suit or coat in just a few hours if possible.

It was way back in 1931, soon after Grandfather broke the world land speed record at Daytona at 245.736 miles per hour – when he also became the first man to drive a car at over four miles per minute, which had been his pet aim. He arrived back in England to a huge fanfare, a government reception at Westminster Hall and then the very next day he was invited to Buckingham Palace to receive his knighthood from King George V.

He was still full of plans to carry on, he wanted to go for 300 miles an hour, but the family were keen to persuade him to give up his dangerous record chasing and settle for something a bit safer. He had no idea what he might do but his father-in-law, Lady Dorothy's father, told him he should be finding ways to show that his talents were not limited to chasing speed records and that he could do a more than useful job either in business or the commercial world. He mentioned to Grandfather that the West Riding of Yorkshire was desperately trying to boost its woollen textile trade and maybe there was something he could do there.

Apparently Lady C's father had also discovered that years before, someone had actually made a coat from scratch in less than a day. It was a man from Oxfordshire, who began to shear his sheep at six in the morning and by late that same afternoon was wearing a coat made from the wool. So the idea was for Grandfather to challenge the wool merchants in Bradford to break that record.

I've been told that Grandfather was a bit dubious about the scheme but that the word 'record' sold it to him! He agreed to go to a meeting of the Bradford Rotary Club, where he told them that his speed records had achieved worldwide publicity, and suggested they needed to do the same for the wool trade. He told them the story of the Oxfordshire farmer and challenged them to go one better. Two companies took up the challenge – one agreed to make the cloth and a firm of tailors said they would then make a suit – and grandfather agreed to return to watch the whole thing.

But then came the hitch. On the day he was supposed to go back to see it all happen, he flatly refused to go. In Lady C's book about him, *Malcolm Campbell, The Man As I Knew Him,* she said he was in 'one of his inexplicably awkward moods' that day, although since then other people have told me he'd had a row with the missus. Lady C said he could be as temperamental as a film star.

Anyway, everybody was furious of course and my grandmother had to go instead. She gave the go-ahead for the shearers to begin at 10 in the morning and just over two and half hours later, the suit was ready. Needless to say, Grandfather was not the most popular man in Bradford even though they had set a new record. The story was later included in the BBC2 Playhouse drama *Speed King,* which was shown in the 70s and featured Robert Hardy as Sir Malcolm.

Unlike my grandparents, I had never been to Bradford when I moved north but I had a very dear friend called Richard Ackroyd, whom I met through Jaguar when I was powerboat racing. He was from Huddersfield and I loved to hear him talk about his home town, the Pennines and the north because he was very proud of his roots. He later went to work for Aston Martin.

I had also visited Harrogate once, funnily enough with Tonni, who was looking for business opportunities in import and export. The idea was to try to run his business alongside the coffee shop to bring in some extra cash but nothing ever came of it. I remember walking along the road near the Spa and buying some little ornate glasses, which had a stained glass window effect, in a jeweller's and gift shop. We stayed in the Swallow Hotel.

When I first moved to Leeds, I used to divide my time between there and Lymington, usually driving down late on Friday to work in the coffee shop Saturday, Sunday, Monday. I soon realised that the accounting was not all it should be – the weekends I was down there, I knew how much money we had taken whereas on the weekends I wasn't there, they said business had been really slow and they hardly had any customers. It was obvious something was wrong because the cash & carry bills were the same. I always say that if you put temptation in front of somebody, you can breed a thief. Of course that doesn't apply to everybody but it was clear something was not quite right.

Eventually, I decided to put The Lentune on the market but it was not the easiest place to sell. I'd paid £250,000 for it so I was looking to get my money back. But while it had been the perfect place for me to buy, people with that kind of money in those days didn't want to work 18 hours a day. Yet it wasn't profitable enough for someone to own it and put someone else in charge to run it. Then it had the house upstairs, which wasn't big enough for a family. So it fell between lots of stools.

Finally I had an offer from a Turkish family who had leased next door and ran it more as a greasy spoon café. Their intention was to buy both places and make them into one. They'd previously had a bed and breakfast down the road and worked really hard to make it a success.

When I finally accepted an offer from him – this was a few years after my move to Leeds – to speed things up we agreed to share a solicitor, who had an office in Lymington High Street. We walked there together and I noticed he was holding a carrier bag, which I assumed held his bits and pieces. But when the solicitor told us both rather solemnly that we had agreed a ten per cent deposit, which must be paid immediately, he picked up the carrier, turned it upside down and all this cash tumbled out on her desk. I'd never seen so many notes, it was hilarious. The solicitor turned her nose up and said: 'Oh, I can't possibly take that.' There was a second's pause before I said: 'Well I can!' and started scooping it towards me. I'd been on a knife edge hoping that the deal would go through and there was he, staggering up the High Street with a carrier bag full of all this cash. I didn't take it there and then of course, she had him take it to a bank next door. But the sale eventually went through – I was at Moor Allerton Golf Club when my phone went and it was the solicitor to say the deal had been completed.

I spent the first few weeks in Leeds looking for somewhere to live, as opposed to staying in a hotel, which is not real life. I pretty soon found a flat in Roundhay Park on the northern outskirts of the city and I'd drive around, familiarising myself with the area, go to Ilkley or Harrogate for the day. And I'd often drive over the tops – over the Pennines – to see a friend in Colne, a woman called Dorothy Teasdale. She was a teacher but in her spare time she had been the secretary of my stepmother Dorothy's fan club when she was the presenter of a successful BBC entertainment programme called *Quite Contrary*. It was a live variety programme and Dorothy used to sing and dance and recite poetry. She was actually on air when the telegram arrived to say my father had broken the water speed record in September 1955 at Lake Mead in Nevada and until then nobody knew of her connection to him.

Dorothy Teasdale often used to drive up to Coniston to see my father and Dorothy, because it's not far from Colne, and because she was star-struck. My dad continued to invite her up there even after Dorothy went back to New Zealand and she remembered me there as a little girl. She told me she used to watch me jump into the icy cold water and swim like a bloody little fish from one pier to the next – it must have been after Leo taught me on the way to the States. She said I'd set myself an enormous goal for a scrambly doggy-paddle – now I regard myself as a rather good swimmer. She was often left in charge of me.

Once when I was at Lymington, she asked me to go up to the school where she taught and talk to all the kids in assembly and then at lunchtime talk to just some of them about motivation. I stayed the night with Dorothy and her partner Lesley who was an art teacher. She had made a beautiful sculpture of The Four Horsemen of the Apocalypse which I admired and when Lesley died, Dorothy gave it to me, which was so kind.

But because my partner was running his business full time, I pretty soon began to get bored on my own in Leeds. I spent an enormous amount of time with his mother who had been widowed for many years. She loved to go out in the car so I would take her to Skipton, to Harrogate, Ilkley, Otley, where we'd have a cup of tea and a sandwich and drive back. Then, because my partner and some of his chums played golf at Moor Allerton in Leeds, I decided to have a few golf lessons with Richard Lane, who was the pro there at the time. I think she was a bit upset because it meant I was not quite so free to take her places.

It was springtime and I booked six lessons but after just two, I was hooked. I went straight to American Golf and bought a set of clubs, whether they were the right ones I didn't know and didn't care. I wanted my own kit. I would have thought I was quite wealthy then, I still had the business and I knew I could treat myself. I was in charge of my own money, I had a little but it felt a lot compared to where I'd been before.

The pro told me that with some very hard work and determination, I could play the game. I was very keen and if someone tells me to do x, I'll do x, and if it works I'll do it again. And then again and again. If it doesn't work, I'll try to work out why. I'd go on to the practice field after my lesson and hit and hit and hit balls until I felt proficient enough to take up a membership, because Moor Allerton is a difficult course. I joined the ladies section and in those days you started with a handicap of 36*P – which meant you had been given the highest handicap possible, although really you should be more than 36. First you had to work off the P and then the star.

We've got ladies who have been at the club 20 years who started out at 36 and are still 36 – and some of them still can't play to it. But that's the essence of the game; I could play against Tiger Woods and the handicap would allow us to compete but I couldn't play tennis against Roger Federer. That's what attracted me to golf…and the fact that you cannot blame anybody else if things are not going well. It's you and the course.

I was pretty naïve at the start, I'd never been a member of a golf club before. I didn't know all the protocols, the rules and regulations, the procedures you have to follow. Everyone assumes you know all this although nobody explains it to you. But as soon as you step out of line, they soon let you know, or give you the complete blank screen treatment. I couldn't believe how, at that time of life, I had to learn a whole new set of behaviours: what you can wear, what you can say, when you can stand, when you can sit, when you can clap, when you can cry. And the whole time I just wanted to be good at it.

Most ladies at the club were delightful, some were difficult, a few horrible to me because they saw me as a threat. I was often in the papers, on the radio, on television and they didn't like it. But I was up on the practice field one day when two ladies came over and introduced themselves. One was a beginner called Avril Hamburg and the other was a good player who suggested Avril and I should play together. We arranged to meet most weekday mornings at eight before anyone else arrived, so we could play when there was nobody to get in the way or for us to get in their way. We had this amazing ability to hit the ball backwards, to bunny hop down the fairway, to miss it completely and then, suddenly, sometimes it would just click. Avril and I have been good friends ever since.

When I was still learning, I went to Ireland to play and took with me a book by David Leadbetter, the famous golf coach who helped Nick Faldo win six major championships. It was called *Faults and Fixes*. I didn't even understand the terminology – when he said to do this and do that, I didn't know what the hell it meant. But you read it and read it and slowly you make some sense of what it means. So when I was back home, I used to take my book, dozens of practice balls and go on to the practice field at Moor Allerton and start at page 1 – the grip. I'd follow his instructions, make sure it was spot on, club in the palm of the hand, not through the fingers. I would diligently go through each stage. People up there must have thought I was crackers. But that's how I am, that's my Virgo trait.

My handicap came down quite quickly, not because I was playing better than my handicap but because the committee were taking off six shots at a time. I think women at the club totally misjudged me at first – they thought I was fiercely competitive and wanted to win all the competitions. But I'd done all the beating in my water sports, my world speed record. I'd had all that, it's just that if one hole is a par four, I want to do it in a four, if I take five, I'm frustrated.

My handicap now is 11 and I'll never get any better. It has been ten, but not for very long. Considering I took it up in my late 40s, I haven't done badly to reach that level and I can still hack my way around. I've been through quite a few sets of clubs and damaged a few clubs. God, I have wrapped some round trees and posts, stamped on them, thrown them at my trolley out of sheer frustration, although I haven't done that for a long time.

During my first year, we spent three months in Florida, renting a house at the PGA National Golf Resort in Miami, owned by the American Professional Golfers' Association, which is a fabulous place to stay in the winter. It is a typically American gated-style community covering four or five square miles, with around 3,000 homes and five tournament golf courses. The Ryder Cup has been played there, the PGA Championship, the Seniors Tour and it's very beautiful, very Florida. Homeowners rent out the places when they do not wish to use them and we from the frozen north love to go there in the winter months to have some sun.

We first learned about it from some golfing friends at Moor Allerton, who eventually bought a house there, and ironically the first time we rented, we were just three doors away from them. Each neighbourhood, as they are called, has a theme and ours that year was Italian, so our house was in the district called Villa D'Este.

Two friends from our club joined us and another couple of lady golf club members were staying nearby. One morning when we were all playing golf and I'd obviously just hit a good shot, I overheard one woman saying to the other: 'She's soon going to be the best player in our club.' I'd only been playing for a few months and I obviously wasn't meant to hear that but my little brain box said to itself: 'Yes, she is.' So I strived and strived and strived until I had the lowest handicap among the lady members of the club – and then I lost interest. Well, that's not quite true but it was a bit like that. Once I had broken the world water speed record, that was it. I have never been in a fast boat since. I'm still up there at the golf club, number two, three or four but that's purely because I don't play that much now.

Over the years, I've played all over the world – I've played often in the south of France at Cannes-Mougins, which is a golf country club, and at Saint Donat golf club between Cannes and Grasse. I've also played in Germany, America, Australia, New Zealand, Chile and a place called Ushuaia in Argentina, the world's most southerly golf course. We were on a cruise across Drake's Passage and on to the Antarctic Peninsula when we stopped there. There was snow on the mountains and glaciers and yet when we were playing, we had to take our sweaters off it was so sunny.

Golf has given me an enormous amount of pleasure and after years of playing, I just about know what to expect. I know very well that if a strange person appears at the club, all the women in particular will peer, look them up and down, check out what they're wearing. Before I was even a member, just having lessons, one woman said to me in a snooty tone: 'If you ever become a member here, you cannot wear trousers like that.' And then there were those who always started by saying: 'Can I just tell you as a friend...' I wanted to tell them where to go. But in fact, Moor Allerton has become a lot less stiff and stuffy since then; you can even wear jeans in the clubhouse...as long as they're not shredded.

Chapter 17

YOUR MOTHER DIED THIS MORNING

I was in Florida when my mother died just before Christmas 1998. We were spending part of the winter there, renting a house again at the PGA National Golf Resort in Miami. We had been there for about three weeks when the call came and we had two golfing friends from Leeds staying with us for Christmas.

It was one of the friends who answered it – he's a total insomniac so always up early. I heard him call 'Gina, phone,' and I went down, a bit hazy. I think it was around 6am. He was having a cup of tea and said it was somebody called Mrs Shaw, which was my mother's married name so it didn't dawn on me for a few seconds that I was not talking to her, but to the woman who acted as her housekeeper, her cleaner and carer. She just said: 'I have to tell you that your mother has died this morning.' I suppose it's a surreal moment in anybody's life, when you think, 'Oh my God'. I asked about Owen and she said he was distraught because this was a man who daren't get up out of the chair without my mother's permission. He was just not in a fit state to talk to me on the phone right then. Apparently my mother had started to prepare the breakfast while he went to take the dogs for a walk and he came back to find my mother slumped in the chair.

I don't remember crying – I don't cry easily – at least not about events which affect me personally. I can shed bucket loads of tears at sentimental movies like *Bambi* or *Lassie*, it can be embarrassing, but not when it's real life. Isn't that strange? My father hated crybabies, he always thought you should stand up and face anything difficult, so maybe that's why.

Her death came absolutely out of the blue for me. I had spoken to her on the phone since we'd been in Florida, just three or four days before.

It turned out that she died of a heart attack and a few weeks later, her doctor rang me to say my mother was found to have had very high cholesterol and he suggested I had mine checked. Sure enough mine was high too – and not from eating any of the usual culprits like butter and cheese. It just is in my DNA apparently so now I take medication to keep it stable.

I said at the start that I am sure my mother never loved me and I never spent one night under her roof after my parents parted. But I always knew that although I did not hold her in high esteem, at the end of the day she was my mother and I owed her some respect. However she'd treated me, I always tried to do the right thing. So many times I tried to start afresh with her, to establish a more normal mother/daughter relationship, but she did not want to know. She could be sugary sweet with my friends but never missed an opportunity to criticise me behind my back. I once went down to see her with my friend June and afterwards June confided that my mother had taken her to one side and told her that although she might think I was a certain type of person, in fact I had a lot of unpleasant traits. June couldn't believe it.

Why did she treat me like this? I've asked myself many times. I can only think that she could no longer hit back at my father – so took it out on me instead. She knew I held a torch for my father – I know he wasn't perfect, but that's how I felt. I really don't know but it must be terrible to bring a child into the world and then feel unable to show it any love.

I went back upstairs and told my partner, who was fairly nonplussed. I knew he'd be working out what the implications were. I think it was December 19 or 20 and within a few hours I was able to speak to Owen myself and again the next day and the next. He eventually told me that the funeral was arranged for New Year's Eve in Devon, where they still lived.

My first instinct was that I would go to the funeral so I sat down and looked in great detail at the logistics. It was enormously complicated. If we both went, we would not be allowed to leave our friends in the house; that was part of the rental agreement. Then there were the implications and the cost of flights, even if I could find one at that time of year. It was high season for Miami and they were not so readily available. Would

I be covered by insurance? Probably so as it involved my nearest and dearest. I'd have to go back to Leeds first to collect suitable clothes and my car, which was laid up for the winter in the garage, untaxed, only insured third party. Somehow I would have to get down to Devon, which meant I would have had to leave almost straight away to make it for December 31. There was a huge mix of reasons why it was difficult – it could hardly have been more complicated.

Of course if she had been a normal, loving mother I would have moved heaven and earth to get there. But she had been far from that. And once I started to put everything into the mix, suddenly my common sense told me: 'It ain't going to make any bloody difference to her, to me, to anybody else whether you're there or not.' Even so, it wasn't just a quick, callous decision on my part. I've never regretted not going, I don't see regret as a very positive emotion.

My mother was cremated and I found out afterwards there were only four people at the service – that's the kind of legacy that she left behind. I believe in the local community she had become a bit of a laughing stock. Apparently almost every week she would write a letter to the local paper about this or that – the birds or the bees, anti-hunting or some such issue, the council should do this and that, this was wrong, that was wrong. They were always negative, never positive, because that was my mother.

She was a meddler, loved meddling in other people's lives including mine, but only when it suited her. She was an amalgam of characteristics as a lot of us are. She never wanted to be there to form my life but once it was formed, she wanted to interfere and rearrange it, which is a bit rich. For most of the time, she was never constructively helpful and yet, because she wanted to be centre stage at my first wedding to Cliffy, she took it upon herself to make the arrangements.

But then when I was married to Philip, she chose to tell him I was having an affair with Michael – how dare she take that upon herself! That was wicked, meddlesome, vindictive. She always seemed to want to come up trumps when my life was in the shit, but when it was all smooth and hunky-`dory, she didn't want much to do with it.

Once when she was on the telephone trying to tell me what to do when I was living in Ashstead with Michael, he picked up the phone and told her to mind her own bloody business, which did not go down well.

And another time I was sitting in our little study one weekend reading the *Sunday Times*, I think around 1986, when I found an interview with my mother in which she was hugely critical of my father. She said he had always lived in his father's shadow, that he was totally in awe of Sir Malcolm and that he would have been nobody without his father's name. She said that was why my father always called himself Donald Malcolm Campbell and even signed his name the same – DMC.

Maybe the press had gone to her but I was so angry, I called her to tell her she was so wrong and how could she be so cruel. When the conversation ended – on a very bad note – I opened the window and threw the cordless phone outside taking great delight in watching it shatter into a thousand pieces. I didn't speak to her again for a long time.

There was always huge animosity between my mother, Dorothy and later Tonia although it's not as though my father left any of them for either of the other two. But there was this loathing between the three of them, they all hated one another vehemently. It was jealousy over my father of course and maybe even jealousy over me, although I never thought of that at the time. I knew I meant something to Dorothy and I spent more time with her than with my mother but I never thought I meant much to my mother. I don't remember her being in my life at all, I never lived with her, never stayed in her house. It was always 'inconvenient dear.' She was really like a stranger to me.

If I was ever speaking to my mother on the phone when Dorothy was staying with me in England, or calling her from Dorothy's in New Zealand, I couldn't bring myself to mention Dorothy's name to her. It happened once when I was living in Lymington when Dorothy had come over to the UK to see me. What a good lass she was. My mother rang out of the blue while Dorothy was there to say that she realised times must be hard for me – mortgage interest rates were a whopping 15% – and would £250,000 help me out? Like, wow, would it not just? She was sure she could sort out the money from her father's trust, which was eventually intended for me anyway.

She took my hopes right up there with her promise, I thought that all my wildest dreams were about to come true. Dorothy was more sceptical and told me it wasn't going to work. And sure enough, a few days later my mother called again to say that it was proving too complicated and it would be impossible to release the money. What she really meant was that it was going to reduce her income, because she drew the interest on the capital and that provided an income for her and Owen. Dorothy showed complete disdain and implied that she would never have expected anything different. Because that was my mother – a carrot woman. She'd dangle it before you but as soon as you reached for it, the carrot disappeared. That's how she was throughout my life – pick me up, push me down, pick me up, push me down. My father used to say: 'Please God that you never end up like that woman.' I think that's why he used to beat me so much because he was shit scared I was going to be like her. It was his one abiding wish for me, he'd grown to hate her so much, which in itself is quite sad. But then she hurt him. At the time I didn't understand but now… dear God, I do and I just hope I am not…

There would be great long periods in my life when I was barely in touch with my mother. When I lived in Denmark I think we phoned one another occasionally and when I was in Lymington, I would ring one Sunday and she would call the next. It was while I was in the coffee shop, around Christmas one year, that I received a card from her with a note inside saying: 'Do call me, I'm going to have my leg amputated.' Of course I rang but could never fully understand why she needed to have that operation. I knew she had had a couple of toes removed but didn't know the details of what exactly necessitated this life-changing experience.

I always questioned whether this incredibly dramatic stance had to be taken but because she wasn't in my life, I couldn't ask. I drove down to Devon with Tonni to see her after she had the operation, and there she was, sitting in a wheelchair with this funny little stump above the knee. She wanted me to look at it and touch it, so I had to get those spooky things over with. But it was gross and yet she was buoyant.

Owen was probably a very nice man but totally devoid of any independence from my mother – he'd never move without her permission. She had this power over men – I call it power but I'm not sure what it was. But it's obviously why a marriage to my father could never have worked. She controlled Tony, her second husband, in the same way as Owen, it was as if she drained their own personalities and initiative out of them and made them into her own little lapdogs.

My father always told me that she was an extraordinary attention seeker but around negative things. He once told me that when they were together in the early days, my mother desperately wanted a new dog, but my father said they could only have one. It was not long afterwards that she arrived home in floods of tears and said the vet had put their dog down. But when my father next saw the vet, he said sorry about the dog because there was nothing wrong with it. But my mother had told him she wanted him to do it so she could have a different type of dog. It sounds pretty fanciful now but I'm sure he was telling the truth. That always stuck in my mind.

But to try to put her life into some sort of context, my father told me my grandmother, Mrs Calvert, lived in a big house in Hampstead with her husband and they were both dinky little people. They had a lodger, Mr Harvey, who was an enormous man, six feet plenty with an enormous girth and he travelled abroad a lot. Mrs Calvert had two children – my mother who was the spitting image of her parents and another daughter who was enormous, totally different, my aunty Pat. When Mr Calvert died, Mrs Calvert promptly married Mr Harvey and he adopted both girls, who took his name and he brought them up as his own.

Apparently Mr Harvey showered more affection on my mother's sister and even as a child, you don't have to be Einstein to sense something like that. She never said anything to me – she was a closed book – but it might explain why she had hang-ups about family life. My mother was riddled with jealousy which probably stemmed from seeing her sister getting more than she did. Mr Harvey died before my grandmother and when the booty was divided, it included a hotel in London, the Savoy Court on Granville Place behind Oxford Street, which Pat inherited. My mother once took me there for lunch. It was a strange place, almost more like a residential home than a hotel because some people actually stayed there permanently. It was a kind of 'arsenic and old lace' hotel so when I walked in – I was probably around 20 –

everyone turned and stared. I was the youngest person there by miles and that included the staff! I cannot imagine how much it would be worth as a piece of real estate.

Her childhood experiences might explain her behaviour. It's not an excuse but a reason for her strange lack of compassion, being able to discard me. Aunty Pat had four children: the eldest Susan, who has died, was the cousin I met at The Warren, then twin girls Sally and Jane, and one son, Charles, all my cousins. They all live in the Bahamas now.

Before I received the news of my mother's death, the four of us in the house in Florida had arranged to play golf with two more friends on New Year's Eve. The three women were going to play together and so were the three men and the golf was booked accordingly. However, the night before the funeral, I decided that out of respect for my mother, I should instead sit and reflect a little on my life with her. It didn't seem quite appropriate to be out there concentrating on my golf. The others accepted it and rearranged so that the two ladies would play without me.

The next morning dawned beautifully and my partner said: 'Oh come on, it's a lovely sunny day, don't sit here and mope all on your own.' I decided he was right and knew it wouldn't make any difference to my mother what I did. He went downstairs and told our friends that he'd persuaded me to play, assuming of course they'd be pleased. But instead, it was the totally opposite reaction. Stuart was always a volatile character and he just exploded and said that now I was going to mess up all their new arrangements. The upshot was a terrible row between the four of us – I can see them now sitting at the breakfast table shouting at me, not an ounce of sympathy for the fact that my mother had just died. It was absolutely awful and the result was that the two of them packed their bags and moved out into a hotel.

Never in my life have I experienced such an extraordinary reaction merely because they thought I was messing up their plans. They were our house guests, remember, and needless to say it was the end of the friendship for a good while, although we later started to see them again. The irony was that my partner and I went to play golf and were teamed up with a German couple who became very good friends. We've visited them in their home in Germany and they have stayed with us in England

and we've played golf with them all around the world.

We stayed in Florida until mid-March and I went to visit Owen when we were back in England. Bizarrely he, too, had to have a leg amputated about three or four years after my mother for a condition called gas gangrene. He inherited everything from my mother – she didn't leave me one penny even though she had always told me she had some of my grandma's belongings which were intended for me. I don't believe my name was even mentioned in the will – I asked for a copy but I never received one. I could have chased it up but I couldn't be bothered.

When Owen died in February 2004 he left a list of the people he wanted at his funeral and my name wasn't one of them, even though I had visited him quite regularly after my mother died. I once went up from London when I was down there for a couple of days after he had his leg amputated. I did see a copy of Owen's will, but again he left nothing to me, not a bean. He left the house and 90% of everything he had inherited from my mother to the cleaner girl who tended to him. She'd done a good job for him after my mother died and I bear no malice towards her and the inheritance. I've no idea of my mother's wealth – it was obviously considerable at one time but so much money must have gone through her hands. Owen even left some money to Specsavers of all things and my grandmother's Victorian sewing box to some obscure person.

I inherited my due from the trust – my mother couldn't do anything about that – and I didn't really expect anything else. It riles me in one respect – after all most children expect they will inherit from their parents. Fortunately as a child I never expected anything because if I did, I ended up disappointed. Like the train set my father brought home one day which I thought was for me. He set it all up on the dining table and we were playing with it when one of his pals, Peter Carr, turned up. Because he had two or three sons, my father promptly gave the whole lot away to him. So I learned never to expect and whether that's been a lifesaver for me or not, I'm not sure.

But I did treat myself to an Aston Martin – second-hand – from my inheritance. A few years before I was invited to spend the day at the factory in Newport Pagnell in the days after the entrepreneur Victor

Gauntlett put a lot of money into the company. Of course it had been owned by David Brown, my father's buddy, who also made the gearboxes for the Bluebirds. It was a fascinating day, I loved it, seeing British engineering at its very best. The sheet metal comes in through this door and it travels and travels and travels and comes out that door in the most fabulous piece of motoring, which in those days was made by hand from scratch. As an honoured guest I was walked through the entire production process, watching the sheet metal arrive, the panel beating, the engine room. At that time each engine was built entirely by one man, who had his name on a plate fixed to it – I don't know whether it's still the same.

Then I was treated to lunch in the boardroom with Victor and afterwards, as if by sheer coincidence, there's always a new car just waiting to go out for a test drive, unpainted, just in its primer coat. I sat alongside the test driver as he drove round Milton Keynes which is all speed limits – but he's not obeying them. When I asked him how he got away with it, he said: 'We have an understanding, my dear. They know me and I know them,' and obviously they turned a blind eye. Who knows whether he was joking or serious, but it was a good story. It was a super day, a really super day looking round their various museum pieces as well as the new cars. But what was so touching was that men could still make cars like that then, I don't know whether we still can or do or whether all such cars are made by robots now.

At the time I visited, it was way out of my scope to own an Aston Martin. They were very expensive motor cars, always have been and always will be, but what struck me when I saw the workmanship which went into them was how they could sell them for that price and still make money. Obviously as the years went by, they simply could not do it. When I finally did have some money, I treated myself to one so at least my mother made that possible.

Chapter 18

I'VE FOUND IT! I'VE FOUND IT!

I was never aware of people looking for *Bluebird*, no-one ever told me they were searching, so when I got that call, it came completely out of the blue. Over the years I had come to accept that my dad and the boat were at the bottom of the lake and I almost thought it was right that he was there. I only ever thought about it if I went there and when I did I often used to be ill – I always seemed to throw up or get the runs – and the weather used to do strange things. One minute it was a nice, sunny day and then a black storm would come down the lake, like the time I was filming with Melvyn Bragg.

We were always told that he was fairly sure to be in one piece because otherwise the divers who searched for him would have found something – a foot, an arm, whatever.

And for a long time a buoy marked the spot, but people kept on nicking it so in the end it was not replaced. We all knew the boat was there – it was only because the lake was so full of silt and sediment, so deep and so cold that *Bluebird* had never been found.

I think it was 1996, almost 30 years after Dad's accident, when I received the phone call from Bill Smith. God knows how he found my number – I was living in a flat in Roundhay in Leeds – and in his strong Geordie accent he told me his name, said he was an amateur diver who was very keen to find my dad's boat.

'And when I find it,' he said, 'would you like a piece?' I was furious. 'How dare you?' I asked him. 'If you find it, it is not yours and you do not go carving bits off it for anybody, least of all me.'

He was obviously shocked and started to apologise. He said he thought he would be doing me a favour and now he realised that was all wrong, that he had offended me. He just kept saying how sorry he was.

And that was the last I heard of Bill Smith for over three years. I never met him after the call, I never even thought about him in between.

Then in December 2000, he called again – this time almost shouting down the phone: 'I've found it, I've found it, I've found it.' It took me just a moment to realise who he was and what he had found – my dad's boat. What do you say – well done or what? In the end it was something like: 'OK, what now?'

Bill was clearly excited, emotional – remember he had been searching for years. He told me that on one of his last dives, something touched him in the dark. He turned and there was the tail fin of the boat. I'm pretty sure he had found the boat some time before he called me because by then, he had already been in touch with the BBC, who wanted to make a documentary about his incredible find and I know that kind of decision is never made in a hurry.

When I arrived up there, his find had already broken in the press. One of Bill's divers had ended up in hospital after suffering the bends and news had leaked out. It's hardly surprising that a group of people on Coniston weekend after weekend should raise more than a little interest. At the beginning he suggested he was carrying out an official survey of the lake's fish!

That initial news and my visit to the lake were surreal. Everyone knew the boat was there and the people of Coniston had come to love the myth. Visitors would arrive and ask local people to point out the spot where *Bluebird* disappeared. Local boatmen would ferry them out on a launch. It was macabre in one way, but I used to think: 'Three cheers that people still care so much about my dad.'

When I arrived, Bill took me out on his boat to where a new buoy now marked the spot. I'd taken some flowers which I threw on to the lake and had a little weep. It was emotional but it's hard to describe exactly how I felt. But I told Bill that now he had found Bluebird, he must bring her up as soon as possible because the moment the BBC showed their documentary about *Bluebird* being found, every amateur diver in the north of England would be up here searching. I knew they would take bits off her as souvenirs. That was entirely my decision, I made it there and then and I took a lot of flak for it from other members of the family. But I didn't want a committee with each of them having their say. He was my father, I loved him and I felt qualified to decide.

That was the first time I met Bill Smith, who was wearing his trademark hat – an awful blue woolly affair in the shape of a dinosaur which one journalist described in the paper as 'a silly hat.' He was eloquent and quite charming and I guessed he had anticipated my remark about raising *Bluebird* because he didn't seem shocked. To me it was perfectly logical that that's what they had to do.

I also said quite clearly that if Bill lifted the boat, he had to find my father, because the two could not be separated. Bill was 100 per cent certain that he would. My father was not in the boat because the front of *Bluebird* was virtually demolished – he would not have known a thing about it.

A few weeks later a BBC producer involved in the documentary rang me to say they already had some underwater footage and asked me if I'd like to go up there and discuss with them what they had in mind. I knew they were going to make the programme anyway so I decided I wanted to go.

It was at that time that I drove the Aston Martin which I'd bought with money I inherited from a trust after my mother died. It was a second-hand model which had belonged to Peter Ridsdale who was first a director and then chairman of Leeds United from 1997 to 2004 when the team was in the Premiership and doing really well. It was a V6 and I knew they'd just brought out a new V12 model so I rang the JCT 600 garage in Leeds and said I was looking to exchange mine for one with a bigger engine. The garage offered to loan me a demonstrator to drive up to the Lakes to meet the film crew, knowing full well that once I'd driven the V12 I wouldn't want to stay with the smaller engine. Mine was burgundy but when I arrived to pick up the new one, it was green – an absolutely taboo colour in our family who all believed it to be unlucky. But I took it anyway – I tried to kid myself it wasn't really green, it was turquoise!

When I got up there, I went out on the lake with Bill and the producers – it was a filthy day again. They dropped a remote camera down and you could see the tail fin quite clearly. It was quite spooky –

we're sitting up there and over 150 feet down was *Bluebird* lying there. I found it quite emotional. I think I took some flowers. It was then I said to Bill, now you've found that and you've got these guys filming it, you can't leave it. The documentary was called *A British Legend: The Search for Bluebird* and it went out on election night, June 7, 2001.

In fact I was not there when the boat was raised on March 9, 2001. I was in America when Bill was finally ready and he wanted to delay the actual day until I arrived home. But it was during the foot and mouth outbreak and with the disease spreading rapidly across Cumbria, he was told he must bring her up as soon as possible and not wait until the weekend, when he might attract more visitors. So can you believe I was actually on a transatlantic plane, flying almost over the lake, when the boat was brought up. By the time I next drove up there, *Bluebird* had already been taken to Bill's place in North Shields where everybody has been so supportive of him and the restoration.

The first time I saw the *Bluebird* was at Bill's place – it's housed in a light industrial unit in a courtyard of lock-up units – it looked horrendous, smaller because the front end was missing. There was a little piece of seat belt attached to a bolt as fat as my finger which broke right behind my dad's seat. Bill took it off and gave it to me. I've still got it along with the Lloyds metal Tonnage Plate.

She was sitting on a dolly trailer and because it didn't really resemble her, I couldn't really see her as *Bluebird* at first. I was much more emotional years later when I went to Records Week at Windermere in 2011 and saw an exact replica of the *Bluebird* which someone had built.

The back end, the main part, was semi intact and you could see the blue colour very clearly and the tail fin with the Union Jack painted on. Bill had the engine covers off and there it was, all corroded of course.

Then Bill took us upstairs into his office suite and what serves as his boardroom. I couldn't believe it – there were hundreds of different pieces of Bluebird and a big chart on which he'd marked where many of them had once fitted. He could take a piece, barely recognisable to most people, and say, for example, that's come off the air intake on the left port side. Quite staggering. He had two spars for the sponsons – I don't know how he got them up because the sheer weight of them would have made it so difficult. Then there was the cockpit area and it was very moving to look in there, thinking of my dad. But at that stage Bill had never actually said that he planned to rebuild her. That was my idea, after they had found my father's body eleven weeks after they raised *Bluebird*.

Bill knew there were official procedures involved in the finding of a body and I think he had a quiet chat with the coroner explaining that, if he found my dad, he wanted to bring him up in a dignified manner. He did not want to involve police divers whom he said might just shovel the body into a bag. It was kind of hush-hush. He asked whether there was anything he should look for on my dad and I immediately told him my dad would have his St Christopher round his neck, on a cord. I can even remember my father replacing the cord many years before, exchanging a very well-worn one for a new, clean piece that was long enough for him to lift over his head. I said he would also have a signet ring on his finger.

I didn't tell Tonia at that stage because I didn't want to add complications and I felt I was qualified to make the decision. I was old enough and in a position to say that's what I felt was right. I didn't want to bring other people into the equation, have people ringing Tonia saying 'Gina's doing this, Gina's doing that', involving the papers and then no doubt another family argument. I just wanted to get it done.

It was May 26, 2001, when Bill found my father's body. He rang me late that afternoon and said they were going to bring him up the next morning, to give me time to be there. We left home around 5am and arrived to see Bill with the launch, a coffin-shaped box and the Union flag. I waited on the shore. Bill had already raised my father's body and he went out on the Lake and returned with it in the launch.

Bill came back in the launch to Pier Cottage. There was nothing discreet about it – I was there and the coroner, a couple of police officers, a BBC film crew, journalists, onlookers – news had spread quickly. Bill and his divers lifted the box on to the grass to wait for the coroner's vehicle which was delayed for some reason. After he brought my father ashore there was emotion, relief, a sense that this is right.

Once back at Pier Cottage, Bill put his hand in his pocket and brought out the St Christopher. I couldn't believe my eyes…I was thrilled. It was shiny and bright as if it had just been cleaned and the cord was totally intact and as strong as the day it had first been put there. On the back, inscribed in clear, bold engraved handwriting were the words 'To Donald from Daddy Nov 1941'. It had been given to my father by his father, Sir Malcolm – I have never known the significance of the date except that Britain was deep into the Second World War. My grandfather was working in Whitehall where the reality of where everyone might end up hit home and he wanted his only son to be kept safe. But who knows? My father wore it every day and took it off at night.

It became and remained one of my special possessions until that dreadful day 11 years later when I lost it, goodness knows where. I played a golf match that day, July 4, 2012, and decided to 'take Dad with me' or, in other words, to wear it as a good luck charm. I won the match and I know that it was still there when I finished because I showed it to the lady I'd been playing against. We were having a coffee afterwards, when she admired a brooch I was wearing and then I showed her Dad's St Christopher. When I left the golf club, I drove home, had a look in my garden and when I came to get changed, it just wasn't there. It had been tied tightly round my left bra strap and tucked in, as always. I was devastated, I still am. I hunted everywhere at home, turned the car inside out, reported it to the police, rang the club, the story was on BBC Radio 5 Live, local radio, local TV and in newspapers, but nothing. The golf club emailed all visitors that day, searched the car park but nothing. Somehow, even now, I feel it will be found – and there is a reward of course. If not, I cannot explain how much the loss means to me.

Also in my dad's pockets when he was found were his Dunhill lighter, silver, inscribed around the top casing with 'Bluebird 403.1', his speed when he broke the land speed record at Lake Eyre in Australia in 1964. It is now on display at Dunhill's in Jermyn Street in London. There were also a few coins in my dad's pocket which I now have – some pennies and a couple of half crowns. Finally, there was a leather key fob, also with a St Christopher on it, which I gave to Bill there and then. It was an instinctive gesture on my part by way of thanks for fulfilling his side of the bargain. I know Bill has had it cleaned and mounted and he now wears it on a chain round his neck, as his own keepsake and for good luck. I hope it brings him lots.

To say I didn't feel very much is not to belittle the occasion. My father had been dead for a long, long time and in a way this just confirmed that fact. And then it was just a roller coaster of interviews, being asked the same questions and trying to think of something intelligent or emotional or exciting to say…and I couldn't really. You fluff around and say it brings closure, but frankly, that had happened a long time before.

When my father's body was finally recovered, still inside his suit, there had to be DNA testing, even though we had established it was his St Christopher and lighter. A policeman came to my house and took a mouth swab and the result came back that the chances of our not being related were at least two million to one.

His funeral was legally Tonia's responsibility because she was his widow. But families are extraordinary things – Tonia is not my family, she's someone my father married. I don't wish her any ill but I'm so different from her. She wanted my father cremated – she said my father had always hated funerals and burials. But I think it was because it was quick, easy and cheap. I said absolutely not – my dad was far too important to both me and his multitude of fans and admirers to leave his final moments to 'British Gas'! I was not going to have him burned into a little box of ashes, blown away in the wind. I was adamant there had to be a place for him because there were too many people who respected and loved and admired him and there are more kids to come who will go through all those emotions. So after much letter-writing and discussions with Tonia, who was in California, she agreed I could have my wish and do what I thought was right and respectful – and that I paid for it.

But first I had to write to my father's lawyer Victor Mischon, later Lord Mischon, accepting that I would take responsibility. So I did write and I did take responsibility.

Setting about planning a funeral such a long time after his death was almost surreal. I thought I knew what I wanted but I discussed it with a handful of people who had been close to my father. They included Anthony Robinson, known by everyone as Robbie, who had lived in

Coniston all his life and was a big friend of my dad's. He started out as Dad's gofer even though he was just a kid at school and then became a member of the team, a timekeeper. They were very, very close and he was on the jetty on the day my father was killed. I wanted Robbie to be an integral part of the funeral, to give the address. His parents used to run the Black Bull in Coniston and then moved to the Sun Hotel where Dad and his team used to stay. Robbie's mother Connie was a guest when Dad appeared on *This Is Your Life* – she was played by the actress Rosemary Leach in the film *Across the Lake*.

It's amazing how these things come together. I wanted my father to be buried in Coniston. I knew the people who lived there wanted that too – they wanted something to replace what had now disappeared from the lake. They never said anything to me but privately among themselves, they felt that now the boat had gone, the myth had gone and were wondering what was left — even though I publicly promised on my life that the boat would go back one day.

The vicar of St Andrew's parish church, the Reverend Mark East, agreed my father could be buried there – because after all he was not a true resident – and we chose a plot, as near as possible to Connie's grave. It was a nice, sunny spot under the wall and she could look over her shoulder at Donald.

From May when the body was found, I started to choose a few hymns for the funeral – I called it 'A service of prayer, thanksgiving and celebration'. Some of them had been sung at my father's memorial service held at St Martin-in-the-Fields in Trafalgar Square on February 23, 1967.

I wanted a male voice choir and I wanted them to sing "Unforgettable", originally sung by my father's favourite singer Nat King Cole. It involved getting copyright permission for it to be sung by the wonderful K Shoes Male Voice Choir – from the company which made the famous shoe brand in Kendal.

And Bill Smith had told me about a song called "Out of This World", quite a haunting song written by a rock group called Merillion, which he said had inspired him to go looking for my dad. The lyrics spoke to my father and *Bluebird*.

The words begin:
'Three hundred miles-an-hour on water
In your purpose-built machine
No-one dared to call 'a boat'.
Screaming. Blue.
Out of this world
Make history
This is your day.'

But I needed to hear the music, to speak to the lead singer Steve Hogarth, because I wanted him to sing that song in the church. We became friends down the telephone and I remember asking whether he had a safety pin through his nose or Idiot stamped on his forehead! But he assured me that apart from slightly long hair, he didn't look punky or heavy metal or heavy rock. And when he came to see me to bring me a disc, he was just gorgeous. How lucky for me that Steve is wonderful, that he agreed to do it for me. Later he told me it was the most nerve-racking performance he had ever done and yet he'd performed at so many rock gigs in front of thousands.

I spent weeks organising it with the vicar and all the local dignitaries – I wanted to know what they felt would be appropriate and listen to how their ideas fitted with my own. The lovely village church seats 200 at a push and there were so many people who had to be there, so many who wanted to be there to pay their respects to a man they regarded as their 'hero.' So I had to draw up an official guest list, send out invitations, arrange for the Order of Service to be printed. In each one I placed a small plate with an enamelled bluebird, a replica of the mascot which first my grandfather and then my father always carried, screwed to the dashboard of their racing craft. It bore the date of the funeral.

And then we chose the date. It was going to be the 11th or 12th of September and we went for the 12th – the very day after the world as we knew it was changed for ever. And it was for no reason other than it being more convenient for Robbie, the vicar and myself.

In fact I was in Coniston on September 11. Standing by a Sky television wagon, I somehow had a feeling 'things' would not work out as hoped – they never did, so why change the habits of a lifetime! First of all I saw the long-range weather forecast for the following day and it was awful – not just bad but awful – it was going to rain in torrents from 10 o'clock in the morning.

All the major media and TV networks had approached me to cover what they knew was a very special event and the church and village hall were all wired up with the necessary equipment, which took a huge amount of effort from so many people.

The day before, I went to Coniston to put the final touches to everything, and to do various interviews. I was talking to a television journalist and I could see myself on one monitor inside and then I could see film from New York appearing on another. I said: 'What's going on, they're showing a feature movie.' Like so many people I thought it looked like a film until the guy told me, no, it's real, it's live footage. Well, that was it, we just stared. Suddenly the impact those tragic events would have on my dad's day struck home. I was heartbroken, in more ways than one, of course. It was surreal, it still is and it's changed our lives.

The next day at 10 o'clock, the heavens opened and it absolutely poured with rain, bucketed down. In the morning, Dad's coffin, draped in the Union flag, was taken from Pier Cottage, which he loved and from where he last departed alive, on to a launch to where the accident occurred and back again. It rained so heavily, the launch was almost swamped. That was a journey for the pall-bearers – Bill, the divers and my cousins. I waited on the shore. The launch went to the Bluebird Café and then the coffin was transferred to a horse-drawn carriage.

As we walked up to the church, there were schoolkids, including some handicapped children in wheelchairs, lining the route in the pouring rain. Some wanted to see Mr Whoppit, my dad's little teddy bear mascot, which was found at the time of his accident and which I was carrying. Tonia had been staying at Robbie's little hotel – she didn't come down to the shore – and she joined us on the walk to the church.

The service had to be by invitation only, with a few people standing at the back. They were family and friends and Robbie helped me with those people in Coniston who had to be invited. Some friends of my dad could not be there – they were elderly and could not make the long journey from the south. The choir came from K Shoes and they filled the choir stalls. I insisted Tonia and I sit together at the front.

She heard the Marillion song which was beautiful and which had inspired Bill Smith to find her husband, the man she said she loved beyond words; it did not seem to touch her at all. I never saw her read her Order of Service. When we left the church, there was one on the floor where she had been sitting. Other people asked me to sign their copies, they wanted to keep them as mementoes. Soon after I know one sold on eBay for quite a price.

When I was thinking about what to wear, I knew Tonia would choose pale blue and I thought we would look silly in the same colour. I wore grey and pink – pink skirt with black polo neck and black shoes, grey jacket. I never wore it again and only recently I gave it away to a charity shop. It was very expensive and normally I am practical about these things and wear outfits again, but somehow this one left a psychological mark.

The service ended with the choir singing "Unforgettable". When we came out of the church, the streets were closed and there were thousands of people in the village. And still it rained, it monsooned. Everyone had arrived in their best bib and tucker, many of them with fancy hats, only to be huddled under umbrellas, desperate to keep dry. All the men were absolutely drenched.

My father's body was taken to the graveyard – the actual burial ground within the churchyard is full – and he now has a beautiful resting place below The Old Man of Coniston, the fell which dominates the village and the lake. The headstones are all local stone and the majority are the same size, but because I wanted something special, I had to have permission from the church. I submitted a design to them with the top of the stone carved in the shape of *Bluebird*'s outline and they agreed. It's still not quite as definitive as I would have liked, but I am happy with it.

On the day of the funeral, we merely placed a marker stone by the grave. Later, when the proper headstone was complete, the marker stone was moved to the lakeside.

I didn't want the wording on the headstone to be schmaltzy or for it to include a list of his wives or even my own name. It's my father's grave not mine, I merely said: 'Donald Malcolm Campbell CBE Queen's Commendation for Brave Conduct, whose achievements in world speed records depict his courage in life and death'. Each time I go to the Lakes, I visit the grave and take some flowers in blue and yellow, *Bluebird*'s colours.

There is a proper pathway leading to the grave now, thanks to a young man who lives in Coniston who's known by his nickname, Novie. He's an amazing man who just loves everything about my father. He describes himself as an official *Bluebird* observer and he has made it his job to tend the grave. If he knows I'm coming up, he'll give the stone a special scrub with a toothbrush, leaving it looking so cared for and like a new pin. He raised the money for the path through sponsorship by taking part in the 14-mile Coniston run, which is right round the lake. He sweated buckets training for that run because he was not particularly fit but so determined to complete it. So the path makes it easier for people visiting and lots of the coach trips stop there.

After the burial, we all went back for lunch to the Windermere Motor Boat Racing Club, where my father was a member. It is affiliated to the Royal Yachting Association who supplied all the timekeepers for his record attempts. And in the evening, I had arranged dinner there for around 30 of Tonia and my close friends who had come up to support me. I hardly remember anything about it. It's a bit like your own wedding day – it's all going on around you but you feel in something of a daze. It was a relief when the day was over. It was all so overshadowed by the atrocities that had occurred the day before, the grief that was suffered as a result. None of us would ever be the same again. Many of the press and TV people had been pulled out to cover those events and only a handful were left. But I knew I had done everything in my power to make this a very special day for my dad and judging by the letters I received afterwards, other people thought I had succeeded.

The next day I had arranged a golf tournament at the Windermere Golf Club for the Donald Campbell Memorial Trophy, which I had commissioned. But it had rained so much, the course was closed and the whole day was a wash-out. I still have the small silver plate trophy at home – I have presented it a couple of times for different competitions but then the winner has returned it to me after their year.

It seemed typical of what had happened to my dad during his life. When I look at old newsreel and pictures of my grandfather making records attempts at Daytona Beach or Pendine Sands, the route would be lined with thousands of people, maybe 50-deep, all men in tweed jackets, collars and ties, flat caps. How the hell they all made the journey there, I don't know, but they obviously made a huge effort. And similarly, film of Sir Henry Segrave shows that when he was racing or attempting records, you could not see the shores of Windermere for people.

Yet my father's attempts were often only watched by a small group of well-wishers and people who just happened to be on holiday there, or walking in the Lakes, and decided to take a look. There was often just an insignificant number, never the lake thronged with people. In fact my father always attracted his biggest crowds for his record attempts in America – they seemed more interested and generous than the Brits. So it seemed extraordinary that that dreadful day in New York happened the day before the funeral – it came along and totally overshadowed my father's final day. And rightly so.

Chapter 19

SHE WAS ALWAYS 'ON STAGE'

My relationship with Tonia has never been easy and that was true at the time my father's body was recovered. Since then, I've probably seen her three times, all in America, and although it is an easier relationship now, she can still be, at best, lukewarm towards me.

I first met her in 1958 when my father brought her to my school one Sunday – yet another glamorous woman for me to meet. We went out for lunch but I had no particular awareness of who she was. But when I got back to school, some of the older girls had recognised her as a singer and cabaret artist. I didn't know what the words 'cabaret artist' meant. The next time I saw her was at Caxton Hall Register Office on Christmas Eve when she married my father.

They met at The Savoy where Tonia was performing for a three-week season and my father was in the audience. By then my dad was divorced from Dorothy and before you knew it, he was marrying for a third time.

My relationship with Tonia has always been difficult and we've had lots of clashes. But she's still singing at her wonderful age so you've got to hold your hat out to her. She's an incredible self-publicist, full of self-belief, but there was never any continuity in the way she behaved towards me.

She's often self-absorbed and didn't really have much time for me when we were living at Roundwood. She'd not a clue about me really. She'd suddenly say: 'I think I should curl your hair today', probably the last thing I wanted. I was a real tomboy and yet I have some pictures of myself after I'd obviously had my hair curled. She'd put lipstick on me and find a pretty dress and I probably still looked like a clumsy oaf. Then she'd think 'I'm not getting anywhere with this kid, I'm never going to make her into a doll' because I'd be off back in my jeans, with the ponies. Extraordinary.

But she was always 'on stage'. There would be flashes of sincerity but suddenly it would disappear – very unsettling. It was sad for me at a young age, when you should be terribly innocent, that I was already able to read these undertones.

It was only after my father died that I found out Tonia had said she was pregnant when we lived at Roundwood. I was totally unaware of it at the time because I was away at school. I thought she had once told me that she could not have children because she had a congenital heart condition and yet the woman has such tenacity and the constitution of an ox.

Apparently she told my father she was pregnant as they drove home to Roundwood from the airport after they had flown back from America, the year after they married. She said she felt sick in the car and because he was unsympathetic, she blurted out that she was pregnant. But just a few weeks later, after her first trip to Coniston, she had a miscarriage. I have to say it surprised me to hear that she was pregnant because I never thought of her as the maternal sort.

Tonia was born in Belgium where she spent her childhood at her father's hotel and nightclub called The Carlton in Knokke-le-Zoute which was a very smart Flemish resort where Frank Sinatra and Marlene Dietrich both performed in their day. The hotel is a block of flats now because Knokke is now very chi-chi and it was worth more as real estate than it ever was as a hotel.

When she was married to my dad, he used to fly us over there in his own plane to visit her father who was a big, heavy man who lived opposite the hotel in a block of flats with Tonia's stepmother Annie. They were a nice couple, but didn't speak any English. When we needed a new housekeeper at Roundwood, she brought Louis and Julia Goossen over from Belgium.

She had three brothers – Daniel was her favourite but he died quite young. The eldest was Pierre who owned a nightclub, and it was his son Ludo who came over to spend some time with us when we lived at Roundwood. He was a big lump of lard who hardly spoke any English. I was about 12 or 13 and he was a few years older than me and he made my life a bloody misery. I had to move out of my room so he could have it and my father bought him a brand new bicycle while I had to make do with this grotty 50-bob machine. I thought he was spoilt rotten, a Johnny Come Lately, and everyone was out to impress him and so impress the new wife's family. I was locked in a bedroom on my birthday when he was there for my bad behaviour, so what did I do? I climbed out of the window and ran away – I always seemed to be running away. I took his bike, cycled miles across the Surrey Downs to my aunty Jean's house but unfortunately she was out. But I knew she'd be picking up my cousins from school so I cycled on to Downsend Prep School at Leatherhead and there she was sitting in her car waiting for Malcolm and PJ. You should have seen her face!

Over the years Tonia has been in and out of my life. As I said earlier, after my father's accident, when I came home from Arosa, there she was lying on a sofa in the Dolphin Square apartment surrounded by people wiping her eyes, bringing her whatever she wanted. She knew how to play the grieving widow all right.

Then ten years later, she invited me to Portugal when I was married to Cliffy and later still she let Michael and I move into Prior's Ford for a while after I left my second husband, Philip.

It was when I was living with Michael in the early 80s, after we'd moved into his house at Ashstead, that Tonia very magnanimously gave me a pair of candelabra which had been a wedding present to her and my father. She said something like: 'You can have these, I never liked them and anyway they're ugly.' They were silver plate on a heavy base, inscribed to Donald and Tonia on the occasion of their wedding, December 24, 1958, from Graham Adams and the family. Graham ran a motor engineering business in New Malden and he transported all my dad's boats and cars around the country, as his father had done for Sir Malcolm.

I wasn't excited about it but she made the gesture and I accepted – at various times she had given me other little bits and pieces which had belonged to my father. Some while later, maybe a few years, I woke up one morning and decided to take a few things down to an antique shop in Dorking, a town well-known for antiques businesses, to raise a bit of cash. We were always short of money. I cannot remember what the dealer gave me for them, but I took it and he then obviously displayed them in the window. The next I knew there was a story all over the *Daily Mail*, with a picture of Tonia looking tearful, accusing me of selling her candelabra, a beloved wedding present. If she'd liked them so much, why did she give them to me in the first place? Apparently someone had spotted them in the shop and instead of contacting me, had got in touch with her and she'd gone straight to the press. She never said anything to me and we never spoke about it at the time or afterwards. But that's typical of me, I'd rather avoid confrontation and I've never done tit-for-tat discussions because suddenly the whole point is lost.

She did the same again, ran to the *Daily Mail*, when I once decided to put Mr Whoppit and few other items up for auction at Christie's, but as it happens, I changed my mind and I've still got him. And yet, years later, she gave me a beautiful Dunhill lighter in the shape of a handbell, another wedding present to her and my father, this time from her own father. Maybe she was having a moment of conscience. But that's Tonia, one minute she's fine with me, the next she's having a go.

It was over 20 years after my father died that Tonia this time married again to the actor Bill Maynard, who played the character of the loveable old rogue Greengrass in Yorkshire Television's *Heartbeat* from the early 1990s through to 2001. Before that he'd had small roles in the Carry On films and was the star of another YTV programme, a sitcom called *Oh no, it's Selwyn Froggitt*. And one of his more unusual claims to fame was that he stood as an independent Labour candidate against Tony Benn in the Chesterfield by-election of 1984. He finished fourth.

Tonia had met Bill years before when she appeared on one of his television shows but I had no idea they were in touch again. They were married in 1989 when I was living in Denmark with Tonni and the first I knew of the wedding was when I picked up a paper there. I sometimes used to drive into Copenhagen to a hotel to buy an English newspaper and on one such day, I opened the paper and saw a photograph of Tonia and Bill under the headline: 'Bill takes Tonia to the dogs for their honeymoon.' Apparently he took her dog racing after the wedding. I think it was a rather more low-key affair than when she married my dad

– Hinckley Register Office in the Midlands and a honeymoon in Jersey I think, compared with Caxton Hall, The Savoy and Courchevel which was much more my father's style.

Bill lived in a modest 1930s' red-brick bungalow in a cul-de-sac in a small village off the M42 in Leicestershire. Tonia later told me the story of how they both went grocery shopping a few days after they were married, with Bill pushing the little trolley round. Tonia loves chicory which is quite expensive here, so when she spotted some she picked it up and threw it in the trolley along with this and that, things she liked, with Bill looking on askance. When they get to the checkout, Bill unloads the stuff he wants, puts the barrier down, meaning the rest is Tonia's – and hers to pay for! That did not best please Tonia who would not like anything as unclassy as that. And that's pretty unclassy, isn't it? I don't believe they ever lived together for long – she must have married him on the spur of the moment. I used to call her Mrs Maynard – like the wine gums – because Bill always said he'd taken that name as his stage name after he saw a poster advertising Maynard's wine gums.

I went to visit her there soon afterwards and she was hating it. They came to visit me at my house and they both wanted to be kingpin, each one trying to tell a funnier story than the other. I think he thought life with her was a bit of a nightmare and Tonia certainly wanted to get out. She went back to the States after a short time and I'm pretty sure Bill never visited her in America – Tonia said he was too mean to pay the fare. She said he only went on the bus once he had a bus pass! But I don't think he was short of money – he must have made some from his career. They're divorced now.

The next time I saw her was when I was spending the winter in Florida and she came to stay with us for a week. How about this for a story? The week she came, it was unseasonably cold and she had only brought frilly blouses and summer clothes so I suggested we went to Loehmann's where you can buy really nice designer stuff at ridiculously cut-down prices. Tonia was wearing her trademark Elton John-style-cap, a bit like a tam-o'-shanter, which she stuffed full of her hair, but which she took off while she was trying on clothes. All of a sudden I look down and say: 'My God, there's a sapphire and diamond eternity ring on the floor – look at this.' So Tonia replies: 'Oh, I thought I'd lost that a month ago.' I didn't know what she was talking about. But it turns out that a few weeks before, she'd arrived home, taken off her hat, thrown it down on the bed, taken off her rings and put them in the cap. Next morning she'd scooped up the rings, at least the ones she could see – her eyesight was appalling until she had laser treatment more recently – put on the hat and off she went. She soon realised she had lost the eternity ring, the one my father gave her, but all the time it must have been tucked up inside her hat and it happened to fall out in the store and I happened to find it. Amazing.

Then in 2003, we went to stay with Tonia at her home in the San Bernadino mountains in California. We had been with two friends on a cruise through the Panama Canal which finished in Costa Rica. The friends flew home and we flew to Los Angeles, picked up a rental car and drove to Tonia's – it's exactly 100 miles from the airport. Once you turn off out of the valley, it's a fabulous road, snaking up, heading for the Big Bear Mountain ski resorts. Tonia lives in a small town called Crestline in a house built on stilts on the side of a hill, overlooking Lake Gregory. I imagine in spring or summer it's very pretty but this was November and everything was looking a bit brown. But it's also an area which has lots of landslides and forest fires – Tonia has been evacuated more than once but her house has always survived. It is also home to snakes and goodness knows what.

Hers is a neat, dinky house and the stairs from the garage up into the house are so narrow that you couldn't walk up there with your suitcase. We had to leave our cases in the garage so every time I wanted a clean pair of knickers I had to run downstairs and root around in my bag. But she made us very welcome.

The first thing she did was to take us for a drive in her white saloon Jag. She climbs in behind the wheel, wearing that same Tam o' Shanter, the driver's seat about as far back as it will go, her legs outstretched to the pedals and off she goes, foot down, crashing through the gears, telling me: 'Your father taught me how to drive.' Let's just say I drove for the rest of the time we were there – I thought it would be safer.

She had decided to throw a party for around 20 of her pals who she wanted to introduce to me. So she booked a pre-prepared turkey meal – it was not long after Thanksgiving – which we had to collect but was all ready to put in the oven. We picked it up the day before the party and that night we all went out to dinner, this time in our rental car, because once you are out of town, the roads are all narrow, running through gulleys and ridges and heaven knows whether you are on the right one or not.

So we have dinner – we pop out now and then for a cigarette and notice first that it's starting to rain and then sleet and it's turning very cold. So by the time we leave it's snowing. We pile in the car and I drive back to Tonia's, she reaches down to the floor where she's put the remote control to open her garage so all she has to do is bend down and pick it up, open the door and we all go in. She's feeling around in the dark, but there's no remote, so then we all start to search on the floor without success. Tonia's wearing this shaggy coat, which should really be a carpet, like the Afghan coats of the 60s and she decides the remote must have got caught up in the long hairs when we were at the restaurant. So we head back there – by now it's 11 or 12 at night, pitch black, snow still falling. We reach the restaurant, explain what we've lost and we hunt and we search and we look, but there's no sign of the remote.

Back in the car, I'm driving, Tonia in the passenger seat giving directions but by this time it's snowed quite a lot, there's not a street light to be had and the roads are getting whiter. Tonia would say: 'Turn here' and then: 'No, I think it should be that one,' so goodness knows how we got back, but eventually we did. I cannot remember how we got into the house – I think she must have had a spare key for a different door but she was desperate not to have lost the remote. We all piled into bed quite exhausted, ready for the party the next day, only to wake up and find that three feet of snow had fallen and nobody could move an inch let alone come to the party or go anywhere, not least because all the roads around were closed.

How this deck of hers held up under the weight of snow, I'll never know. It felt like the whole thing was creaking and about to collapse. When I walked out on to it, I sank up to my waist in snow! We'd come off a cruise so we only had Panamanian-style clothes, hardly appropriate for thick snow. I put on a pair of socks and flip-flops – hardly the most suitable – and tried to shovel the snow to relieve some of the weight.

Even more worrying was the fact we were supposed to be leaving for Las Vegas the next day. I had booked tickets before we left home for all three of us to see Celine Dion and we'd reserved rooms at the Bellagio. I was starting to think: 'Oh my God – what happens now?'

We'd planned to drive up there, I think on the Wednesday to see the show on Friday. By some miracle, we managed to get out on the Thursday although we had to go a long way round to Las Vegas because of the snow, adding another 100 miles to the journey. I was driving, Tonia was in the back, right in the middle, leaning forward, talking, talking and talking some more, she never stopped the entire way. It was 'Well, Celine Dion is all right, but she's not pitch perfect, she's no personality, she needs this and she needs that,' to the point where I'm thinking of asking whether we should tout the tickets at the door.

We had booked into the Bellagio, beautiful rooms, but ironically, although we had a suite and Tonia a room, she had the most wonderful view of the hotel's famous fountains which we could not see at all. I'd booked expensive tickets online at the Caesars Palace Colosseum which were only eight rows from the front – the place holds 4,000 people – and Tonia sat there spellbound by Celine Dion, and so did I. I couldn't take my eyes off her, I thought she was the most exquisite thing I've ever seen. She moved around the stage like a feline, like a wild cat, so graceful, elegant, beautiful movements and there was so much going on with people riding bicycles on wires, people flying across the stage that it was really magical. I just stared. When she finally came off stage she came down to where we were sitting – we had three seats at the end of a row – to meet a young disabled girl in a wheelchair. It had obviously been pre-arranged but it meant that we got up pretty close and personal to her.

We stayed a couple of nights before we drove back, again Tonia never stopped talking, and we then decided that as it might snow again, we better grab our things, head into LA and book into a hotel there. So that's what we did and in fact the next time we saw her was a year later in Los Angeles when we were on a cruise which stopped there for a day. She drove down and had lunch with us. It must have been 2008 and that was the last time I saw her.

At least when we've been together recently as adults, we can now talk as equals and discuss things woman to woman. It's a much easier relationship now but sometimes she can be just lukewarm.

When I rang her and said the man I'd lived with for 18 years had finally left, she said: 'My dear, he was such a common man, how could you have been with him, you shouldn't have even been with him for his money. I told you he didn't have any class.'

But that was it – she wouldn't follow it up asking how I was coping and I haven't heard from her since. I sent her postcards from New Zealand from my latest trip, but didn't hear a thing

But she is pretty fantastic for her age, still performing, and she will go on till the day she drops. On her website she listed her bookings for 2012, one at The Cathedral City Center near Palm Springs and another on the Grand Princess during the two-week Mediterranean cruise in May. So although I hate to admit it, I do have tremendous respect for her. Even though I don't have to like her, I sometimes wish I could attack life with that same verve.

Only last year, in 2011, she crashed her famous white Jag and spent the night in the car. When she came off the road, she managed to climb out, walked up to the road, but unfortunately no cars came past. She'd heard all about mountain lions and the like so she decided she'd be safer in the car till next morning, so she climbed back in and fell asleep. Amazing.

I've always wondered how Tonia survives financially – I've fantasised that she has had a sugar daddy somewhere but who knows? I cannot believe her performances at tea dances and Jewish suppers are big payers so maybe she invested the money from Prior's Ford extremely wisely, or else she keeps selling off bits and pieces. It's not for me to question it. In one way she's a bit like me – when she's had money she's spent it and when she didn't, she managed without or sold something, assuming something would come along.

Chapter 20

I THREATENED TO SELL HER ON EBAY

What next? *Bluebird* was now out of the water, safely installed at Bill Smith's workshop but what was to happen to her now? That was just to be the start of literally years of discussions, arguments, meetings, reports which went on for years.

One of the first shocks was when a man called Paul Foulkes-Halbard who lived in Sussex suddenly claimed that he was the legal owner of *Bluebird*. This was just about a week after she was brought up from Coniston and it came right out of the blue. He didn't come to us, he went straight to the papers and, of course, it was a big story. He claimed he had bought *Bluebird* from the insurers for a nominal £1 for salvage and had the paperwork to prove it. It was the first we had heard of it.

We knew the man – he'd been a racing driver himself known as 'the flying farmer' apparently – and he lived in a medieval manor house called Filching Manor near Eastbourne. Oddly enough I'd heard his name mentioned when I was in Australia, in Perth because he originally dealt in old exotic, high-end cars – Bugattis and the like – but over the years he had created a kind of Campbell museum, lots of memorabilia that he had collected and stored and displayed in a series of sheds around the place. My *Agfa Bluebird* boat is still there, stuck in his chicken sheds. He even created what he called a memorial go-cart track there and he invited me down with my cousin Donald to open it when I was in Lymington. Some people say his place was a bit of a shrine to my grandfather and father and he used to offer guided tours, but giving all the money he charged to charity.

The family knew that *Bluebird* had been insured but the details were hazy. It was suggested that Dad had negotiated the insurance in return for sponsorship which could well have been the case. But whatever the details, we'd never heard the suggestion that this Foulkes-Halbard owned it.

He even said he planned to take a trailer up to Coniston to collect the *Bluebird* and take her back to his place. He claimed that because *Bluebird* was conceived and built in Sussex, she should go back there at least so he could find out why she crashed.

By then certainly Tonia and I felt that *Bluebird*'s rightful home was at Coniston and everybody who lived there wanted the same. This man never produced any paperwork to prove his claim but nevertheless the family decided we had better involve the lawyers before we started planning what to do next. So we consulted Mischon de Reya, the lawyers for the Campbell estate, who brought a High Court Action in May 2001. They stated that the Campbell family, including Tonia, wished the boat to be kept in Coniston, ultimately at the Ruskin Museum.

Of course the case dragged on and on as everything involving lawyers always does, till eventually on September 7, just days before my dad's funeral, Mischcons issued a news release. The formal wording was that a Consent Order had been lodged with the High Court stating that the executors of my dad's estate – Lord Mischcon and Tonia – were declared the rightful owners of *Bluebird*. It also said that they had arranged for her to be transferred to the Campbell Heritage Trust and that the family intended the *Bluebird* to be based at the Ruskin Museum. Tonia gave the boat to the family trust with certain caveats, the main one being that the Trust inherited the legal bill. How wise was that! Originally the bill was close to £50,000, which they generously reduced to £31,000! Certainly Mr Foulkes-Halbard never challenged it again and in fact he died in October 2003. I think his son closed the museum, although you might still be able to visit by arrangement.

The Campbell Trust was made up of my father's sister Jean and my three cousins, Malcolm and Peter Hulme, her sons to her first husband, and Donald Wales, her son to her second husband – and me. Sadly aunty Jean died in June 2007. All through this time there were stories in the papers about family rifts – aunty Jean did not want either the *Bluebird* or my father's body to be recovered from the lake. She felt so strongly about it that she would not attend my father's funeral. Of course they were huge decisions but I always knew that once Bill had found the *Bluebird*, he had to bring her up otherwise every diver in the world would be searching and taking bits of her as mementoes. And then once she had been brought out of the lake, it was only right that Bill tried to find my father's body. I didn't want him at the bottom of Coniston now that his *Bluebird* was no longer there.

But there was still the question of what was to happen to *Bluebird*. We'd always promised the people of Coniston they could have her – many of them were peeved that they'd lost their boat. There was some bad feeling – after all the boat tours used to point out the exact spot on the lake where *Bluebird* made her final plunge, stopping to tell visitors that she lay beneath where they were. But I knew what Coniston had meant to my father and how so many people there had been a part of his life. I felt the people of Coniston should never have to pay to see her again. I had an idea that she should be rebuilt and set into an enormous piece of perspex on the lake shore so that everybody could see her. But of course that would have been totally impractical because I'm sure the Lake District National Park would never allow it and the perspex would eventually go green so you couldn't see anything inside. But it was a spontaneous suggestion on my part.

It was not long after dad's funeral, certainly before the end of 2001, that the Trust agreed we should write a letter of intent to the Ruskin, offering the Museum the long-term loan of *Bluebird* – say 99 years with an option to extend – once they had built an extension to house her.

The county council wanted to commission what they call an 'options appraisal' to look at the best ways of preserving, restoring and displaying *Bluebird* – it was obvious that it would bring thousands more visitors to the museum and so benefit the whole tourist bit. Jura Consultants of Edinburgh prepared a business plan, all 66 pages of it, some of which I disagreed with. To my mind, they completely underestimated the number of people *Bluebird K7* would attract – when I look back at it now I see I scrawled a pencil note to say I'd give them £1 (one pound) for every visitor under 100,000 in any one year! I just knew it would attract people, literally from around the world.

All the time there were meetings with the Heritage Lottery Fund people, early ones seeking their advice on how best to make the application. We had meeting after meeting and my cousins Don and Malcolm came up to Manchester to meet them a few times. Then you get a change of personnel and you have to start dealing with new people who come at it from a different angle. The bottom line is the Lottery refused the first application but suggested we reapplied, approaching it in a slightly different way.

That meant another load of meetings. Meanwhile Vicky Slowe, the director of the Ruskin Museum, managed to get planning permission from the Lake District National Park for a building to house the *Bluebird*, as long as she raised the funds which she eventually did because she is an amazing woman.

Finally the Ruskin made the application – which is the size of an encyclopaedia itself – for the 'acquisition, restoration and display of *Bluebird K7*' – and in 2005 the Heritage Lottery rejected it! I could have punched their lights out. Why didn't they say at the very beginning: 'This is not for us.' As far as I can remember they'd had a panel of three so-called experts – I think one's main interest was Roman underwear, another some sort of sculptures. They had no concept of what *Bluebird* was and what it meant to so many people.

I was furious, so angry I threatened to sell her on eBay, even to put her back in Coniston. We had wasted all the time and money and I was well aware of some of the obscure projects the Lottery throws money at. They even conceded that the *Bluebird* and the Campbell family story 'has a special place in our history', yet they said that an expensive rebuild 'did not represent good value for money.' They wanted *Bluebird* to remain partly as a wreck. To me that would have been like putting on show the crashed car in which Princess Diana was killed. It was ghoulish. If people went to look at it as a wreck, they'd only go once and they'd hate themselves when they walked out and they wouldn't want their kids to see it because it's all too gory. To me, it would have been the height of bad taste. But I was in the minority.

The Lottery people said there were three issues which led to the rejection – the approach and conservation, volunteer involvement and value for money. I thought it was bollocks.

OK they said they were still talking to the Ruskin about other ways of telling the Campbell story, or in their words: 'We have advised ..... that a conservation-led approach towards the restoration of *Bluebird K7*, leading to an interesting display in controlled conditions..... celebrating the achievements she represents, is more likely to attract HLF funding in the future.' What the hell did that mean and how much longer was this all going to take? Already over five years had passed since Bill found *Bluebird*.

So as the 40th anniversary of my father's accident approached, the family talked about where to go from here with the restoration and we decided to actually give *Bluebird K7* to the Ruskin Museum, which is a charity owned and managed by the people of Coniston. We all agreed and it was on the condition that Bill Smith continued to restore and rebuild her and that the Museum raised the funds to build an extension to house her.

Bill had been involved every step of the way and was always called on to make presentations of what he planned. No-one ever questioned his experience and expertise. But his work was kind of on hold until we knew about the Lottery money.

Once they'd turned us down, he got cracking and gathered volunteers from all over the UK willing to give up their spare time to have a part in the Bluebird Project as we called it. They were mostly guys with engineering experience and all through 2006, 2007 and 2008 they slowly and carefully reconstructed the shattered hull. They had a trial assembly of her in September 2008 and a couple of months later invited me up to ceremonially fix the first rivet. It was exciting of course but also strange for me to see the *Bluebird* which had been such a part of my life, taking shape again.

Meanwhile the Ruskin and its fantastic director Vicky Slowe never gave up on the huge task of raising the money to build an extension. They managed to secure gifts and grants from all kinds of organisations – Cumbria Vision, South Lakeland District Council, The Garfield Weston Foundation and other Trusts and inevitably massive local support.

I helped all I could – attending any event designed to raise money for the building, pushing the cause whenever I had the chance. Every few months I drove up to see Bill and each time I could see more of *Bluebird* taking shape. Meanwhile the shiny new extension at the Ruskin, called The Bluebird Wing, was also being built. It was finally finished in 2010 and is now open to the public but of course awaiting its greatest exhibit.

As the years went by, Bill continued his restoration, always refusing to give a definitive date when she would be ready to return to Coniston. He collaborated with Sky on a documentary which was shown in December 2010 when they used new technology to recreate Dad's accident to try to finally say exactly why it happened. They concluded that the *Bluebird* had been designed to travel at no more than 250mph but when the crash happened, she was moving at 328mph on water still choppy from the first run. She started to bounce and on the third bounce, the jet engine cut out. Without its thrust, it was impossible to keep *Bluebird*'s nose down and she took off. Bill spent time at their studios and they filmed at his workshop in North Shields and the programme ended by saying *Bluebird* would be back in the water in 2012.

Sadly some of the people who would have loved to see her restored have died. For example, Ken and Lew Norris, who co-designed *Bluebird K7* and *CN7*, the car in which my father broke the world land speed record at Lake Eyre. Ken died in 2005 and Lew four years later. Another very sad death was that of Carl Spencer, one of the divers who joined the team which set out to find Dad's body and he was a pall-bearer at my father's funeral. He was just 39. Carl was such a lovely man – he was a heating engineer by trade in the Midlands but he was also one of the world's most talented deep-wreck divers, but so modest. When anyone asked him what he did, he used to say: 'I'm just a plumber from Cannock'. And yet he had led some of the most high-profile explorations of famous wrecks.

He died in May 2009, when he was part of a team diving on the Britannic, the sister ship of the Titanic, which sank in the Aegean off Greece in 1916. He suffered an attack of the bends.

I went to his funeral and it's so tragic when you go to a funeral and everyone is younger than you. He left a beautiful young widow and two little children. It's like watching the funerals of servicemen killed in

Afghanistan – his parents were there to bury their son. When I see the bodies of the Afghan war dead being brought back, it's so sad and yet in terms of numbers it's nothing like the Somme where thousands were killed in a day. And look at the difference in their kit – today's soldiers' equipment looks like it's come out of an Action Man box, compared to that of the poor devils who had a tin mug for their head and old hessian boots. I don't know how any of them survived.

In November 2011 a lovely man called David Watt died. He had lived in Coniston all his life and everyone said my dad was his hero. He had scrapbooks and photographs of most of my dad's time at Coniston and was always happy to talk about him to friends or visitors to the Lakes. He ran the hardware shop in the village until he retired and after used to supply my dad with bit and pieces. He lived with his sister and his enormous springer spaniels which you'd see him walking every day. He was there when *Bluebird* went down and the day she was brought out so I know he would have loved to see her restored.

Of course I'm as impatient as anyone to see *Bluebird* back at Coniston – everybody is – but in the end only Bill will know when she is ready.

Chapter 21

HAPPY BIRTHDAY FROM BLUE BIRD, 1938

In 2004, yet another Bluebird came into my life when my partner decided to buy a motor cruiser, a super yacht, after he sold his company and of course, we named her *Bluebird*, but this time *Bluebird of Happiness*. Lots of people have heard the story that it was after my grandfather watched a performance of Maeterlinck's *The Blue Bird*, which was having the run of the season in London in 1912, that he decided to rush home, repaint his latest car blue and christen her *Blue Bird*. The next day he drove her at Brooklands. So we wanted to remember that and, also, there are lots of other boats floating around called *Bluebird*, for one reason or another.

The boat was brand new, 86 feet long, four double cabins, four bathrooms, fitted out as you would a four bedroom detached house – the only difference is, it floats. It has all the power you need for aircon, washing machine, drier, electric cooker, hot running water on tap, showers. And this boat was fantastic – it had the linen, the knives and forks, the pots and pans, the cups and saucers, everything was there. You could literally walk on it in the morning and sail off and live on it for a month.

We took delivery of her in the south of France in early December and we had a berth in Antibes. Because we were keen to try her out, we decided to sail to Portofino for Christmas, and invited two friends to join us. As it turned out, it was not the best idea we ever had. We had a new young crew, a captain and second in command, two lovely English lads, both called Chris.

People think that the south of France is always warm, but believe me, that December, it was anything but. So off we set from Cannes, with an overnight stop somewhere in Italy, and we duly arrived at Portofino, where it was freezing cold and deserted, with not another boat in sight. We dropped anchor, because there are no ground lines there, back up to the sea wall and thought: 'We've arrived'. None of us had ever been to Portofino before: it's a tiny little place, very quaint, and we wandered round the shops, bought a couple of cashmere jumpers, had a coffee, a brandy, you know how you do. We found a restaurant that was opening for Christmas Day, booked lunch and all enjoyed our Christmas meal there.

By the time we got back to the boat, the weather had turned really bad and the crew had to move the boat forward and drop two anchors to lay us off the sea wall – the surge and the swell were so great that we were in danger of the back end of the boat hitting the wall. I remember sitting up all night, in a howling storm, making cups of tea and coffee for the crew – they were so anxious they didn't go to bed. You could see the Christmas tree in the centre of the town square, bending over double in the gales.

Next morning, we decided to leave and head for Genoa, but when they went to pull up the anchors, they discovered one of them was fouled, caught round a chain. It was still pouring with rain and it was a nightmare to try to free it. Eventually a little old man came out in a little old row boat, which looked as though it shouldn't even have been afloat, to help us. He must have been a friend of the harbour master and he helped the crew to drop a line, tie it on and eventually unsnag the anchor. And then we could leave. By then my nerves were frazzled beyond repair.

So off we sailed to Genoa where we felt relieved to be in a port with other boats. We stayed there for a couple of nights, then started to head back to the south of France when one engine began to splutter. We turned it off and then limped into Monaco of all places, radioing ahead to make sure they had a berth. Our friends had to fly back to the UK and we ended up spending ten days in Monaco, between Christmas and New Year and beyond because we assumed that the manufacturers would be on holiday.

It turned out that the fuel tank was contaminated from when the boat was built – the tank had not been sealed and all kinds of rubbish like filings, bolts, nuts, crisp packets, had fallen in. The fuel filter looked as though a dustbin had been emptied into it. So the tank was emptied of fuel, centrifugally cleaned, and refuelled so we could sail back to Antibes to our berth.

And that's when the teething problems really started, when we found all the little things which are snapped, broken, do not work – the top deck around the canopy had not been sealed and when it rained, the beautiful pear wood below was water damaged and had to be ripped out and replaced. There was a two-year warranty with the boat and it probably took that time to make sure everything was absolutely right.

It really shows up the incompetence of some manufacturers today, who are building high-quality, high-end boats with incredible technology, and yet they then have to pay for all that repair work over two years – it makes you wonder how anybody ever makes any money out of it. Then, three months after the warranty ran out, one engine blew. There were two engines, half a million Euros each.

We had some fabulous times on it, as did most of our friends – suddenly you have more mates than you ever knew you had. It bore no relation to anything I'd done before with boats although when I was very young, my dad had a motor cruiser in the south of France, but I have no memories of that. We were as green as grass the first year and it is strange living on board and not being able to open the front door and step outside. Yes, we'd sail into ports and walk off but it's not like walking out of your house – everything had to be arranged in advance. Sometimes I'd feel a bit locked in, confined.

We had golf clubs on board and we'd play at various courses in Provence and we went to the Monaco Grand Prix a few times. We didn't take the boat because it's too expensive and too confining – you are locked in the harbour there for about ten days. So we'd leave the boat in Antibes and take the train. We had friends there and we'd usually watch from our charter agents who have an office on the circuit. I like F1 but inevitably when you're stationed in one spot, you haven't a clue what's happening without rushing to the television every five seconds to see who's in the pits, who's leading, who's crashed out. The noise is intolerable and before too long, you are just begging for the race to end!

I said there were lots of boats out there called *Bluebird* and they include one very special one in particular. We were in St Tropez on my birthday, September 19, one year in the mid 2000s, when my grandfather's boat pulled up alongside us. The captains of the two boats had been talking and obviously ours mentioned it was my birthday that day – the next minute, a bottle of champagne arrived for me.

The boat berthed next door was 100-foot, very traditional, a lovely old gentleman's cruiser, discreetly named *Blue Bird 1938*, the year my grandfather commissioned her. His plan was to sail her to the Pacific to search for buried treasure in the Cocos Islands, but in the end, the bounty hunters sailed in *The Adventuress,* a converted Liverpool pilot boat, belonging to his friend Lee Guinness.

We were invited on board and the moment I stepped on, I realised that its refurbishment was not the handiwork of your average joiner. This was *the* most tasteful refit but all in keeping with its original traditional lines and styling. How often do you step on a boat in the south of France to find an open fire and two Labradors lying in front of the blaze? For a moment you wonder: 'Am I on a boat in St Tropez or am I in a country house in Surrey?' Two gorgeous little blond boys came running through, obviously twins, and the host introduced himself as 'Tara'. In fact, he was Tara Getty, grandson of John Paul Getty, the late oil tycoon. Suddenly it came as no surprise that, by his own admission, he had already spent £15 million on the boat. He was charming and gracious and very proud of the boat which was built for Sir Malcolm in White's Yard in Southampton and which still had the original ship's bell and various plaques. And I think he was actually quite proud that its original owner's granddaughter was on board.

The boat had quite a history. During World War ll she was fitted with Royal Navy guns and joined the evacuation at Dunkirk and, in 2010, she joined the flotilla of ships which sailed to France to mark the 70th anniversary of Dunkirk. I had been aware of her chequered history over the years but had lost track of her latest owner.

A year or two after we first met, Tara Getty wrote to me to say he was publishing a book of dozens of photographs detailing the restoration of the boat – they were taken by Kos, the famous female photographer who specialised in yachting pictures. He asked me if I would do him the honour of writing the Foreword, which I duly did, telling a story my father had passed on to me. He told me that some time after my grandfather's boat was completed, he had a dream that it was going to catch fire and burn out and so the silly man put it on the market and sold it straight away, without setting foot on it again.

After the war, I know she was bought by the Renault family, who gave her a facelift apparently and then in the late 1980s, I was contacted out of the blue by a guy called Bob Harvey George who said he had bought my grandfather's boat which was then way down in the southern hemisphere. His plan was to sail back to the UK to refurbish her and he asked whether I would fly out to the Azores, at his expense, and sail back with him. My first instinct was: 'Wow, what an offer,' but I soon started to realise that I didn't know this man at all and did I want to be stuck on a boat with maybe 12 guys for the long time it would take to sail to the UK? I'd no idea about the facilities on board, plumbing, showers and soon decided to turn it down.

Years later, I kept reading adverts for corporate days aboard Sir Malcolm Campbell's luxury motor cruiser and then one time when I was in Glasgow, I think with Agfa, she happened to be there and the same man invited me to look round. The boat was a bit shabby by then, red flock wallpaper as I remember, reminded me of a chintzy Indian restaurant. After that I would see her advertised for sale in *Motor Boat and Yachting* magazine, every month, right through the early 1990s. I know now that Tara Getty bought her in 2004 and spent three years restoring her to her original glory.

He invited me to a glitzy party in London to launch the book, which is a huge magnificent tome called *Blue Bird – Seven Decades at Sea*. But it was December 2010 and we had already booked flights to Florida before then so unfortunately I had to turn it down. He sent me a signed copy – it's fantastic, but I can hardly lift it!

I've been back on board a few times when we've both been berthed in the same harbour in the south of France and I was always received with great courtesy – we even had a few deliveries turn up on our boat intended for his *Blue Bird*.

We had some good times out there, sailing as far south as Sicily, Barcelona, Mallorca, Minorca – the boat would go as far as you wanted but every 500 or 600 miles you need fuel, an awful lot of it! In the first few years we'd spend two weeks every month out there through the summer, I enjoyed the sun and the warmth and I'd swim in the sea if it was warm enough, water-ski and jet bike, all the trappings of a yacht owner. And yet there is something artificial about life on board and in the last couple of years we spent a lot less time out there. I feel no emotional attachment to the boat and I know I will not miss it.

Chapter 22

AN INVITATION TO THE PALACE

The man I lived with for 18 years – almost one third of my life – walked out one day in September 2011. He was at home when I left early one morning to play in a golf competition – and gone when I rushed home, buzzing because our team had won. He left a 14-line handwritten note on the kitchen table telling me he'd left. Within 48 hours, photographs posted on a social networking site informed me that he was in Venice with another woman. I soon discovered they left there for a Mediterranean cruise. It was an abrupt, sad and very hurtful end to 18 years in which I had been honest, loyal, caring and steadfast. I was deceived. The details are still too raw and too personal for me to talk about here but I wonder whether he ever gave a thought to the impact on me. He was the man who brought me to Yorkshire and at that moment I felt very alone – no parents, no kids, no brothers, no sisters.

So much happened in those 18 years, which changed the course of my life – not least both the *Bluebird* and my father's body were recovered from Coniston. But I also travelled a lot, often revisiting countries I had visited with my father years earlier – the USA, Australia, New Zealand, the south of France. And I visited new countries like South Africa and South America.

When he left, it hit me hard. But, as they say, life goes on. Very soon afterwards I drove up to Coniston for the launch of a book published by my good friend Neil Sheppard, who I first met when *Bluebird* was recovered. He has a lifelong interest in the Campbells – I always call him 'the learned one' because he knows more about the Bluebirds than my father would have done. But before I reached the village, I stopped at the head of the lake – my father always used to stop there. The lake looked fantastic – Coniston definitely had her best Sunday clothes on.

There was a bright blue sky and yet, literally out of that blue, a rainbow appeared and I stood there and wondered at it as it moved up the lake and seemed to stop almost opposite me. It was so beautiful and I managed to capture it in a photograph. Then I drove straight to Dad's grave and as I walked up the path, I spotted a black cat pushing itself against the side of the headstone. By the time I got my camera out it was moving away but I did take a picture – it somehow seemed very poignant. And then, if a robin didn't land on the headstone, just for a few seconds, but it seemed to make up three special moments for me. I don't know what meaning to put on them, but they seemed significant. By the time I walked away, the whole village knew I was there – it always seems to happen like that when I go there.

When people say that every cloud has a silver lining, it's easy to dismiss it as a clichéd proverb. But actually something else happened to me after my partner left to prove there is some truth in it – I discovered that I had more friends than I ever knew. Of course when he left, news spread through the golf club like wildfire and I thought that people might snigger, there'd be lots of nudge, nudge, wink, winks, tittering and so on. But I was so wrong. In fact the reaction of the girls was the exact opposite: dozens of people contacted me by email, text, phone – no sooner did I put the phone down on one person, than another would call. Some arrived at the house with boxes of chocolates and bunches of flowers. OK, maybe a few did contact me for a spot of titillation and a very few may even have thought 'there but for the grace of God'! But the majority by far were wonderful. I used the analogy of a lioness protecting her cubs and it really struck a huge chord with me. So much so that I asked the club secretary if I could put a card on the notice board thanking the ladies for their caring, their understanding and telling them just how much I appreciated their respect. They really did help to keep me sane through those first weeks and have continued to do so for months. I really do love them. Some of the menfolk we knew were a little more wary, after all some of them had spent weekends sailing in Lymington years before when I ran the coffee shop and perhaps realised I had a long memory!

And to lift my spirits, there was another very special surprise waiting for me a couple of weeks later when, out of the blue, I received an invitation to Buckingham Palace.

In fact the beautiful gold embossed envelope, with the Buckingham Palace postmark – second class post – didn't come directly to my home but instead it was sent to the address of a workshop in Cardiff where my cousin Don has his base for his electric car. In August 2011 he had made his latest attempt to break the UK electric land speed record at Pendine Sands, in South Wales but it had to be aborted when he had a mechanical failure. How many times did that happen to the Campbells who went before him?

Anyway, my invitation had been sent to the Bluebird Project, care of an address in Cardiff. The guy there, who is working with Don on his planned world speed record attempt in 2013, emailed me to say he had the envelope from the Palace and should he open it and tell me what was inside. You can imagine my reply. 'F… off, it's none of your business.' When it finally arrived, it said that 'The Master of the Household has received Her Majesty's command to invite Ms Gina Campbell' to a Reception for 'those involved in exploration and adventure' to mark the centenary of Captain Scott's final expedition to the South Pole. I was absolutely thrilled.

I emailed my acceptance because the invitation had taken so long to reach me but also replied formally to The Master of the Household. It was to be held on December 8, which was brilliant for me as I had booked to go away on December 13 and if it had been on that day, I would have spat bricks, as they say. I mentioned it when I was talking to Bill Smith a couple of days later and he reminded me he was a member of the Explorers Club, which was founded in New York over 100 years ago, and that he'd love to go. I said I'd see what I could do. So I emailed the office at the Palace again, explained who Bill Smith was and said that if anybody was an explorer and adventurer, it was him. I gave them his full name and address in case they saw fit to invite him and there were still places. And they wrote back and said they would be delighted to invite him. I rang him straight away and I could hear the elation in his voice, he was like the cat who'd got the cream. I was pleased for my own sake too because it meant I would know at least one person. I don't live in the London social scene, I don't mix in these circles, I no longer go to sporting events so the prospect of walking in and not knowing a soul would be quite daunting. I didn't know whether there'd be 50 people, 250 or 2,500.

The Reception was from 6pm to 8.30pm and I knew immediately what I'd wear – a beautiful pink suit, from Hong Kong, with satin lapels and a little camisole underneath which is discreetly elegant. I'd have preferred comfy shoes but I definitely needed the regulation high heels. At that time you can neither underdress nor overdress but when I arrived, my outfit was bang in the right area. I arranged a haircut, booked my train ticket, asked my friend Neil Sheppard if I could stay the night after with him and his then fiancée Sandra – they've since married – and was all set.

Neil lives in Chiswick where every wall of their beautiful flat is covered with photographs of *Bluebird* – I've never seen so many in one place. Those that cannot fit on the wall are propped up on the floor.

I arranged a hire car to pick me up, it was raining and when we arrived at the gates of Buckingham Palace there were queues of people with their invitations. I was given a card printed with my name and details of what to do and a piece of paper listing who from the Royal family was going to be present. It really was like a Who's Who – the Queen, the Duke of Edinburgh, Princess Anne and her husband, Prince Edward, Duke and Duchess of Gloucester, the Duke of Kent, Princess Beatrice.

I had been to Buckingham Palace more than once since my Investiture, on one occasion when I was invited to a garden party to present the Duke of Edinburgh Gold Awards. But on the day, I was suddenly ushered inside and introduced to the heads of the Award scheme all across the Commonwealth. There was a line of people stretching the length of a very long State room, from Australia, New Zealand, Canada, Gambia, all the Commonwealth countries and a sea of children, waiting to receive their award. I'm not sure why I had never received a briefing, so I was totally unprepared. But fortunately I realised I was standing beneath a huge portrait of Henry VIII and so I was able to start by saying that I felt rather vulnerable beneath the great man's gaze, waiting at any moment for the chop! After that I was fine although I cannot remember a word I said, but I did it.

It's just wonderful to be within touching distance of all those magnificent paintings and that struck me again in December 2011 when the reception was held in the Picture Gallery and the Music Room and Blue Drawing Room leading off it. I was ushered to a doorway leading into the room where the Queen and the Duke were welcoming guests. My card said, 'Gina Campbell, water speed racer,' and Prince Philip took one look at me and, in his distinctive voice, said: 'Water speed racer – a little thing like you…I know you,' and he laughed. Prince Philip knew my dad of course, but that really touched me – the Queen had been very polite but the Duke of Edinburgh's comment was charming and seemed personal. We forget our Royals keep up to date with what we citizens get up to – after all it's their job – and they may well have already attended two or three formal engagements that day.

Bill hadn't arrived but I spotted a few famous faces like Sir Richard Attenborough, who was tiny, and David Walliams, who in September had swum the 140 miles down the Thames. And there was James Cracknell and Ben Fogle and Sir Chris Bonington. Apparently in all there were 310 guests and I felt very proud to be one of those 310.

Then I sat down with a very smart young soldier – he told me he was a bomb disposal officer – who had lost a leg in Afghanistan. He said that he usually wore a prosthetic limb but had a problem with his leg at the moment. We talked about his career and I eventually said to him, 'I bet you guys have a hell of a time out there.' What I meant was that they are so highly trained, kitted out with such fantastic equipment, they must be strung as taut as a violin string, so that to actually get to use all that training, must be a bonus. He smiled and said I was the first person ever to say that to him, that usually people just felt sorry for him and his mates. And he actually admitted: 'It's the best game of cowboys and Indians you'll ever get to play.'

By then Bill had arrived and we both stood talking to Princess Anne. I reminded her about Cherry Hatton-Hall, the instructor who first taught PA, as she was known then, to ride at Benenden. 'A blast from the past ma'am,' I said. Because my school Iford Manor had lots of inter-school riding competitions and events with Benenden, I'd come across her many times too.

I spoke to Prince Edward too and reminded him that I once sat next to him at a dinner organised by the South West Shingles Yacht Club, often called the most exclusive yacht club in the world. It was founded in 1984 by Commodore David Latchford, who always says it was 'born of adversity', and membership is strictly by invitation only. I was invited to join soon after my water speed record attempt at Holme Pierrepont in 1985 which ended with me being catapulted into the lake.

He started it the year after he'd been sailing from Cowes to Poole with his two sons on board, when on a glorious summer day, he managed to crash into the South West Shingles marker buoy. Fortunately none of them were hurt but it gave him the idea of a club for those who had stupid accidents at sea but still came out smiling. In fact the day he founded it, HMS *Jupiter* was 'parked' inadvertently against London Bridge and its Commander, Colin Hamilton, became an early member.

I was invited to join after very publicly turning my boat over at Holme Pierrepont, splitting my trousers and exposing my frailties to the world. I think your misadventure has to be very public. Lots of my pals from boat racing have been invited after some little quirk on the water. I think Prince Edward is an honorary member.

The Club holds dinners at the Royal Thames Yacht Club opposite Harvey Nicks in Knightsbridge and because my aunty Jean's husband Buddy Hulme is a member, I am entitled to stay there. The rooms are called cabins and very delightful they are too. I have been asked to respond to the ladies' toast before now.

Bill wanted to stay at the Palace until the end but I decided to leave a little earlier. My father always used to say that one should arrive last and leave first at public engagements, to show that your time is very precious! When we left it was raining of course, no taxis to be had, so we walked down The Mall to Bill's hotel where we had arranged to meet up with Neil. He and I headed back to Chiswick on the tube, with me teetering along on my killer heels – and boy, they nearly did kill me. My friends call them 'car to bar' shoes! There I was, tripping down the escalators at Westminster Bridge tube station, in my beautiful pink suit, by this time a bit damp from the rain.

A few weeks before my trip to the Palace, I'd spent a couple of days in the Lake District at the annual Powerboat Records Week, which always used to be held on Windermere until they introduced the speed limit in 2005. Since then it's been held on Coniston which people say is the spiritual home of speed records anyway – it's certainly where my father achieved his records. I go almost every year because the K7 Club dinner is held that week at the Windermere Motor Boat Racing Club – it's an important organisation and it's only right and proper for me, as an honorary vice-president, to be there.

Over the last two or three years I'd heard little whispers about a businessman in Lytham St Anne's in Lancashire building something of a *Bluebird* lookalike, but at that stage it was more of a Chinese whisper. Then three or four days before Records Week began on October 31, the boat materialised out of a workshop and I was receiving pictures taken on mobiles of it parked outside a motorway rest area on the M6, obviously on its way up to Coniston, looking identical to *Bluebird K7*. It even had the circle enclosing the infinity sign with the letter K, one big figure 7 and two tiny 7s inside. They called it K, triple 7, but talked about passing it off as an exact replica.

I don't know how long it took to reconstruct but during the whole time, never did anyone involved have the decency or common sense to contact me or my cousin to tell us what they were doing. I was in absolute outrage when I saw the photographs, my little temper was getting hotter and hotter. Meanwhile the pictures kept coming and everybody was asking me: 'Have you seen it, *Bluebird*'s back?' There was one particular guy who I'm sure had some kind of interest in it, who kept trying to pacify me, telling me that it was a tribute boat. But I was fucking furious – if it was a tribute, why not tell us in advance, invite us to come and see it, shake hands, christen it, open a bottle of champagne? Instead it was all done so secretly, which is why I had to doubt this 'tribute' idea. Anything we knew was only coming second, third or fourth hand, never from the people who had built it.

Anyway, as I was driving up early on Thursday morning, I had a call from Bill Smith, his voice full of glee. 'They've sunk the boat, they've sunk the boat.' Sure enough the papers were full of it and all the clichéd headlines came out: You Blew It, Bluebird Sinks Again, Got That Sinking Feeling. When I arrived I knew the boat was at Pier Cottage where my father used to launch his *Bluebird*. So instead I went straight to the main pits area and caught up with all my chums. Sadly Robin Brown, who was chairman through all the negotiations to move Records Week to Coniston, died just before Christmas and it was the first time for me that he had not been there.

But I did meet a new record chaser, a little boy called Ben Jelf from Maidstone in Kent, just 11 at the time, who had become Britain's youngest world speed record holder in a powerboat. He was charming. He approached me, in his little blue race suit and boots, helmet under his arm, and said very politely: 'Excuse me, my name is Ben Jelf and I truly admired your father.' I couldn't believe his grown-up attitude – here was a pint-sized kid who had just set a world record of 43.11 miles per hour. He's the Lewis Hamilton of powerboating at the moment – not many children get that opportunity, but he's got it and is making the most of it too. I spent time talking to him and his mother, who asked if I'd have my photograph taken with him, which of course I did. And she showed me pictures of him at the Union Internationale Motonautique (UIM) Awards in Monaco in his dinner jacket and bow tie, a little scrap of a boy, but so gentlemanly. He blew me away.

Thursday night was the K7 Club dinner but I knew that quite a few other people involved in the replica *Bluebird* were going to be there, including Jim Noone, the guy who had been driving it. I've known his parents for many years, they are a lovely family. Nevertheless, in a fit of pique, I told them I was withdrawing from the dinner – I decided to take the moral high ground, which I felt was mine to take. So instead I had dinner with Neil Sheppard, who had just published a photographic book about the Campbells, and his then fiancée Sandra. They were married a few weeks later.

By Friday morning, everyone was talking about the row between the Campbells and the team involved with the replica, but still nobody from there had approached me. Finally they asked Neil to act as go-between and he told me they'd like to meet me. In the end I thought: 'What the hell.....' and agreed to see him at Robbie Robinson's house, neutral ground.

So I met Mr Charles Morris, a quietly spoken, gentlemanly businessman who was responsible for the replica. He was very polite and although he didn't offer an outright apology, he did admit they had rather fallen short and that he or one of his team should have made contact with our family. He had told the press that it wasn't a replica, yet it was identical to *Bluebird*, a gas-driven turbo hydroplane, and everyone who saw it agreed it was the image of *Bluebird*. I told him we'd kept hearing whispers but nothing official and that we saw it as a replica. He said the project was really that of his three sons and that it was meant as a tribute to the Campbells. We both said what we wanted to say and then he asked me whether I would go to see the boat. Well, how can you argue with someone who says they have built the boat as a tribute to my father? I agreed but said I didn't want there to be any cameras so I drove down to Pier Cottage where Dad used to launch *Bluebird* to watch them prepare their boat.

In typical Campbell style, the weather was grim and no sooner had this replica arrived, than it started hammering down with rain. As I drove round Coniston, the water was grey, the trees grey, the landscape grey, the sky grey, the whole lake was grey and, suddenly, there is this bright blue boat sitting there. It just looked like *Bluebird*. It was like a cinematographer's dream, as if they had fuzzed out all the surroundings and focused on this boat. For me, it was like a ghost, quite incredible, and it caught me in the throat. Dave Aldred, their engineer, who has worked with Bill Smith in the past, spotted my reaction and tried to comfort me.

They had dried the boat out after its swamping from the day before, and they then did a static engine test – it was quite amazing to hear that roar again of the Orpheus engine, to hear it echoing round the hills of Coniston. It must have almost been like a fire or lifeboat siren in the past. It absolutely reminded me of my father's K7. It echoes round the hills, because everything else is so still and so quiet.

They did a couple more tests, all their calculations on power. Jim Noone stood there, blue overalls, of course, ready to get in. And my heart went out to him. He was physically ill with nerves. By then there were cameras clicking off everywhere – how can you stop them when everybody with a mobile phone turns into a photographer? Poor Jim was as white as a ghost and just as he was about to climb in, the heavens opened – and I don't just mean rain, it pelted down, you could see it bouncing off the lake, and before too long water was lapping at the edges of their workshop, in the same place as Dad's. They manoeuvred the boat out and were waiting to fire it up because the organisers were messing about with another boat on the lake, which seemed to break down and they couldn't get anyone to tow it out of the way. Meanwhile, they are keeping *Bluebird* on a tow rope, going round in circles, for what seemed like an age. They had it in their minds to break a record – not an outright world water speed record but, because this was a class of boat for which there was no previous record, any decent speed would set one. They finally fired her up and she moved off but she just didn't have the oomph to lift up and plane, so she was just ploughing through the water. If they were aiming to reach the measured mile like that, it was going to take for ever. And so it was aborted. But, for me, it was a heartstrings moment. They took the boat back to the landing stage, winched her out, drained her and we all went home. Strangely they said they'd keep in touch, keep me up to speed with their plans – but six months on, I hadn't heard another thing from them.

I have heard, again on the grapevine, that they are building another craft, this time not as closely resembling *Bluebird* as this one. I think they want to try for a world water speed record. I left on the Friday – I never hang around these places, just breeze in and breeze out, say what I have to say and go. Only this time, I couldn't quite leave when I planned, because my car wouldn't start! Flat battery. Fortunately someone jump-started me so I could reach the garage where they reset the electronics.

Chapter 23

A WONDERFUL ATTITUDE OF LIVE AND LET LIVE

The plan to spend three months in Florida over the winter, playing lots of golf, as we had done for last few years, was no longer going to happen. So instead I decided to take myself off to New Zealand, to return there yet again, this time on my own. After all that's where the people I feel closest to all live – Dorothy's three children, Max, Lisa and David, who all refer to me as their 'sister.' As soon as I told them I was planning to visit, they all said I must stay with them, spend Christmas with them and seemed genuinely happy that I was going. When I arrived, it was obvious that they were.

I flew out on December 13 and booked my return flight for March 1, so plenty of time to catch up with everybody. As well as Max, Lisa and David, I contacted some of my old pals – boating pals, people I raced with, some I worked with on the water safety campaigns – and every one of them invited me to visit and stay.

The trip didn't get off to such an auspicious start though. A couple of days after that long, 28-hour flight, I was caught speeding – a flipping NZ$180 fine, not far off £90 with the exchange rate when I was there, so a lot of money. I was driving to Taupo on the shores of Lake Taupo in the middle of North Island when I was stopped by a woman traffic cop – a real smart-arse she was.

It was the most unfortunate timing – I'd just lit a cigarette and I'd dropped a Solpadeine tablet, a soluble painkiller, into an opened can of coke wedged between my legs. Bad luck for me that it fizzed up and soaked my shorts with a horrible coloured liquid. When she took my driving licence and started the paperwork, I asked her to be as quick as she could because I was dying to have a wee. There's hardly anywhere at all to stop on their long straight roads. She took one look at my shorts and said: 'I think it's a bit late for that now, dear!' But I assured her it was not!

They are sneaky over there, their speed cameras are hidden as rocks on the side of the road. And the limit is 100ks so it's very difficult to sit at 62 miles per hour on roads where you might not see another vehicle for miles.

But really it was the best thing that could have happened to me because after that, I stuck to the limits. There are some awful drivers in New Zealand – they don't just have minor accidents, they have terrible wipe-outs. Almost every week in the paper you seem to read about six or eight people being killed in one accident. And Auckland's traffic is diabolical, because the city has grown so fast. It's home to almost a third of the whole country's population and over one third of those people were born overseas.

I'd decided it was heaps cheaper to buy a car, under a guaranteed buy-back scheme. For the whole time it cost me NZ$ 2,000 and it would have easily cost me NZ$3000 to hire one for three months. And it was a really nice car – some kind of Mazda GT, go faster 'something', automatic, stereo, aircon, easy to drive.

The last time I saw Dorothy's children was at her funeral in February 2008, but we have always stayed in close touch with cards, letters, emails and phone calls. Dorothy's youngest son David met me at Auckland airport in the pouring rain – I hardly recognised him with his long, wild-looking beard so I told him I couldn't even say hello to him looking like that. He trimmed it the next day! But it was all in good fun, it was as though we hadn't been apart.

Remember, I'd spent a lot of time with him in the 1980s after his father died and Dorothy was so busy working in the theatre. David lives alone now – he did marry, a woman a bit older than him who already had a two-year-old girl whom David adopted. She's always called him 'Dad' – she's 21 now – but David and her mum parted some time ago and she has remarried.

David lives in a lovely, modern house, on three storeys, where he has his own suite of bedroom, walk-in dressing room, bathroom and balcony on the top floor, almost in the eaves. There's another beautiful balcony on the first floor and from there you feel as if you could almost reach out and touch the Sky Tower, albeit it's not really that close but a great landmark when I was finding my way back to David's. It's the tallest man-made structure in New Zealand and from the balcony we could see them bungee jumping down the side of it.

David works for his brother Max who is in finance, forecasting future currencies or some such, so he spends most of his days at a computer. But he took time off to be with me – I spent the first few days with him in and around Auckland and then we headed off in separate cars to Lisa's for Christmas and New Year.

I'd never been there before and it's a five or six hour drive, over 500 kilometres, Auckland to Taupo, Taupo to Napier, then on to Hastings, their nearest town. The roads are amazing, you can go for miles without seeing another car. Their place is so remote it must have taken me about 20 calls on the mobile to her husband Bobby to find my way because every landmark he gave me was another 15 ks further on.

They live in the Napier area of Hawke's Bay on the east coast of North Island, up a track four kilometres from the main road. It's what they call a 'lifestyle unit' out there, not really a farm, a wooden house on the top of a hill with around 20 acres, where they keep about eight sheep and two goats and they're never going to make a penny bean out of it. It's a relaxed lifestyle but they're very happy. People say there are places in New Zealand where you'll never see another house and theirs is one of them. The Tuki Tuki River runs down the bottom of their place and there's a famous vineyard, Craggy Range, over the hill from them. It was developed in the 1990s, a family affair which produces single-vineyard wines and where they have a restaurant and hold tastings. It's their equivalent of what we call our 'local' but of course too expensive to be just that.

The house is not what you'd call beautiful – there are bits of unfinished plaster work and you might find the odd cockroach in the outside toilet – but it's wonderful, made that way by the family.

Lisa and Bobby have two boys, the eldest is Zachary, who is 18 now and Max, 16. I put both boys through private school, Lindisfarne College at Hastings which is one of the best in the country. I did this for Dorothy because she gave me so much. When I made the offer, years ago, she said a very touching thing: 'My family will never forget you for this.' That's not why I did it, but it was something I wanted to do, to give them a good solid education. Zachary has left school now and is at university in Dunedin, where his cousin Christopher, Max's son, is a student too.

Lisa always says she thinks of me as her sister and I spent a lot of time with her, the most I ever have. And I fell in love with their dog Spikey, a grey cross-breed poodle. David and I both spent Christmas with them which was a pretty traditional day – we had a huge Christmas breakfast and everybody had a pressie from everybody else, even if it was only a box of Quality Street. Max is mad on hunting and he has a carbon bow and arrow so I bought him a pair of boots to go with his hunting gear. Then we had the full lunch, turkey, crackers, Christmas pud and afterwards we sat outside in the sun. The weather was good that day although it was very mixed during my stay and there was a lot of rain.

Although they live miles from anywhere, Lisa constantly produces these wonderful meals. They rear their own lambs, send them for slaughter, freeze the meat and sell the wool. Then Lisa cooks the lamb to make absolutely delicious meals.

One night after New Year we had a real scare when an aftershock from an earthquake shook the whole house to its roots. Spikey seemed to sense it before we felt it as he let out a strange noise just milliseconds before we felt the whole earth move. It shook the house to the roots and I was ready to spend the night outside. We suffered no damage but we had no idea of the scale of it until the locals mentioned next day that it measured 5.8 magnitude on the Richter scale. We thought it might have been one of the hundreds of aftershocks which have been felt since the terrible earthquake in Christchurch in February 2011, although the next day one of the locals said the epicentre had been somewhere else, much nearer.

I didn't go to Christchurch but I met a fair few people from there. The sister of my boating pal Blue Derry moved out and up to Blenheim where he lives. Their stories were harrowing and sad – remember 185 people were killed – and they are so weary of the aftershocks, sometimes dozens a day. People have left the city in droves, their nerves shot to pieces. There have been so many now in Christchurch that the city is struggling to rebuild more than a year later.

I took my golf clubs to New Zealand and played a few rounds on different courses, but not as much as I would have liked because I couldn't find anyone to play with. I did manage to persuade Bobby to play but you should have seen his bag and clubs – I think the mice ran out when he picked it up. We played with a friend of his, Hamish, who only has one leg – he wears a prosthetic which just looks like a pole, no foot, no nothing and he plays 18 holes with no problem. What's more he never complains about a bad shot – I guess he knows all about keeping things in perspective. He only lost his leg eight years ago in a motorbike accident so it's not as if he has been used to it from being a child. They took me to one of their local courses which had a wonderful sign listing the Course Etiquette. Would you believe it included the line: 'Alcohol in moderation' which by New Zealand standards could mean quite a lot. I had to take a photograph of that. Can you really imagine such a sign on a golf course in the UK?

In contrast I went to play one of the poshest courses in the world, Cape Kidnapper's on the eastern coast of North island, where there is a gannet sanctuary. It's a beautiful place with fabulous views of the Pacific but it costs an amazing NZ$385, around £190 by my calculations, for a round. Fortunately because I was staying with David, I could pay the residents' rate of NZ$265. Because there was nobody to play with – the place was deserted, just two Japanese in a golf cart – David said he'd walk round with me. And that's what I love about New Zealand – David had on a pair of scruffy jeans, chopped off, and flip-flops and nobody said a word. They have such a liberal attitude, you can do almost anything there. They are very free and nobody criticises you, no-one judges you by what you drive, what you wear, what you eat, what you drink. They have this wonderful attitude of live and let live, unlike in the UK where we seem hung up on image.

After my first stay at Lisa's, I went to visit Max who is definitely the most serious of Dorothy's children. He lives in a beautiful house overlooking Wellington harbour with his wife Anne and their three children. The two boys Christopher, 21, and Andrew, 18, have both grown into fine your men. Chris is at Dunedin university and Andrew looks like taking a career in the police force or the Army, he's an outdoorsy, adventure boy who was just back from an outward bound course when I was there. But they have a seriously handicapped sister, Rose, who has the rare Angelman Syndrome, which is a neuro-genetic disorder which means that she has not developed normally and she only ever says two or three words. And yet she is usually happy and smiling, which is also a characteristic of her condition. Rose is 16 now, she can walk, although she's very ungainly, and in fact Anne walks her off her feet – she walked me off mine. We walked four miles up Oriental Parade, right round to Evans Bay, sat and had a coffee and walked all the way back. Their poodle started off as a Standard and ended up as a Toy!

Rose goes to a school for special needs children and a taxi picks her up every morning, but she was on holiday when I was there. Max had warned me not to be disappointed if Rose didn't recognise me – he didn't think she would remember – but the moment I walked through the door, she rushed towards me. She knew me immediately and never left my side for ten days. She'd climb into my bed, root through my suitcase, follow me into the shower room.

The house has stunning views, with a deck overlooking the majestic Wellington harbour – when people rave about Sydney Harbour that only tells me they have never seen Wellington's because for me there is no contest.

It must be an expensive home to run because, compared to the UK in 2012, nothing is cheap in New Zealand. Food is expensive and therefore restaurants are too, cigarettes are dear, cosmetics and over-the-counter drugs at pharmacies are expensive and the list goes on. I guess it's because their currency is strong.

Then I also met up with some of my boating buddies. I went to stay with my old pal Blue and his wife Debbie, who live near Blenheim on the South Island where Blue has a vineyard. It's in the Marlborough region which is famous for its wines. Blue grows grapes but he sells them, he doesn't make his own wine there. The area usually has a wonderful sunny climate but Blue said it had been a very poor harvest this year because of the weather.

He was a jet boat champion in his day, known by everyone on the boating scene in New Zealand, and he was the man who organised my world speed record back in 1990. Sadly Blue was very poorly and I spent the first few days in tears, seeing the sad deterioration of such a vital man, so obviously in the twilight of his life. It was his 77th birthday while I was there and he had to admit those years had been pretty full-on because New Zealanders really know how to work, rest and play – they work hard, they play hard and they party hard. But Blue was still able to invite me to sit on his knee so he could give me a squeeze! That was a hint of the old Blue. Debbie is much younger than him, just 49, but they've been together for a long time, although they only married six years ago.

We kind of reminisced about our water speed days, but he could not really concentrate for long spells any more. I stayed with them for ten days and I played golf at Blenheim on a beautiful sunny day and for once I managed to meet another couple and play the round with them. It was one of those amazing coincidences – it turned out they came from Yorkshire, from Linton, near Wetherby, a village just a few miles from my home. When I arrived back in England, Debbie emailed to say that Blue had gone into a hospice for some palliative care, although a few weeks later she said he was back home and outside cutting the grass. Sadly Blue died at the end of May. He was an amazing man, but I think he was just burnt out because he lived hard and played hard.

While I was there, I wandered down to Blue's purpose-built barn with an enormous floor space, which used to house all his boats, including my record boat, the hydroplane. After my speed record back in 1990, I went back to Denmark and Blue took the boat to his place which was like a race horse stable for boats – boats he was building, pleasure boats, boats he was working on. Blue had laid out quite a lot of expenses to help me with the record attempt and as I didn't have the cash to pay him outright, we agreed he should sell my engine and keep the money for everything he'd done for me. But he kept the boat and the fantastic trailer which was purpose-built, with hydraulics – it may even have been worth more than the actual boat.

Even when Blue moved house to buy the vineyard, all the boats went with him. When I visited him there on a holiday in the late 1990s, I had a look at my boat – I've got a photograph of me climbing into it.

Then, when I visited in 2012, all the boats had gone, including mine. Instead it was filled with his vineyard tractors, cutters, pruners. Because Blue was ill I didn't want to challenge him about it but I mentioned it casually and he hedged, said he thought I knew all about it, that he'd emailed me but never heard back. Apparently he'd moved my boat out a few years earlier and stored it under a tarpaulin and a young man had turned up in a white 'ute' – their name for a utility vehicle – one day, said he understood Blue had a boat for sale. He said he knew someone who wanted it, they agreed a price and away it went. The man said he'd be back with the money and as Blue is a very honest man and assumes everyone else is the same, he believed him. He never saw him again and never received any money. He had emailed me, he thought I was in touch with this guy, the exact details had all been lost over time. I suppose I can understand it.

He then told me that a year or two later, he received a phone call from a guy in Australia who said he had my boat and could Blue fill in some of its history for him, he obliged and that was last he heard. While I was in New Zealand, I later told the story to a friend called Mike Costello in the New Zealand Power Boating fraternity who in turn got in touch with a contact in Australia, whose passion was hydroplanes. He emailed me once I was back in the UK to say that he had actually traced the man who once had it – but that he had died! And that's really where the story ends.

In a way I feel sad that all my boats have disappeared – well, my *Agfa Bluebird*s are still at Filching Manor, the place owned by the Foulkes-Halbards, along with a lot of other Campbell memorabilia. But the Museum is only open by prior arrangement to groups of ten people or more. I never owned the Agfa boats and when I stopped racing Agfa came to some arrangement with Mr Foulkes-Halbard that he could display the boat at his place.

I realise it would be bit of a headache knowing what to do with them but I'd like them to be on show again. The only piece of memorabilia I do have is the propeller from the little catamaran that was written off at Holme Pierrepont when I set the unofficial women's world water speed record. It's a beautiful piece of stainless steel engineering, sharp as a razor. That's about all I've got to show for what was a big part of my life, except for my memories

One day I drove from Blue's to see Dorothy's brother David, who lives in Nelson, a two hour drive from Blenheim. He told me to take the Wairau Valley Road route, which he said was a beautiful drive and he was right. David is a county court judge and so travels around the country a lot – he's the only one of Dorothy's siblings who is still alive. She was one of six and they were all high achievers: one owned a newspaper, another a top orthodontist and another worked for the World Bank. We talked a lot about Dorothy.

Blue was just one of several people from my past who I really wanted to see again. People like Graham Pike, an old boyfriend and boating pal, a guy I raced with. We went out on the water, went to a couple of boat races and saw more of my old mates. He said he'd love to come to England to see *Bluebird* go back in the water. And Denis Robinson, the man who ran the ad agency involved in the water safety campaign and the guy who knew how to throw a party! He was living in a caravan – not because he had to but because he wanted to and it suited his lifestyle. He published books about New Zealand artists so he moved around the country. He watched them work, wrote profiles on them and compiled lovely books which sell very well because there are some outstanding artists in the country. Denis used his caravan as a mobile office and when I was there it was on a park, two miles off the motorway, yet just 20 paces to the beach and into the sea. Idyllic. He has a daughter in England who he visited every other year and we usually met up. In fact he came over in the summer of 2012, a few months after I returned home, and I took him to Bill Smith's workshop to see *Bluebird*. He was absolutely thrilled. Then he was setting out on what he called his 'great adventure' with another male friend – a cruise from Dover all the way back home to New Zealand. We emailed each other during his trip and he was blogging about the amazing cruise. Then, out of the blue, in the middle of August, I received an email from his daughter to say that Denis had died suddenly on the last day of the trip. I just could not believe it and feel so sad for him and his family. I guess he'd think that at least he went out on a high – and I'm so glad he saw *Bluebird* before he left.

Joanne Ruscoe, whose PR company took charge of ANZ Bank's sponsorship of my campaign, is married now and lives with her husband in Waikanae, a seaside resort north of Wellington. I used David's house as my base and then went off to visit all these friends. I had a lot of fun with her, we laughed and laughed, it was as if we had never been apart. She is still working although I think her business has suffered a bit in the economic downturn. One night she made pizzas in her very special pizza oven on a covered deck at the back of the house. She sets the fire and lets it burn and burn till the ashes are red hot, then she shifts them to one side and puts in the pizza. Delicious and fun.

David was a good host, although I helped him out with one or two chores. He's the kind of man who loves a bargain and while I was there he bought a huge American fridge freezer on Trade Me, their equivalent of eBay, which we had to collect. It didn't look heavy but boy was it! How we managed to carry it up 28 stairs at David's, I'll never know. Even after we removed the door to lighten the load, it was still a struggle, but we managed it. Then we took the old one out, cleaned it up, photographed it and within a few days, he'd sold it, again on Trade Me.

Nothing goes to waste there, it seems to be in their DNA. We have become such a throwaway society, but not there. David has two identical washing machines, one in the kitchen, one outside under plastic. So when something goes wrong with the one in the kitchen, out he goes, bang, crash, wallop, and up he comes with a circuit board or a soap dispenser or a new door or control panel or whatever it needs and he manages to get it working. But then we had water all over the floor, the alarm going off because there's a leak, mop and bucket out and he has to start all over again. Out comes the one under the polythene, up comes another part from it into the kitchen, in it goes and by some miracle it works!

But hey, although I saw New Zealand as an adventure, and other people think a trip like that is all carefree and wonderful, the reality is that when you're always a guest in someone's home, you don't have total freedom. If the people you're staying with want to go to bed at midnight, you go to bed at midnight; if they want to stay up till 3am, you've got to do the same and equally, if they are shattered the next night and decide to go to bed at nine o'clock, you've got to go to bed at nine too. You're a guest in their home

So the week before I left I was looking forward to coming home, but then in the last few days, I grew to dread it because I knew I was returning to that same uncertainty about the future, not sure what direction my life was going to take. At the moment I am facing the prospect of a single life and my friends are telling me to enjoy it while I can, although it's probably not something I want for the rest of my life.

But when I arrived home, not one single friend who supported me after I was left alone, had forgotten me and that has truly lifted my heart. I had never quite learned the value of friendships and how deep they can be – I was never so conceited as to think that so many people thought so much about me. I didn't really think the girls from the golf club – and the boys – would give a toss about my life, but how wrong I was. Now I've really learned a lot about the closeness of friends.

I did feel really at home in New Zealand and I'd love to go back and I will. Lisa's husband Bobby said to me: 'I know you're not ready yet Gina, but when you get old and you need someone to look after you, we will do just that.' How good an offer is that? I'd love to live there but who knows whether it will ever happen.

Chapter 24

GINA'S DOWNFALL –
A JOURNAL

Although New Zealand was simply wonderful in every way, I did have what I would call low times – they were few but none the less, that's how I felt at times. I travelled the length and breadth of the beautiful countryside by car which gave me complete freedom – it housed my travelling wardrobe, my golf cart and of course the golf clubs too. It was amazing – the scenery, the roads, the whole thing is fabulous, but not to share all this beauty with another person just seemed so empty. I've a million photos of all this but there's nobody in the shots…not even me.

I wrote a 'Journal' on and off while I was there – something I have always wanted to do. I'd taken with me a gorgeous chamois-bound book I'd had for years for this very purpose but had never been used. So finally this was the time to put some words, some thoughts and feelings inside its pages. I realised I had been through the complete washer/dryer cycle of emotions over a pretty short period of time…I thought this process would be 'cleansing.'

While I was staying with Max and Anne I wrote: '*I am lonely, or alone (what's the difference?), all these lovely places and sights and no-one to share them with. It's silly, I should be so ecstatic and so privileged to be here, it all sounded so wonderful, but the reality is in fact very different… I am very lonely. In a strange way I don't want to be on my own, to not share all this beauty is criminal, even though I am quite comfortable in my own company.*'

But the main reason for my low spirits was a man I had met just eleven days before I flew out, eleven mad, passionate days and nights which made me feel absolutely wonderful – and loved. I described how we met in my Journal. I called it *Gina's Downfall* and here are a few extracts written during my time in New Zealand.

'I have to ask myself if I'm the very, very worst judge of character of the male species that ever lived, or am I the eternal optimist. Whichever one I am, I am without doubt useless.

Having just been 'dumped' by a man I thought was my soulmate, after 18 years of togetherness, feeling so battered, bruised, humiliated, deceived, lied to, that I walked/ran then headlong at an alarming pace into the arms of another man. This one was I thought a thoroughly nice, decent man, but had I stopped to think, which of course I didn't, never have, never will I suppose – why should such a gem be 'available' and on a dating agency site.

But then I was, and I am, a thoroughly good, decent person but with zero prospects of meeting a man: I only go to Tesco's, short of falling over someone's trolley – no prospects there and certainly no-one to help load or unload my car. Or I go to the Club which is full of rather aged, overweight men…and I did not want to return there – so I had to start looking elsewhere.

So the dating agency seemed the way to go. I have dear friends who met this way and later married and you hear numerous stories of this being 'the way to go' so I was prepared to give it a go…whut the hell So with a little help and encouragement from my friends, off we went.

After spending hours figuring out how to download a half-decent photo - tempted to use an old one, but decided I actually looked better this year than last. Spend hours reading the spiel of all the 'lonely hearts', what is man-talk for – just want a shag, or a carer, housekeeper, or financier, slowly you learn to read between the lines.

You are offered multiple choices to list your likes/dislikes, character, instincts, hair, eyes, tit size, the lot. When you've chosen your pet name – I'm not revealing it here to save embarrassment both to myself and others! - off you set in 'profiling' yourself. Well no one's going to put – I'm a nasty, hateful, difficult to get on with right bitch who'll take you for every penny – you naturally list to the best of your knowledge and belief, all your finest qualities – well, for me of course, there's not enough lines to put them all in! I thought I sounded like Mother Theresa, looked like Zsa Zsa Gabor (but younger), your actual top of the range, most desirable woman in the world.

The first response I got – pet name Ivabigun! – quickly told me what all this was about and that one went in the black-listed box. I decided to subtract two years off my age, as 62 really does sound a bit old and I truly don't want an old man! So – age group 59-65 – my God, though, that's getting on!

I spent hours into the night – I don't sleep well – trolling through these lonely hearts only to become more and more depressed: whilst your erstwhile Zsa Zsa Gabor seemed to attract the very worst of them (the story of my life!)! Their interests, pubs, clubs, darts, football, hiking, camping, tromping, you name it. I had put golf as my main interest, also horse-riding, motor sports and other conventional sporting interests. I couldn't put powerboat racing or record breaking – too much information. Still nothing came my way, so I decided Mohammed had to go to the mountain. So I started being more daring and sending 'winks' (OMG how sad is that, I thought) and writing little notes to possible candidates, that wasn't much better either, really don't know what people are looking for.

But I've since found out that it's the women who make all the first approaches, so there goes the old-fashioned belief that you sit like a wallflower and wait to be approached – how tradition has changed. Day after day I'd get 'alerts' of visitors to my profile but nothing of interest came my way. Then I realised if you didn't subscribe to the 'full monty' in financial terms, your communications were filtered out! Hence they had you! So three months subscription – £40-50 not sure – started to bring some minor results! But subscriptions are hilarious – if you want a laugh or a cry just go and look and read. Get amused or get depressed – both. One even said: 'Please contact me, I only have 1-5 years left, got lung cancer' .... very sad indeed.

I spotted someone whose name left me thinking he was almost certainly a Yorkshireman. I wrote a note, thinking I'd never hear back... wrong. He comes back, later, said out of politeness I wonder. He was in Australia, gave me a rundown on his stay, we questioned – well, he questioned, I answered. I didn't want to give away too much about myself to him, my background would have worked against me I know. So very *cagey, just some bits and scraps.*

I grew to like his contact, even started to long for it, each night we would converse by email and text and got to know each other quite well over about three weeks. He knew I was coming to New Zealand for an extended stay from Dec 13, he was only due back on the 2nd, so only a short time to meet, although we had got deeper and deeper to the extent of flirting online!

I watched his flight traverse the world on the iPad app, I saw with delight safe landing LHR and by midday he's back in Yorkshire. A meeting set for 3.30 at a hotel outside Leeds.

I was there, waiting, excited, anticipation. First glance not what I expected, he was a good-looking man but a bit thinner, says she weighing in below seven stones. I warned him I was tiny – in every sense of the word. We had a coffee, sat by the fire and I knew very quickly he was a really decent man and I very soon thought of intimacy with him, although he doesn't look sexy in the true sense of the word. He looked vulnerable and kissable. I kissed him first briefly, probably out of embarrassment, he waffled about people he knew. He had put 2 and 2 together and decided he knew my background so nothing more to hide there! After coffee I wanted a ciggy, he suggested going out to car for one. Sitting smoking – he said he hadn't smoked in years, I believe him. After while I made a suggestion – he could follow me home. It's dark, it's rush hour so I explained where I lived, he knew vaguely. Arrived at my house, made some drinks, he looked shattered travelled halfway and more round the world. I had to go to a friend's for dinner, so suggested he rested, watched telly, shower, anything he wanted. I rushed out, had a quick dinner, rushed back home. I knew instinctively I could trust him.

We kissed, cuddled and yes, fancied each other like mad. It was so exciting, wonderful to be touched and fancied and kissed – so long for me, I was ecstatic, I thought he was too. Eventually time to move closer – bed – offered spare room – didn't want it! So mine – it was just amazing...

We spent lots of time together over the next few days but eventually I had to pack up and leave for NZ. I was so looking forward to going but the thought of leaving him was hard. But then some time apart was I thought a good thing – he couldn't keep up that intense passion for ever anyway…at the ripe old age of, dare I say it, 62, I was having more passion than a youngster – this was/is too good to be true. I finally left on Tuesday 13th, after we spent the last night together. He had my promise I would return to him – I gave him something very precious to me to prove it – and he promised he would wait for me, that we would be together again.

Three months is a long time to be parted…and I hadn't left Manchester airport and I was already scared that all was never to be the same again, obviously it was only designed to be for those very very, passionate fleeting moments. I shall never forget them. Mr X can be thanked for all of that so if only for fleeting moment in my life I had what I had and thank you Lord for that. Is it better to have loved and lost than never to have loved and be loved at all? Answer – don't know.'

Once in New Zealand, we were in touch by text, email, Skype – sometimes just one line and two kisses from him but that could lift my spirits. Then one day he didn't respond, the next the same and then, for ten whole days, nothing. Silence. I was absolutely distraught and I wrote in my Journal …

'Now I'm heartbroken twice in four months. This is not possible, this is not real, this can't be life, what have I done, why, why WHY!!'

I decided to email his sister – I'd come across her email address by chance on one that Mr X had forwarded to me – to ask initially if he was safe. It crossed my mind that he was lying in a ditch somewhere, nobody would know about 'Us', therefore I should never know if something had happened to him. She assured me he was OK, suggesting that he sometimes retreats in to 'his own cave'. I was torn – I wanted this man desperately, but knew I had more than enough emotional baggage of my own to contend with without taking on someone else's problems.

On Friday 13th of January – was that prophetic – I wrote: *'I can stand no more of this silence, this finality, I have had to make a text but I am sure I shall have no reply – what, why, for how many times have I asked myself this question but with no answer. I shall never know what he is suffering, what he wants, why so sudden a change, why from such 'words', actions of love do I end up with this pain.*

What is it that this man carries through his heart and mind that can shut out someone he professes to love so much, not something that I can understand, maybe because I have in some ways been blessed not to carry such burdens. I do not want to carry such baggage that makes this happen, will not let myself.

How should 'love' feel – I 'love' so many people I have people in my life that mean worlds to me. So this is not love, this is something much more, so different, so soul-searching, passion, arousal. It's almost horrid, I don't think I like it, it's too scary, too hairy, too all embracing. Is this just me or do other people carry this emotion? I think it's unique to me, think it stems from a deep, deep desire to be loved, having never been loved in my conception, birth and childhood – I'm the one that's different. I so wanted the necessary love from my own parents. Neither knew how to show or feel any love for me. The first person to tell me they loved me, I married them. This is what I wanted, just love, love that's never been in my life.

Is this why I need, want, almost demand love? Your erstwhile little Miss Perfect – yes, that's me! It's probably so lucky for my survival that I have a pretty high level of optimism and self belief, otherwise I would have flipped – I would have killed myself and not be the person that I think I am. My life will not be worth living any more.

So if at some point someone reads this and that's what I have done, please don't be angry with me – have faith we shall all be together again – though it will be crowded.

It will be because that's how I shall find my peace, away from the awful loss and the wondrous highs of my life – LIFE-DEATH.

Why do I crave love, respect, care and all the tenderness anyone can give me? I have so wanted all these things but it never comes and stays. Am I too self-absorbed? Why do I want him so much? Yet I also want the freedom of mind, I want to have some time for myself, everything is in place for all this, yet I want to share the beauty of life. I actually don't want to have to care or worry about another, I've done that for too long in my life. I want life for myself and myself alone, some time away from the domestic goddess stuff.

My problem is rejection, I'm sure. I never thought that my extraordinary life could leave me such a mental freak, but I do believe it has. When I get it, I almost don't want it, can't handle it, want not to.'

We did return to each other's arms…I now know and understand so much more. This has been a huge revelation to me too – maybe I should be more in control of myself and my emotions. Take each day, each week…

Chapter 25

THE BEST IS STILL OUT THERE

How do I feel being the last Campbell? At least the last one of this particular Campbell dynasty. Unique, I would say, and lucky, because I don't have to share my legacy with anybody. In a way I've got the whole apple, I don't have to give bites away to other people, it's all mine. My cousins are Malcolm Campbell's descendants and very proud of it, too, but they do not have the Campbell name. Donald Wales, in particular, is fiercely protective of the family name and the one who is continuing to chase speed records. He's a lovely boy and I love him very much.

I think bearing the name has been something of a weighty responsibility because I realise that anything that has gone a bit haywire or ugly in my life does not only carry my name, but carries the Campbell label too. If I make a mistake, I don't just have to live with it as Gina, but as Gina, daughter of Donald, granddaughter of Sir Malcolm. And I do not want anything to reflect badly on the great reputation of my forefathers – I can carry it, I made the mistakes, they didn't.

But if anyone wants to know how proud I am of the Campbell name, they need only look at my number plate K7 DAD. Only this year a company called Registration Transfers came up with it for me – I think it's brilliant.

And then there is the aspect that as soon as people know my name, they change immediately. When I was first married to Cliffy, I took the name Percy and many people we met after that had no idea about my family. I always remember competing at a horse show in Somerset, held on the estate of Edward du Cann, a Government minister in the 1960s, who was a friend of my father. As I came into the showjumping ring, I heard the announcement on the public address system: 'Next into the ring is Gina Percy, formerly Gina Campbell, daughter of the late Donald

Campbell.' It took me aback because I hadn't heard it before at those events. Within five seconds of coming out of the ring, there was Edward Du Cann, waiting to introduce himself, telling me he was a pal of my father. Let's face it, he would never have appeared had I been just Gina Percy but it took me till much later in life to realise the enormity of the name.

It's also the case that when people hear my name, many of them believe I must be loaded, just because my father and grandfather lived in the public eye. Maybe that is the case today – just look at Mr and Mrs Beckham and the like. But in that day and age, publicity didn't gain you those financial rewards. Then it was just a privilege to be recognised for your achievements. And remember it was an era when news could take days and weeks to filter through, even when something as important as a world record had been broken or achieved. Yes it's true they still became huge, iconic figures but today their whole lives would be PR-managed. They would be appearing on every talk show, every this, every that, judging the *X Factor*, and being paid handsomely for all of it.

Imagine if my grandfather was sailing to the Cocos Islands to search for buried treasure today – he would have a satellite TV crew and a journalist on board, a helicopter overhead, the whole journey filmed and transmitted into our living rooms within hours. Every detail of his and my father's lives would have been broadcast – every wedding, every time they appeared at an airport, every record attempt, not a stone left unturned.

It's pretty surprising that I am the one and only Campbell, with no brothers and sisters, when you consider that my mother and my father each married three times – once to one another and then twice more. It must be pretty rare for only one child to be born of five marriages in total.

And yet I too have been married three times and I do not have any children. There was my accidental pregnancy to Cliffy and Philip and I talked about kids, but that's as far as it went. Now I'm so glad I never had children because I don't see myself as a mother, never have, which is not to say I'm not caring, because I am. I think there must be a legacy of my own childhood in there somewhere, being the product of a mother who showed no love or care. How awful to bring a child into the world and not love it – that's not a risk worth taking. My mother didn't even like me most of the time, let alone love me, so I know my feelings are a legacy of being brought up as an unwanted child.

According to my father, my mother despised being pregnant, and he probably took one look at the baby and thought that as it wasn't born with a tassle, he was not very interested. I'm pretty sure that if I had been conceived a few years later, I would not have been born.

And as I grew older, I somehow must have known that my life was going to be topsyiturvy, that I'd have to make decisions on the hoof – decisions I'd have to make on my own – and you cannot do that if you have children. I must have had an idea all along that I was going to live a life full of turmoil, emotionally and physically, and that a child or children would just not fit in. I just wouldn't have been able to make the life-changing decisions that I've made, when I made them and how I made them. No, I've absolutely no regrets about not having children.

Lots of people ask me whether my life is somehow a mirror of my father's. I suppose that although in some ways it has been, I don't completely see it that way. I've been left with a fair bit of his spirit and influence, also some of his tenacity. As the Campbells would tolerate anything but failure, I will not attempt anything unless I know – or at least think – I shall succeed, although I do know my limitations. I knew I couldn't be a brain surgeon, so I never tried! But I am made of stern stuff and I will always see a job right through to the finish. I am capable and I have proved that both to myself and to others.

My father was also a stickler for the truth and my backside bore testament to this only too well! I'm not saying that I'm a George Washington with his famous, 'Father, I cannot tell a lie' statement, 'cos for sure I've made up little excuses and little fibs (if there is such a thing). But I am honest and believe in the truth, to the point where some may call me stupid. It may be why so many 'bloody noses' come my way, but at least I can look into the mirror and know that I am happy with what I see…well except the natural ageing process!

Although I am very capable of being on my own, I have always been taught to share and this is still with me today. It started when I was a tiny tot, right through my school days and on into adulthood. My father was always a team player and he instilled this spirit into me. I think I am an excellent team player and I have always held this value, I have never been selfish.

I did always consider that I was a pretty good judge of character. But I have to admit honestly that I'm useless, probably a bit like my father, who after all had three wives. Too many people in this life are not what they seem, not what they say they are, sometimes not even who they say they are. It's been proven too many times, but still I fall into the same pit. I get bitterly disappointed but you can't change what you are. I keep coming back for more. It's because I so believe that other people have the same thoughts and beliefs as myself and I trust everyone…big mistake! And yet I still carry on believing it – how naive can one be? I am so open, to my own detriment for sure, but I've had a bit of fun on the way. You pick yourself up, dust yourself off, but really, I have to 'smarten up'!

Yes, I have been very let down in life by others who haven't had the same morals, values and attitudes, but everyone has the right to do what they wish, even though that means that at some stage they will, without doubt, ride roughshod over someone in the process. Yet still I think you have to love people as they are and not how you want them to be – very noble words, but not always easy to live up to. We are all guilty of trying it on…and sometimes it has been worth it!

I have made some very deep friendships over the years, which have held me together. The unconditional love of another human being is in fact the most fundamental and important emotion – the touch, the smell, the breath, the feel of love is my desire.

But love, life, honesty are just not integral to everyone. I am too straightforward, honest, trusting, loyal and caring…and others just ain't! But you cannot change – I shall no doubt go to the grave with all of these beliefs and feelings and no doubt get taken to the emotional cleaners again before I do.

I know that I am hugely romantic and full of romance, not just the loving, smoochy side of life, but the spiritual side, too. I am a great dreamer, day and night, always thinking about how, when, where and what life will hold in store for me. I can lie and dream and think about past and future events for hours, plotting and rearranging my movements, but I am by nature a very positive person and realise that life is for now.

And I don't think that I have lost any of my joy for life and for whatever a new day brings. I am the eternal optimist and I still find so much pleasure in just smelling the grass, watching the flowers bloom, the trees blossom, the hills, the valleys, the mountains and in my utter fascination with water, lakes, rivers, streams, ponds, brooks and eddies…and of course the sea.

I've had a pretty turbulent life, full of ups and downs, just like everyone else. But now, at 63 years old, I am a totally free spirit and will map out my closing years for myself. I shall no doubt make a few poor turns, but at least I shall do it with my own will, and be responsible for the consequences. No longer shall I have to please anyone else, no longer worry if they don't like my cooking, no longer worry if I am doing or saying the right thing just to massage another's ego, so I am FREE…free of the encumbrance of all that worry. I can even have sex – forgive me! – to a degree as and when and how I would like it, without feeling I have to please someone else, just ME. Only now do I realise that I've spent the majority of my life trying to please others, but there are no more worries in that direction now. No worries, mate!

It is rather late in life to be in this position, but at least it's been worth the wait; it's not all a bunch of roses but at least all the blooms are for me and the thorns I can dispense with at my leisure. I do believe that the best that life has to offer me is still out there for the taking.

Where am I heading? Who knows – wouldn't we all like to have that crystal ball? But we are told never to put off till tomorrow that which can be done today, as tomorrow, we know, is promised to no-one. I still have mountains to climb, seas to cross, although what they are and when I shall do it, I do not know. But sometime soon, in line with my total philosophy on life, I shall grab and run with my instinct. In other words, here comes trouble…!

Would I like to have my life all over again, to do things differently? Answer: very, very few things. Naturally I'd like to make sure I didn't repeat any hurt I have caused to others and I do feel remorse for the hurt I have inflicted. But I am the person I am and I've woven a very thick tapestry through all of my life. I've taken the ups and the downs on the chin but even now, I always believe that the best is yet to come. So bring it on!

And I certainly feel proud of myself for sticking to my guns about the restoration of *Bluebird*, despite a lot of criticism. Everyone involved can feel proud to uphold my father's and *Bluebird*'s memory as two of the greatest record-breakers that ever existed. And we can all be proud to be British (for once, lately). The spirit, will and endeavour of so many like-minded people has made it possible; people like Bill Smith, who will write his own account of his efforts, like Vicky Slowe, Director of Coniston's Ruskin Museum, Anthony (Robbie) Robinson and Novie Dizanora, both from Coniston, who have spent their lives watching the Bluebird story unfold, and Neil Sheppard, a huge Campbell enthusiast who has written his own book about *Bluebird*, and his wife Sandra. They are just a few of the people who shared this vision, who backed it to the hilt from the very beginning. They are the Bluebird Gang (a good gang) the team that has given and helped in every way possible to get us here, to return *Bluebird* in all her finery to her home, to write this final chapter. Nobody could have achieved all this alone.

How shall I feel when Bluebird finally makes it back on to the water, and we can all stand and be thrilled by her fineness? I shall feel huge relief, relief that the decisions I made, mostly against the wishes of others, were the right ones and that all the hard work, passion, brilliance of so many people have achieved so much. The effort and sheer dedication of others to reach this point is just a testament to what the Brits can do when the chips are down. So much has been done by so many individuals that never seemed humanly possible.

DONALD'S MANUSCRIPT

Donald Campbell started to write his own memoir, thirty-eight foolscap pages of neatly typed autobiography filed in an orange folder. The title *The Eternal Challenge* is handwritten on the front cover with his name, D.M.Campbell, underlined beneath. The manuscript remained unfinished.

Inside the folder are pages entitled *'Fast and Loose'*, which appear to be a synopsis of the book he intends to write. It begins:

'It was 1940. The place was Central London. The time was two in the morning. The setting was pretty hellish. Bombs were falling, guns were blasting and the walls of the Kit-Kat Hotel in Jermyn Street were visibly shaking.

The scene in one of the double bedrooms was almost as dramatic. I was a twenty years old aircraftman. Life was for living. There was no point in planning for tomorrow, because no-one knew if there was going to be one. Life was for living today and I was living it.

The girl was beautiful. That night I loved her to a background of noise that was unbelievable. Suddenly there was a deafening crash. I felt a violent blow on the back of my head. Stars of all colours flashed before my eyes. The bed collapsed and I rolled on the floor. So this was the end. I thought we had had a direct hit and faced the inevitable with equanimity. Five minutes later, I realised I had a very sore head but otherwise I was very much alive. I picked myself gingerly off the floor. The girl was lying beside me and then I saw what had happened. The double bed had a large wooden bedhead which had broken apart from the bed. As the top half of the bed collapsed, the bedhead fell and hit me on the back of the head. It was a terrible anti-climax.'

He talks of his early days and memories of his father. *'A great father and a wonderful man.'* And of inheriting his father's passion for speed after his death. *'I had got the bug. It broke up my marriage. My wife could not understand my dedication...My second marriage was also sacrificed on the altar of speed. It was the only thing that mattered to me.'*

He writes that he will *'tell of my marriage to Tonia (*his third wife), *one of the most glamorous cabaret entertainers in Europe. The clash of wills that almost ended our marriage.'*

Although there is no mention of his daughter Gina in this 'synopsis', in an early chapter he describes his first marriage to her mother, Daphne Harvey, and then he writes:

*'After a pleasant honeymoon in Devonshire, we returned to Surrey and bought a pleasant little three-bedroomed house in Kingswood. We happily settled down to married life, daily driving to and from London, pursuing the career of an Insurance Broker. Twelve months later our daughter Georgina was born; again this happy event was surrounded by the tempestuous aurora (*sic*) which always seem to attend the family Campbell.*

The child was due to be born in the private wing of a London hospital; however on arrival at 5 o'clock in the morning, we were horrified to learn from the Sister in charge that there had been a mistake in the dates and that no private room was available. We telephoned our local Doctor and immediately drove home arriving in time for breakfast. Dr Binney, our Family Doctor for more than ten years, turned up trumps: Daphne was as happy as could be and Georgina was safely delivered in the afternoon.'